DISCARDED BY

MACPHÁIDÍN LIBRARY

CUSHING-MARTIN LIBRARY
STONEHILL COLLEGE
NORTH EASTON, MASSACHUSETTS 02357

INTELLECTUAL FREEDOM AND CENSORSHIP

•

An Annotated Bibliography

•

FRANK HOFFMANN

The Scarecrow Press, Inc.
Metuchen, N.J., & London
1989

British Library Cataloguing-in-Publication data available

Library of Congress Cataloging-in-Publication Data

Hoffmann, Frank W., 1949-
    Intellectual freedom and censorship : an annotated bibliography /
by Frank Hoffmann.
        p.   cm.
    Includes index.
    ISBN 0-8108-2145-1
    1. Censorship--United States--Bibliography. 2. Freedom of
information--United States--Bibliography. 3. Libraries--United
States--Censorship--Bibliography. I. Title.
Z658.U5H64   1989
016.3633'1'0973--dc 19   88-18811

Copyright © 1989 by Frank Hoffmann
Manufactured in the United States of America

TO CHARLES BUSHA

whose guidance as a teacher and friend
inspired a lifelong involvement with
intellectual freedom.

CONTENTS

FOREWORD

In today's society, the concern with access to knowledge and to the information on which it is based has a significant importance. Having just celebrated our 200th birthday of the Constitution and the First Amendment we are reminded of just how precious access to information and the importance of intellectual freedom is in this society. With the growth of knowledge and information sources, our dependence on complex sets of institutions and mechanisms to supply it becomes greater.

At the time this republic was founded, when the spread of information was oral or through private presses, it was the Federal government that had the power to suppress access to information and knowledge. The constitutions of most of the new states prohibited their legislatures from denying freedom of speech or of the press, and the First Amendment of the Federal Constitution did the same for the national Congress. Freedom to express one's views effectively required not only freedom from government suppression, but also the opportunity of access to the materials and tools that had become the vehicles to reach the people.

Up until the 1950s, federal, state, and local authorities felt free to deny the right to publish or disseminate printed materials (especially films) on the grounds that they were obscene, even with the presence in the Constitution of the First Amendment. Prior to 1950 the courts were rarely asked to review any laws that restricted access to information, although the mere presence in the Constitution of the First Amendment had no doubt inhibited public authorities from censorship of print. In a series of landmark decisions in the 1950s, the Supreme Court defined quite rigidly what was indeed the acceptable basis for prosecuting publishers of printed materials or the producers of films on grounds of obscenity.

For the most part, censorship today is aimed at the purchase of materials by libraries or their use as textbooks. Pressures from both right and left and from religious, ethnic, and other concerned groups are a problem for textbook publishers and selectors. There has been a significant rise in the number of censoring actions during the 1980s. Several groups concerned with the rise in restricting access to information reported recently that during the 1986-87 academic year there was a 21 percent increase over the prior year and a 168 percent jump since 1982.

John Buchanan, of People for the American Way, attributes the national increase in restricting freedom of information to the televised preaching of Christian evangelists and the greater activism of conservative religious groups. Buchanan pointed out "that censorship is on the rise because you have militant national groups that are stimulating cases (and) because every time you turn on a television set you can hear a Pat Robertson, a Jerry Falwell or a Jimmy Swaggart talk about the evil of 'secular humanism' in public education."

This rise of censoring actions has for the time being been dealt a setback by recent federal court decisions. In one case a federal appeals judge overturned a lower court ruling that Christian fundamentalist children in Hawkins County, Tennessee, had their rights violated when school officials used reading texts that discussed feminism and pacifism. In another case an appellate court reversed a ruling that banned from Alabama schools 44 textbooks said to promote secular humanism as a religion. In Arkansas the statute mandating the teaching of "creation science" has been held unconstitutional.

It should be noted, however, that public pressures with regard to the selection of materials for libraries and textbooks come from people located along the political spectrum, are found in all areas of the country, and cover nearly all kinds of subject matter.

It is difficult to overcome one's own upbringing and value systems and assume a totally neutral stance in the selection of materials for inclusion in libraries. The Office for Intellectual Freedom of the American Library Association has in many of its documents adopted the concept of diversity in collection development as a goal libraries should be aiming toward to best serve this country's pluralistic society.

Despite an overall trend toward greater openness of access to materials as evidenced by the recent court rulings, private censorship is very much a live issue. If we are to continue to guarantee our rights under the First Amendment of the Constitution, we must continue our vigilance of those attempts at restricting access to information and intellectual freedom.

In this book, Censorship and Intellectual Freedom: An Annotated Bibliography, Frank Hoffmann has put together a document which will serve as a source for those charged with that vigilance.

Dr. William Pichette
Sam Houston State University

PREFACE

This reference volume is intended to act as a general introduction to the field of intellectual freedom and censorship. It is aimed at students in high schools and institutions of higher learning (i.e., junior colleges, colleges and universities) as a means of preparing assignments as well as more intensive research. Instructors and general readers interested in the subject should also find the book to be of value.

The majority of materials--predominantly books, periodical articles, and legal materials--cited in the work can be located in the collections of medium- or large-sized public libraries as well as in most academic libraries. In addition, the average high school library collection is likely to contain a substantial portion of the book's entries. The harder-to-find titles--e.g., articles in law journals, older monographs--can be obtained through either interlibrary loan or personal visits to larger libraries located in the majority of urban centers and university communities (particularly those with law schools, library schools, and criminal justice programs).

The book is divided into five parts, each of which provides a different perspective on the field of intellectual freedom and censorship. The parts are further divided by a system of subheadings; the material included is organized alphabetically by main entry--i.e., author or title--under each of these headings. Users who find that the Table of Contents does not direct them to the information they need are encouraged to consult the index at the end of the book.

All materials relevant to a particular subject are designated by means of a code number. These numbers are arranged consecutively in the main text of the book, thereby facilitating ease of location. Each entry includes basic bibliographic data--for books: author(s)/ book title/edition/volume/place of publication/publishers/date of publication; and, for journal articles: author(s)/article title/title of journal/volume and number of issue/date of issue/pagination of article. The citation is followed by a concise descriptive annotation. The annotation serves as a means of determining whether or not the user might wish to consult the original source. It should be noted that the annotations are evaluative in the sense that the overall volume has included only those materials which possess (1) utility for research; (2) a reasonable degree of depth in their treatment of the subject matter; and (3) a lucidity rendering them easily understood by the typical lay reader. A premium has also been placed upon items which are considered to be either milestones in the literature or representative of a particular point of view. As previously noted, the general accessibility of the source is also given serious attention.

For those users desiring to explore particular topics beyond what is included in the book, additional examples are provided in the introductions to parts II, IV, and V. It should be noted that many of the sources cited in the book possess comprehensive bibliographies of their own. The most notable of these works is Ralph E. McCoy's Freedom of the Press. This source, which includes a supplementary volume bringing the coverage up through 1977, is a truly comprehensive annotated bibliography devoted to all facets of intellectual freedom and censorship. It--and other works of its kind--are highly recommended to those interested in further study of the topic.

The book concludes with two indexes: Personal Name and Subject. Both include page numbers (for non-entry sections) and citation numbers (referring directly to particular entries). Page numbers have been underscored to distinguish them. A key word approach has been employed, omitting only generic terms central to all or most entries; e.g., United States, the First Amendment, various courts (except the Supreme Court). Material in bibliographies and the appendixes in Part V have also been omitted from the indexes.

Frank Hoffmann
Sam Houston State University
Huntsville, TX

PART I:

THE THEORETICAL FOUNDATIONS OF CENSORSHIP AND INTELLECTUAL FREEDOM

The Intellectual Freedom Newsletter succinctly delineates the inter-relationship of censorship and intellectual freedom.

> In basic terms, intellectual freedom means the right of any person to hold any belief whatever on any subject, and to express such belief or ideas in whatever way the person believes appropriate. The freedom to express one's beliefs or ideas through any mode of communication becomes virtually meaningless, however, when accessibility to such expression is denied to other persons (i.e., the intrusion of censorship). [1] For this reason, the definition of intellectual freedom has a second, integral part: namely, the right of unrestricted access to all information and ideas regardless of the medium of communication used. Intellectual freedom implies a circle, and that circle is broken if either freedom of expression or access to the ideas expressed is stifled. [2]

The importance of intellectual freedom to our nation's founding fathers was such that they made it the essence of the First Amendment of the Bill of Rights. This commitment did not then--and should not now--signify that intellectual freedom is an American brighright, sufficiently ingrained into our character so as to be more or less taken for granted. As noted by Robert B. Downs,

> The framers of the U.S. Constitution of 1787 were educated, highly literate, and widely-read men intimately acquainted with the centuries of struggle between tyranny and freedom that had been going on in England and more recently in America. The long record of oppression and suppression formed a backdrop as the leaders proceeded to build the government of the United States on the sovereignty of the people and their rights as citizens of a republic. [3]

Downs goes on to note that the Bill of Rights was challenged

almost immediately by various elements of American society. In 1798,
Congress enacted a series of Alien and Sedition laws in reaction to
the threat to social order posed by the developments abroad in the
wake of the French Revolution. In 1835, Congress defeated a proposal by President Andrew Jackson to enact legislation prohibiting
the use of the mails for "incendiary publications intended to insti-
gate the slaves to insurrection." In more recent times we have
witnessed the internment of Japanese-Americans in concentration
camps during World War II and the specter of "McCarthyism" in the
early fifties. While the examples cited above fall into the political
realm, a number of other areas have also been characterized by fre-
quent censorial attacks: social values and traditions, sexuality (more
specifically, obscenity and pornography), and religion. In short,
every generation since 1790 has--in varying degrees and intent--re-
defined and reinterpreted the First Amendment.

> Though the language is clear and explicit, "Congress shall
> make no law ... abridging the freedom of speech, or of the
> press," Congress, the courts, and executive powers have
> repeatedly done, or at least attempted to do exactly that.
> One theory used to circumscribe or circumvent the Amend-
> ment was use-abuse or liberty versus license. Under the
> notion, a distinction was made between right and wrong use
> of speech and press, i.e., liberty as against license. Super-
> seding that doctrine to some extent was Justice Holmes'
> 'clear and present danger' test, according to which liberty
> of press and speech would remain unrestricted as long as
> public safety was not imperiled.... A new theory that has
> come into vogue in more recent judicial decisions is 'balanc-
> ing of interest,' as between public and private rights and
> welfare. All of these theories, it should be noted, infringe
> on the unqualified guarantees of the First Amendment. [4]

The materials cited in this chapter will assist in delineating
core intellectual freedom concepts--e.g., censorship, the First Amendment, obscenity and pornography--as well as providing a historical
framework (see Table 1) and an assessment of relevant research.
The application of these concepts to practice-based settings are
covered in the remaining sections: (II) the courts; (III) selected
professions; (IV) individuals and groups either undercutting or upholding First Amendment rights; and (V) the mass media.

TABLE 1: Milestones in the History of Censorship in the U.S. [5]

1735   John Peter Zenger, owner of the newspaper, The New York

TABLE 1 (cont.)

Weekly, is charged with seditious libel. The case's
legacy includes: (1) the establishment of truth as a defense
of libel; (2) the institution of the right of the Jury to decide
libelousness; and (3) the realization that free expression cannot be at the pleasure of the government as it is incapable
of deciding what is truthful and what expression has merit
to be allowed to be exchanged in the marketplace of political
controversy.

1787   The institution of the U.S. Constitution and Bill of Rights.

1815   Commonwealth of Pennsylvania v. Sharples represented the
first reported case of importance involving a battle over freedom in sexual literature and art. Jesse Sharples was convicted of exhibiting "a lewd, wicked, scandalous, infamous,
and obscene painting, representing a man in an obscene, im-
pudent, and indecent posture with a woman, to the manifest
corruption and subversion of youth, and other citizens of
the commonwealth." The case indicated that obscenity was a
common-law offense in England at the time of the American
Revolution and hence became part of the common law of Pennsylvania.

1868   The adoption of the Fourteenth Amendment to the U.S. Constitution. The new law signified a recognition of the federal
government's responsibility to protect citizens from abuses
by state jurisdictions. Section 1 states,
    "All persons born or naturalized in the United States, and
    subject to the jurisdiction thereof, are citizens of the
    United States and of the State wherein they reside. No
    State shall make or enforce any law which shall abridge
    the privileges or immunities of citizens of the United States;
    nor shall any State deprive any person of life, liberty, or
    property, without due process of law; nor deny to any
    person within its jurisdiction the equal protection of the
    laws."

1873   The Comstock Act of 1873 was a product largely of the pressures applied by crusader Anthony Comstock. The Congressional ruling had the practical effect of controlling the use of
mails to disseminate obscene materials. It represented one
of the earliest--and most far-reaching--examples of censorship
at the hands of the federal government.

1913   In United States v. Mitchell Kennerley and Hagar Revelly, the
defense protested the 1868 Hicklin Rule on Obscenity--a landmark case which determined the test of obscenity to be whether
the tendency of the matter in question is to deprave and corrupt those whose minds are open to such immoral influences--

TABLE 1 (cont.)

indicating that it was not relevant within the context of the understanding and morality of that time.

1930   The Tariff Act of 1930 modified an earlier ruling which had forbidden customs officials from allowing the works of such classic writers as Voltaire, Rousseau, and Boccaccio to be brought into the U.S. Henceforth, the importation of classics and books of recognized scientific and literary merit was permitted.

1934   In United States v. One Book Called "Ulysses", the Federal District Court of New York ruled that Joyce's novel was not legally obscene, thereby halting efforts to prevent its entry into the country. The case was pivotal in its use of the "literary merit" argument as a defense against prosecution; it is seen as a forerunner of later judgments which achieved protection on free speech grounds (e.g., Commonwealth of Pennsylvania v. Gordon et al.).

1939   The American Library Association adopts the Library's Bill of Rights, the precursor of the present Library Bill of Rights, the profession's basic policy statement on intellectual freedom involving library materials.

1940   The American Library Association establishes the Committee on Intellectual Freedom to Safeguard the Rights of Library Users to Freedom of Inquiry (currently known as the Intellectual Freedom Committee). Its main function has been to recommend policies concerning intellectual freedom as well as to promote the concept to librarians, patrons, and the public at large.

1949   Commonwealth of Pennsylvania v. Gordon et al. represented the first notable effort by American courts to address whether or not sexual expressions, like political or religious expressions, might be entitled to First Amendment protection. Accordingly, the suppression of literature alleged to be obscene could only be tolerated upon showing that there existed "a clear and present danger that the book will cause criminal behavior"; this was to become one of the primary constitutional approaches taken by the American Civil Liberties Union and other lawyers in subsequent efforts to do away with obscenity censorship.

1953   The Freedom to Read Statement is drafted by a group of librarians, publishers, lawyers, businessmen, authors, journalists, and educators. The document was endorsed officially by the American Library Association on June 25, 1953, and subsequently by the American Book Publishers Council, American Booksellers Association, Book Manufacturers' Institute,

TABLE 1 (cont.)

and other national groups. Its essential point was that the
freedom to read is essential to our democracy.

1957   In Roth v. United States, the Supreme Court convicted the
        publishers and distributors of literature (including the periodi-
        cals American Aphrodite and Good Times, A Review of the
        World of Pleasure) held to violate the postal law. This land-
        mark case required that laws directed against obscenity "safe-
        guard the protection of freedom of speech and press for ma-
        terial which does not treat sex in a manner appealing to
        prurient interest." As a result, publishers, authors, editors,
        police officials, prosecutors, and judges are still straining to
        see the limits of the constitutional law protecting sexual ex-
        pression.

1962   In Manual Enterprises v. Day, the Supreme Court reversed
        the lower federal court actions which had refused to give in-
        junctive relief against the Postmaster General's ban on the
        mailing of certain magazines featuring photographs of nude
        males designed to appeal to homosexual interests--Manual,
        Trim, and Grecian Guild Pictorial. Justice Harlan observed
        that the "magazines cannot be deemed so offensive on their
        face as to affront current community standards of decency--a
        quality which we shall hereafter refer to as 'patent offensive-
        ness' or 'indecency.' " This case also allowed the Court to
        rule for the first time that the "community" embodied in the
        test for obscenity, certainly when a federal scheme of censor-
        ship was involved, was not local or parochial, but "national"--
        taking in "all parts of the United States whose population re-
        flects many different ethnic and cultural backgrounds."

1963   In Ginzburg v. United States, the defendant--publisher of a
        magazine (Eros), a newsletter (Liaison), and a manual of sex-
        ual information (The Housewife's Handbook on Selective Promis-
        cuity)--was found guilty by the U.S. District Court of Phila-
        delphia of distributing obscene materials through the U.S.
        mail. The defendant, Ralph Ginzburg, was sentenced to five
        years in prison and a fine of $28,000. On March 21, 1966,
        the Supreme Court upheld the conviction. The unexpected
        factor in the Court's decision was the introduction of a new
        determinant of obscenity, one involving the promotion and
        advertisement of the works in question. The works of Ginz-
        burg and another publisher, Edward Mishkin (Mishkin v. New
        York), were the first the Supreme Court ever found to be
        obscene.

1964   In Jacobellis v. Ohio, the Supreme Court reversed Ohio's con-
        viction for the distribution of a film called The Lovers. With
        Jacobellis, the Roth formula for identifying obscenity came to

TABLE 1 (cont.)

involve a three-pronged test; i.e., the material had (1) to
have its dominant appeal to the prurient interests of persons;
(2) to be patently offensive to contemporary national community
standards; and (3) to be utterly without any kind of social
importance.

1966   In A Book Named John Cleland's "Memoirs of a Woman of
        Pleasure" v. Attorney General of the Commonwealth of Massa-
        chusetts, the lawyer, Charles Rembar, was able to persuade
        the Supreme Court to strengthen the proposition that only
        material empty of value could be brought within the scope of
        obscenity laws. Justice Brennan clarified the implications of
        Roth's social value rule, as extended in Jacobellis:
            "A book cannot be proscribed unless it is found to be ut-
            terly without redeeming social value. This is so even
            though the book is found to possess the requisite prurient
            appeal and to be patently offensive. Each of the three
            federal criteria is to be applied independently; the social
            value of the book can neither be weighed against nor can-
            celed by its prurient appeal or patent offensiveness."

1969   In Stanley v. Georgia, the Supreme Court found that, while
        the First Amendment does not protect obscenity, it does pro-
        tect the right of an individual to possess obscene material
        for private use. The court modified its treatment of hard-
        core pornography, indicating that for many persons, doubt-
        less most, it is unedifying but harmless. Accordingly, the
        Georgia state law rendering it a crime to "possess" porno-
        graphy is unconstitutional.

1970   The release of the Report of the U.S. Commission on Obscenity
        and Pornography, originally established by the Johnson ad-
        ministration to conduct a study and "recommend advisable,
        appropriate, effective, and constitutional means to deal effec-
        tively with [the] traffic in obscenity and pornography."
        Stanley Kauffmann notes that, as little as ten years ago, the
        recommendations of the Report "would have been read only
        in the most liberal journals."

1973   The Miller v. California decisions modified the guidelines for
        the determination of obscenity: (1) whether the average per-
        son, applying contemporary community standards, would find
        that the work, taken as a whole, appeals to the prurient in-
        terest; (2) whether the work depicts or describes, in a pat-
        ently offensive way, sexual conduct specificially defined by
        the applicable state law; and (3) whether the work, taken
        as a whole, lacks serious literary, artistic, political, or scien-
        tific value. The decision further stated that "to require a
        state to structure obscenity proceeding around evidence of a

TABLE 1 (cont.)

national 'community standard' would be an exercise in futility
... people in different states vary in their tastes and attitudes
and this diversity is not to be strangled by the absolutism
of imposed uniformity."

1986   The Government Printing Office published the Final Report
        of the Attorney General's Commission on Pornography. The
        Meese Commission, by its conduct and by its report, was
        criticised in many quarters for revealing little regard for the
        First Amendment. Maxwell Lillienstein termed the Commission
        as "officially inspired vigilantism." Christie Hefner considered
        the ultimate failure of the report to be that "it misdirects
        sincere people's attention away from thinking about the real
        causes of violence and abuse."

NOTES

1. The information within the parenthesis was supplied by the author.

2. Intellectual Freedom Manual, compiled by the Office for Intellect-
    ual Freedom of the American Library Association. 2nd ed. Chi-
    cago: American Library Association, 1983. p. vii.

3. Downs, Robert B. "Freedom of Speech and Press: Development
    of a Concept," In: The First Freedom Today, edited by Robert
    B. Downs and Ralph E. McCoy. Chicago: American Library
    Association, 1984. p. 5.

4. Ibid., p. 6.

5. Table 1 has employed material in Edward De Grazia's Censorship
    Landmarks (New York: Bowker, 1969); Martha Boaz's "Censor-
    ship," Encyclopedia of Library and Information Science, Volume
    4 (New York: Marcel Dekker, 1970); Anne Haight's Banned
    Books, 4th ed. (New York: Bowker, 1973).

A. BACKGROUND READINGS ON THE
FIRST AMENDMENT

1. Anastaplo, George. Constitutionalist: Notes on the First Amend-
   ment. Dallas: Southern Methodist University, 1971.
   Anastaplo analyzes the practical implications of the First
   Amendment on contemporary life.

2. Barron, Jerome A., and C. Thomas Dienes. Handbook of Free
   Speech and Free Press. Boston: Little, Brown, 1979.
   The work is intended to provide the legal profession with a
   short but comprehensive discussion of the central issues in the
   contemporary law of free speech and free press. The major
   headings include: (1) Controlling Speech Content: Clear and
   Present Danger; (2) The Doctrine of Prior Restraint; (3) Speech
   in the Local Forum; (4) Commercial Speech: Old And New; (5)
   Symbolic Speech; (6) The Rise of the Public Law of Defamation;
   (7) The New Public Law of Privacy; (8) The Newsgathering
   Process and Constitutional Privilege; (9) Free Press and Fair
   Trial; (10) Obscenity.

3. Bartlett, Jonathan E. The First Amendment in a Free Society.
   New York: Wilson, 1979.
   An analysis of the protections provided by the First Amend-
   ment.

4. Bosmajian, Haig A., ed. The Principles and Practices of Freedom
   of Speech. Boston: Houghton Mifflin, 1971.
   The anthology incorporates notable legislation, writings, and
   court cases concerned with First Amendment rights. Includes:
   Milton's Areopagitica, Mill's Of the Liberty of Thought and Discussion, the Alien and Sedition Acts of 1798, Roth v. U.S.
   (1957), Ginzburg v. U.S. (1966), and Thomas Emerson's "Towards a General Theory of the First Amendment."

5. Brennan, William J., Jr. "Guaranteeing Individual Liberty,"
   USA Today. 115:2496 (September 1986) 40-42.
   Brennan argues that "the task of achieving the constitutional
   ideal of liberty and individual dignity protected through law must
   be the work not just of judges and lawyers, but of all of us."

6. Dennis, Everette E., Donald M. Gillmor, and David L. Grey,
   editors. Justice Hugo Black and the First Amendment. Des

Moines: Iowa State University, 1978.
The collection of essays analyzes Black's interpretational posture on the Bill of Rights, specifically in the area of communications law.

7. Doctorow, E. L. "A Citizen Reads the Constitution," The Nation. 244:7 (February 21, 1987) 208-217.
An adaptation of a talk delivered by the renowned author at Independence Hall in September 1986. He examines the U.S. Constitution as a composition; that is, the implications of its literary characteristics with respect to its applications to everyday life.

8. Downs, Robert B., and Ralph E. McCoy, editors. The First Freedom Today: Critical Issues Relating to Censorship and to Intellectual Freedom. Chicago: American Library Association, 1984.
A collection of essays reviewing the continuing debate over the nature and scope of freedom of speech, the press, and access to information.

9. Emerson, Thomas I. "Statement on the First Amendment," In: The First Freedom Today, edited by Robert B. Downs and Ralph E. McCoy. Chicago: American Library Association, 1984. pp. 38-43.
Emerson sets forth a general theory on freedom of expression, the core concept being that "a fundamental distinction must be drawn between conduct which consists of expression and conduct which consists of action." The second half of the essay, "Application of the Theory to the Publication of Classified Information," consists of testimony before a U.S. Senate Judiciary Committee subcommittee looking into questions on freedom of the press.

10. Emerson, Thomas I. "Freedom of Expression," In: The First Freedom Today, edited by Robert B. Downs and Ralph E. McCoy. Chicago: American Library Association, 1984. pp. 36-38. Reprinted in: The Bill of Rights Today. New York: Public Affairs Committee, 1973.
Emerson notes the scope and limits of the First Amendment as it has been interpreted by the courts.

11. Emerson, Thomas I. Toward A General Theory of the First Amendment. New York: Random House, 1966.
Emerson looks at the practical applications of the First Amendment as well as its theoretical foundations. He notes that the Supreme Court is more hesitant to grant First Amendment protection to speech, writings, etc., of a potentially troublesome nature.

12. Harris, Richard. Freedom Spent. Boston: Little, Brown, 1976.

Harris argues that while the myth of freedom has been
pounded into our heads since birth, the reality of freedom remains an elusive entity. He attributes this to the fact that
the judiciary "nearly always serves the interests of the state
rather than its citizens." He lends credence to his thesis by
outlining the experiences of three different individuals who found
themselves involved in drawn-out legal struggles after exercising what they had thought were their constitutional rights.

13. Pilpel, Harriet F. "Freedom of the Press--American Style,"
     In: The First Freedom Today, edited by Robert B. Downs and
     Ralph E. McCoy. Chicago: American Library Association, 1984.
     pp. 43-49. Reprinted in: Publishers Weekly. 203 (March 12,
     1973) 26-29.
        Pilpel, a New York lawyer specializing in First Amendment
     cases, discusses the constituent parts of freedom of the press:
     (1) freedom to speak, (2) the right to listen, (3) the right not
     to speak, (4) the right not to be forced to listen or see, (5)
     the right of anonymity, (6) the right to know, (7) the right of
     access, and (8) against whom to apply this constitutional guar-
     antee.

14. Rembar, Charles. Perspective. New York: Arbor House, 1975.
        A compilation of essays concerned with the role of the First
     Amendment in upholding the individual freedoms in American
     society.

15. Van Alstyne, William W. Interpretations of the First Amend-
     ment. Durham, N.C.: Duke University Press, 1984.
        An insightful apology for the First Amendment divided into
     the following topics: (1) Interpreting This Constitution; (2)
     A Graphic Review of the Free Speech Clause; (3) The Con-
     troverted Uses of the Press Clause; (4) Scarcity, Property and
     Government Policy: The First Amendment as a Mobius Strip.
     The author is a law professor at Duke University and consul-
     tant to various Congressional committees on constitutional issues
     concerned with the First Amendment.

History of the First Amendment

16. Brant, Irving. The Bill of Rights; Its Origin and Meaning.
     Indianapolis: Bobbs-Merrill, 1965.
        Brant devotes a sizeable portion of the book to the evolution
     and interpretation of First Amendment rights in American history.

17. Downs, Robert B. "Freedom of Speech and Press: Development
     of a Concept," Library Trends. 19:1 (July 1970) 8-18. Re-
     printed in: The First Freedom Today, edited by Robert B.
     Downs and Ralph E. McCoy. Chicago: American Library As-
     sociation, 1984. pp. 2-8.

A historical survey of the evolution of First Amendment
rights in America. Precedents in England--going back as far
as the High Middle Ages--are covered.

18. Downs, Robert B. "Issues of the Past Decade," In: The First
Freedom Today, edited by Robert B. Downs and Ralph E. Mc-
Coy. Chicago: American Library Association, 1984. pp. 17-
27.
    Downs reviews and analyzes the vital issues relating to in-
tellectual freedom during the 1967-1977 period. The headings
employed are: Pentagon Papers; Classified Information; Prior
Restraint; Press Gag Orders; Fair Trials vs. Free Press; Pri-
vacy; Rights of Special Groups; Obscenity and Pornography;
1970 Commission on Pornography and Obscenity; Textbooks.
Based on the Foreword to Ralph E. McCoy's Freedom of the
Press: Ten Year Supplement (1967-1977), published by the
Southern Illinois University Press in 1979.

19. Haiman, Franklyn S. Freedom of Speech. Skokie, Ill.: National Textbook Company, 1979.
    The work is primarily concerned with reviewing the judicial
precedents relating to freedom of speech in the twentieth century. The author notes that while the focus is on speech, defined as the communication of ideas and feelings through such
media as public speaking, rallies and marches, leaflets and
picket signs, armbands and flag burnings, plays, movies, radio
and television, the principles covered are applicable to the print
media.

20. Hentoff, Nat. The First Freedom. New York: Delacorte, 1980.
    An expansive survey of the First Amendment's history.
Hentoff focuses on the vital role it has played in forming the
underpinning of American democracy.

21. Konvitz, Milton R. Expanding Liberties; Freedom's Gains in
Postwar America. New York: Viking, 1966.
    A scholarly examination of the growth of individual rights
in the areas of religious freedom, freedom of association, academic freedom, and obscene and pornographic publications since
World War II.

22. Levy, Leonard W. Freedom of Speech and Press in Early American History; Legacy of Suppression. New York: Harper, 1963.
    Levy dispels the myth that freedom of thought and expres-
sion was cherished in colonial American society.

23. McCoy, Ralph E. "The Evolution of the First Amendment,"
In: The First Freedom Today, edited by Robert B. Downs and
Ralph E. McCoy. Chicago: American Library Association, 1984.
pp. 28-36.
    McCoy delineates some of the changing concepts of the First

Amendment as the public and the courts have confronted new
issues in politics, religion, sex, and personal libel. The application of the First Amendment to mass media such as films,
radio, and television is also covered.

24. McCoy, Ralph E. "Freedom of the Press and Unbelief," In:
The First Freedom Today, edited by Robert B. Downs and Ralph
E. McCoy. Chicago: American Library Association, 1984. pp.
8-17.
   McCoy surveys the evolution of First Amendment rights in
England and the U.S., beginning with the evolution of the
printing press up through the Moral Majority movement.

25. Roche, John P. "American Liberty: An Examination of the
'Tradition' of Freedom," In: Aspects of Liberty, edited by
Milton R. Konvitz and Clinton Rossiter. Ithaca, N.Y.: Cornell
University Press, 1958.
   Roche's essay is particularly valuable for its analysis of the
Fourteenth Amendment as a safeguard of First Amendment rights.
He notes that, "the growth of federal power has led to the im-
plementation of a principle of national protection of individual
liberty against the actions of states or municipalities by the
judiciary and to judicial decisions excluding the states from areas
of jurisdiction of vital significance in civil liberty." (p. 156)

26. Tedford, Thomas L. Freedom of Speech in the United States.
New York: Random House, 1985.
   A historical survey of the development of freedom of speech,
designed to serve as a textbook for a course on this topic.

Religion and the First Amendment

(See Also: Advocates of Censorship)

27. Combee, Jerry H. "Evangelicals and the First Amendment,"
National Review. 38:20 (October 24, 1986) 40-42, 61-62.
   Combee focuses on the "practically forgotten" fact that we
owe separation of church and state in America today at least
as much to the influence of evangelical Christianity as we do
to the so-called rationalistic Enlightenment and Madison and
Jefferson. His revisionist stance argues that the gulf between
Evangelicals and Enlightenment thought may not have been
nearly as great as supposed by contemporary intellectual history.

28. Hale, John P. "Where He Started & Where He Stands; A Case
Against Charles Curran," Commonweal. 114:2 (January 30,
1987) 47-51.
   Hale, a Manhattan-based trial lawyer who regularly advises
and represents the Archdiocese of New York City on public

policy questions, argues that Father Curran stands far removed
from his church as he challenges the fundamental teachings not
only of the popes, but of the Old and New Testaments.

29. Komonchak, Joseph A. "Issues Behind the Curran Case; The
     Church & Modernity: From Defensiveness to Engagement,"
     Commonweal. 114:2 (January 30, 1987) 43-47.
         Komonchak, a theologian at the Catholic University of America,
     attempts to provide a philosophical framework for Father Cur-
     ran's brand of scholarly dissent. He considers it unfortunate
     that a deeply Catholic effort at a creative and critical engage-
     ment with modern culture appears likely to be postponed yet
     again.

30. "Religious Intolerance--1986," Newsletter on Intellectual Freedom.
     36:1 (January 1987) 8, 22.
         Excerpts from a report on religious intolerance in American
     politics, with specific reference to the 1986 election campaign,
     released in October 1986 by the People for the American Way.
     Most instances fall into the category of a candidate claiming to
     be chosen by God for political office, and/or identifying an op-
     ponent with Satan.

Professions and the First Amendment (See: PART III)

Rights of Youth Under the First Amendment

31. Archer, Jules. Who's Running Your Life? A Look at Young
     People's Rights. New York: Harcourt Brace Jovanovich, 1979.
         A primer for young adults; it is intended to provide them
     with an awareness of their constitutional rights.

32. Broderick, Dorothy. "Intellectual Freedom and Young Adults,"
     In: Library Lit. 9--The Best of 1978, edited by Bill Katz.
     Metuchen, N.J.: Scarecrow, 1979. pp. 346-358. Reprinted
     from: Drexel Library Quarterly. 14 (1978) 65-77.
         Broderick determines the sources behind attempts to limit
     the rights of young people. She concludes that, "the role of
     the library as an information agency is to buy and publicize
     the materials that will allow young people to make informed de-
     cisions about their own lives."

33. Farley, John J. "The Reading of Young People," Library Trends.
     19:1 (July 1970) 81-88.
         Farley discusses the complexities involved in rendering intel-
     lectual freedom a meaningful concept in the lives of young people.
     He concludes that, "the liberal ideal of the free marketplace of
     ideas, for all of its near-impossibility of perfect realization, is
     ... a viable ideal; indeed its maintenance as an ideal may very

well be a condition for the continuance of any worthwhile civilization."

34. Rollock, Barbara. "Caveat Lector: A Librarian's View of Controversial Children's Books," Catholic Library World. 46 (October 1974) 108-110.
   An apology for the rights of children "to a wide and varied scope of the best available materials."

35. University of Wisconsin, Madison, Wisconsin, June 14-18, 1976. The Young Adult & Intellectual Freedom: Proceedings, edited by Mary L. Woodworth. Madison: University of Wisconsin School of Library Service, 1977.
   Nineteen presentations have been included, covering the following areas: (1) censorship--an overview, in film, science, humanities, and schools; (2) legal aspects; (3) realistic adult novels; (4) transitional novels; (5) evolutionists vs. creationists; (6) portrayal of ethnicity and ethnic groups; (7) strategies in dealing with administrations and school boards; (8) resources outside the community; (9) reports on two censorship and intellectual freedom institutes; and (10) results of an intellectual freedom study.

Research and the First Amendment

36. Barbour, Alton B. Free Speech Attitude Consistency. Denver, Colo.: University of Denver, 1968. Ph.D. dissertation, available from University Microfilms, no. 68-17,836.
   The study found that 93 percent of the respondents professed to believe in free speech; however, with respect to practical applications, the subjects indicated an opposition to free speech as outlined in Supreme Court cases.

37. Barbour, Alton B. "Survey Research in Free Speech Attitudes," In: Free Speech Yearbook, 1971. New York: Speech Communication Association, 1971. pp. 28-35.
   Barbour summarizes the published literature dealing with free speech attitudes. He states that, "on the basis of literature available about free speech attitudes it is reasonable to conclude that Americans are poorly informed about their constitutional rights of free speech, and that a large number of Americans, young and old, are willing to restrict the free speech of others, particularly with regard to threatening issues."

38. Beach, Richard. "Issue of Censorship and Research on Effects of and Response to Reading," In: Dealing With Censorship, edited by James E. Davis. Urbana, Ill.: NCTE, 1979. pp. 131-159.
   Beach reports the following conclusions based upon his survey of the literature: (1) readers' responses are highly unique

and vary considerably from one book to another; (2) differ-
ences in readers' age, personality, values, sex, literary training, and previous reading result in highly unique meanings for
different readers; (3) there is little short-term change in values
or attitudes from reading certain books; (4) there is little or
no evidence of any relationship between reading and deviant
behavior; (5) exposure to sexual material may be an integral
part of normal adolescent sexual development, providing information about sex not available elsewhere--conversely, adolescents deprived of such material do, in some cases, experience
deviant social development; (6) when a book is not available,
desire for that book is not reduced, but enhanced. The article
includes an exhaustive bibliography.

39. "New Survey Finds People Oppose Censorship," Newsletter on
Intellectual Freedom. 35:6 (November 1986) 202-203.
      According to a poll conducted by Penn & Schoen Associates
of New York for Americans for Constitutional Freedom (ACF),
more than 80 percent of Americans oppose restrictions on access
to lawful books and magazines. Another survey, however, com-
missioned by the Freespeech Committee in Minnesota, indicates
that a large minority, and, depending upon the issue, a majority
of Minnesotans, support restrictions on free expression. A
breakdown of the findings of both studies--along with interpre-
tative analysis--constitutes the bulk of the article.

40. "Report Finds Censorship on Rise," Newsletter on Intellectual
Freedom. 35:6 (November 1986) 203.
      A summary of the findings of the People for the American
Way's fourth annual study of censorship, Attacks on the Freedom to Learn, 1985-86, reveals that censorship of books and
public school curriculums has been increasing dramatically; the
number of incidents has risen 35 percent during the past year.
Most significantly, the nature of the attacks has shifted from
the targeting of "dirty books" to targeting ideas with which the
would-be censors disagree. While censorship efforts don't origi-
nate solely with the political and religious right, the survey indicated that almost one half of the incidents reported were organized by such groups as Phyllis Schlafly's Eagle Forum,
Beverly LaHaye's Concerned Women for America, Pat Robertson's
National Legal Foundation, and the Citizens for Excellence in
Education (a component group of the National Association of
Christian Educators).

B. CENSORSHIP

(See also: Advocates of Censorship)

41. Abraham, Henry J. "Censorship," In: International Encyclopedia

of the Social Sciences. Volume 2. New York: Macmillan, 1968.
pp. 356-360.
   A historical survey ranging from classical antiquity to the
present day. Abraham cites the rationale most frequently used
by censors to justify their actions.

42. Anastaplo, George. "Censorship," In: The New Encyclopaedia
     Britannica. 15th ed. Volume 15: Macropaedia. Chicago: En-
     cyclopaedia Britannica, Inc., 1986. pp. 634-641.
        Concise survey of the topic. Headings include: Concerns
     Relevant to Censorship--the Status of "Individuality"; Require-
     ments of Self-Government: "Freedom of Expression"; History of
     Censorship; Character and Freedom; Bibliography.

43. Berger, Melvin. Censorship. New York: Franklin Watts, 1982.
        Berger offers a concise, objective study of censorship--
     emphasizing its past in America as well as delineating current
     issues surrounding the concept--ideally suited for students who
     are new to the subject.

44. Beth, Loren P. "Censorship," In: The World Book Encyclo-
     pedia. Volume 3. Chicago: World Book, Inc., 1985. pp. 257-
     258.
        Beth provides a concise orientation to the topic. Four types
     of censorship--moral, military, political, and religious--are
     identified and discussed. Methods of censorship are also covered.

45. Boaz, Martha. "Censorship," In: Encyclopedia of Library and
     Information Science, edited by Allen Kent and Harold Lancour.
     Volume 4. New York: Marcel Dekker, 1970. pp. 328-338.
        A concise introduction to the topic, utilizing the following
     headings: Historical Background; Censorship and the Law;
     Recent Cases; Pressure Groups; Tolerance and Intellectual Free-
     dom.

46. Censorship: 500 Years of Conflict. New York: New York Pub-
     lic Library/Oxford University Press, 1984.
        A collection of essays documenting the unending struggle
     between expression and authority. The final three chapters--
     Joel Wiener's "Social Purity and Freedom of Expression," Joan
     Hoff-Wilson's "The Pluralistic Society," and Stephen Spender's
     "Thoughts on Censorship in the World of 1984"--are most rele-
     vant with respect to the American arena. The text is inter-
     spersed throughout with illustrations from the exhibition held
     at the New York Public Library, June 1-October 15, 1984.
     The illustrations from the exhibition which are not included in
     the text are reproduced at the rear of the work, along with
     bibliographic data for all entries.

47. Censorship: For and Against, edited by Harold H. Hart. New
     York: Hart, 1971.

The collection of essays by prominent writers, critics, lawyers, politicians, and clergymen addresses the pros and cons of
censoring books, magazines, films, theater, and government
information. Contributors are Hollis Alpert, Joseph Howard,
Judith Crist, Carey McWilliams, Charles H. Keating, Jr., Eugene
McCarthy, Rebecca West, Ernest van den Haag, Arthur Lelyveld, Max Lerner, Charles Rembar, and Nat Hentoff.

48. Daily, Jay. "Censorship, Contemporary and Controversial Aspects of," In: Encyclopedia of Library and Information Science,
edited by Allen Kent and Harold Lancour. Volume 4. New York:
Marcel Dekker, 1970. pp. 338-381.
     Daily focuses upon the complex issues related to the practice
of censorship. He develops a strong philosophical case for the
defense of intellectual freedom.

49. Hoyt, Olga G., and Edwin P. Hoyt. Censorship In America.
New York: Seabury, 1970.
     The book analyzes the forces attempting to control American
cultural life, including radio, television, film, theater, and fine
arts.

50. Kirk, Russell. "Censorship," In: Collier's Encyclopedia. Volume 5. New York: Macmillan Educational Company, 1985. pp.
629-631.
     A concise survey of censorship, including the following
topics: Church Censorship; State Censorship; Private Censorship; and Current Problems.

51. McClellan, Grant S., editor. Censorship in the United States.
New York: Wilson, 1967.
     The compilation attempts to show how our First Amendment
rights are affected by censorship activities, public or private.
The essays--contributed by such luminaries as William J. Brennan, William O. Douglas, James Reston, Henry Steele Commager,
and Richard Nixon--are organized under the following headings:
(1) Censorship: The Current Debate; (2) The Supreme Court:
More Freedom or Less?; (3) Censorship and Politics; (4) Censorship and Intellectual Freedom; (5) Censorship and Education.

52. McCormick, John, and Mairi MacInnes, editors. Versions of
Censorship: An Anthology. Garden City, N.Y.: Doubleday/
Anchor, 1962.
     The compilation provides a multi-faceted view of the various
strategems employed by the censor.

53. McKeon, Richard. "Censorship," In: The New Encyclopaedia
Britannica: Macropaedia. 15th ed. Volume 3. Chicago: Encyclopaedia Britannica, Inc., 1974. pp. 1082-1090.
     Excellent survey of the topic; includes selective bibliography.

54. Widmer, Eleanor, ed. Freedom and Culture: Literary Censor-
     ship in the 70s. Belmont, CA.: Wadsworth, 1970.
         In the words of Widmer, the work "attempts to bring together
     some of the points of view that both vex and excite our current
     thinking on censorship, in its literary, social, and political con-
     texts." The compilation is intended for courses in literature,
     communications, and the social sciences. Contributions are ar-
     ranged under four units: (I) Principles of Literary Censor-
     ship: Arguments and Counterarguments; (II) Censorship and
     the Young; (III) Case: Censorship and the Novel; (IV) The
     Cultural Context of American Censorship.

55. Widmer, Kingsley, and Eleanor Widmer, editors. Literary Cen-
     sorship: Principles, Cases, Problems. Belmont, Calif.: Wads-
     worth, 1961.
         A book of readings which emphasizes the problematic, open-
     ended nature of intellectual freedom issues. The work is di-
     vided into three major sections: the first presents general
     arguments for and against censorship, followed by an in-depth
     exploration of three specific cases, and concluding with several
     diversified views of the cultural context of contemporary cen-
     sorship. Substantially revised--and retitled--as Freedom and
     Culture: Literary Censorship in the 70s (1970).

                   C. OBSCENITY AND PORNOGRAPHY

56. Anastaplo, George. "Obscenity and Common Sense: Toward a
     Definition of 'Community' and 'Individuality.'" St. Louis Uni-
     versity Law Journal. 16 (Summer 1972) 527-556.
         Anastaplo delineates the tug of war between community in-
     terests and individual self-expression with respect to obscenity.

57. Astor, Gerald. "No Recession in the Skin Trade," Look. 35:13
     (June 29, 1971) 27-36.
         The article surveys the growth of pornography in an increas-
     ingly permissive society.

58. Bosmajian, Haig A., editor and compiler. Obscenity and Free-
     dom of Expression. New York: Franklin, 1976.
         A collection of approximately 100 legal decisions concerned
     with the tension between constitutional rights and obscenity in
     society. The time span covered is 1868 to the mid-1970s.

59. Brown, Phillip. "South Dakota Voters Reject 'Parrish law,'"
     Newsletter on Intellectual Freedom. 28:1 (January 1979) 9,
     15-17.
         An in-depth report of the events leading up to the defeat of
     a proposed obscenity law by South Dakota voters on November

7, 1978. Key provisions of the Draconian bill are cited; it is
noted that opponents found parts which seemed to violate the
First, Fourth, Sixth, Eighth, and Fourteenth Amendments.

60. Burgess, Anthony. "What Is Pornography?" In: Perspectives
on Pornography, by Douglas A. Hughes. New York: St. Martin's, 1970.
      Burgess questions the assumption held by many that porno-
graphy causes tangible harm to its consumers. He notes that
"didactic works" like Mein Kampf and Das Kapital have had more
influence than books "which merely represent life, no matter
how onesidedly."

61. Christenson, Reo M., and A. S. Engel. "Censorship of Pornography?" The Progressive. 34:9 (September 1970) 24-30. Reprinted in: Current. n.123 (November 1970) 31-38.
      Two members of the Political Science Department of Miami Uni-
versity debate whether or not pornography should be censored.

62. Clor, Harry M., ed. Censorship and Freedom of Expression;
Essays on Obscenity and the Law. Chicago: Rand McNally,
1971.
      An anthology focusing on the controversy regarding obscenity
and censorship. The first two selections provide a legal context
from the perspective of American judges who have dealt with
the constitutionality of obscenity censorship. The subsequent
essays present diverse viewpoints on the constitutional issues
and opposing arguments about the dangers of obscenity and the
propriety of censorship as public policy.

63. Fleishman, Stanley. "Censorship: The Law and the Courts,"
Library Trends. 19:1 (July 1970) 74-80.
      A concise survey of court decisions since 1949 which have
influenced American obscenity laws.

64. Gilmore, Donald H. Sex, Censorship, and Pornography. 2
volumes. San Diego: Greenleaf Classics, 1969.
      An historical survey of censorship and obscenity law.

65. Hartogs, Renatus. Four-Letter Word Games: The Psychology
of Obscenity. New York: Dell, 1968.
      A somewhat sensationalized study of the social and psycho-
logical implications of obscenity.

66. Jeffries, John A. Legal Censorship of Obscene Publications:
Search for a Censoring Standard. Bloomington, Ind.: Indiana
University, 1968. Ph.D. dissertation, available from University
Microfilms, no. 69-7,690.
      Jeffries focuses on the issue of "whether the threatened dan-
ger posed by allegedly obscene publications is sufficient to war-
rant use of police and judicial power for its suppression."

67. Kaplan, Abraham. "Obscenity as an Esthetic Category," Law
     and Contemporary Problems. 20:4 (1965) 544-559.
         Kaplan compares pornography to a black mass. His analysis
     of the genre is largely philosophical in tone.

68. Moretti, Daniel S. Obscenity and Pornography; The Law Under
     the First Amendment. London: Oceana, 1984.
         Since obscene material is not protected by the First Amend-
     ment and judicial efforts to find an acceptable definition of ob-
     scenity remain elusive, this work acts as a guide to determin-
     ing what is or is not obscene. Landmark legal cases are dis-
     cussed both in relation to society as a whole and with respect
     to specific areas such as the broadcast media, motion pictures,
     and the telephone. Also includes many useful appendices; e.g.,
     states which have adopted or judicially incorporated the Miller
     test for obscenity, state child pornography statutes, and a
     Model Cable Pornography Statute.

69. Zimmer, Steven L. "How One Southern City Faced the Obscenity
     Standards Issue," Christian Century. 91 (September 25, 1974)
     884-886.
         Zimmer profiles the Jefferson County (Kentucky) Commission
     on Community Standards Related to Obscenity.

PART II:

KEY COURT CASES RELATING TO CENSORSHIP AND INTELLECTUAL FREEDOM

A. AN INTRODUCTION TO THE LEGAL LITERATURE

Legal citations take a form which deviates substantially from the bibliographic material most familiar to the majority of readers. However, they are easy to decipher once the user becomes acquainted with a few rudimentary rules.

A bibliographic entry (or citation) for a court case consists of the following elements:

(1) Name, or style, of the case; e.g., Smith v. Jones.

(2) Publication where the case is found. This information is given in the form shown below:

VOL. NO./PUBLICATION ABBR./PAGE NO.

The publication name is always abbreviated. A list of commonly cited abbreviations is provided in Table 2.

(3) The court that heard the case (if not the United States Supreme Court). The court information is also abbreviated. If the court in question is a district court, the information appears as follows: "N.D. Calif.," where tne "N" represents "north" (other compass points are also used, as is "M" for "middle") and "D" stands for "district." It is important to note that the abbreviation for the state where the court is located is not the standard two-letter scheme employed by the U.S. Post Office.

(4) The date of the decision. With respect to district court cases, the full date is given (e.g., Aug. 14, 1978). In all other cases, only the year is cited.

The citation for a law consists only of element #2 above, with the exception that pagination is replaced by a section number.

Unlike other bibliographies, legal listings are arranged chronologically, starting with the most recent case. The rationale for this practice is that current legal interpretations of the laws can only be ascertained by reference to the most recent cases. Cases are further subdivided by the level of the court handing down the decision; in other words, U.S. Supreme Court cases are listed first, followed by Court of Appeals (circuit court) cases, and then District Court cases.

Legal materials can be obtained in an array of settings. The most comprehensive collection of legal source materials will be located in law school libraries. Most law schools will permit nonstudents to use the library without check-out privileges. Many government depository libraries possess copies of the Supreme Court decisions as well as federal laws and statutes. Large academic libraries will frequently own these sources, particularly in cases where the parent institution offers criminal justice and/or business law courses. Large and medium-sized public libraries usually include federal laws and statutes within their respective collections; in many cases, they can also provide access to case materials. Most counties in the United States have a county law library. The county law library not only possesses these resources, but is open to the public at large. In addition, the information included within the aforementioned materials is available through commercially disseminated data base systems such as LEXIS and WESTLAW.

TABLE 2:   Legal Abbreviations

Cir.	circuit
D.	district
F.2d	Federal Reporter, 2d series (West Publishing)
F.Supp.	Federal Supplement (West Publishing)
S.Ct.	Supreme Court Reporter (West Publishing)
	These cases are also contained in the U.S. Reports, published by the Government Printing Office.
sec.	section
U.S.	United States Reports (GPO)
U.S.C.A.	United States Code Annotated (West Publishing)
	This information is also included in the United States Code, published by the GPO.

B.   CENSORSHIP AND THE LEGAL LITERATURE

The majority of censorship cases involve a violation of someone's First Amendment rights. Due to the vast number of cases concerned with First Amendment violations that have appeared before the state and federal courts, it is possible to list only the most important examples in this chapter. The prime criteria for inclusion were (1) sociopolitical significance, as reflected by reference to the respective cases in both the legal and nonlegal literature, and (2) to illustrate the wide range of activities protected by the First Amendment as well as those falling outside its embrace.

The cases included here are arranged as follows: (1) cases that allege direct First Amendment violations, arranged by subject matter, and (2) cases alleging that a certain federal statute is unconstitutional. With respect to Part 2, an explanation of the statute involved is initially provided, followed by annotations of cases that resolve the question. For those interested in pursuing legal research beyond the annotated entries cited here, a partial list of other First Amendment cases, listed alphabetically by case name, is included at the end of the unit.

TABLE 3:   The First Amendment

"Congress shall make no law respecting an establishment of religion, or prohibiting the free exercise there-
of; or abridging the freedom of speech, or of the press;
or the right of the people peaceably to assemble, and
to petition the Government for a redress of grievances."

C. INDIVIDUAL COURT CASES

Cases that Allege First Amendment Violations

a. Association and Assembly

70. Anderson v. Celebrezze, 460 U.S. 780 (1983)
An independent Presidential candidate challenged the constitutionality of Ohio's filing deadline. Ohio requires that independent candidates for President file intentions by March in
order to be included on the ballot for November's general election. The Supreme Court held that this early deadline places
an unfair burden on the candidate and his supporters and violates their First Amendment rights of association.

71. Brown v. Socialist Workers '74 Campaign Committee (Ohio), 459
U.S. 87 (1982)
The committee brought class action charging that Ohio's Cam-
paign Expense Reporting law, requiring disclosure of names and
addresses of contributors, was unconstitutional. The Supreme
Court held that application of this law to Socialist Workers Party

members violated their First Amendment rights by possibly sub-
jecting them to harassment for their political beliefs.

72. National Association for the Advancement of Colored People v.
     Claiborne Hardware Company, 458 U.S. 886 (1982)
         The NAACP boycotted white merchants in Mississippi. Al-
     though the pickets and demonstrations were peaceful in nature,
     merchants sought restitution for lost business. The Supreme
     Court held that peaceful demonstrations were protected by the
     First Amendment and participants could not be held responsible
     for loss of business.

73. Keyishian v. Board of Regents of the University of the State
     of New York, 385 U.S. 589 (1967)
         The instructors at a state university were dismissed for re-
     fusing to sign a certificate stating that they were not Communists.
     New York required this certificate as a means of preventing the
     appointment or retention of a "subversive" in state employment.
     The Supreme Court ruled that the statute as written was vague
     and overbroad and unconstitutional under the First Amendment.

74. Gay Student Services v. Texas A&M University, 737 F.2d 1317
     (5th Cir. 1984)
         Texas A&M University denied official recognition to a gay
     students' group. The students charged the University with the
     violation of their First Amendment rights. The court found
     that the University's denial lacked justification to be allowable
     under the First Amendment tenets.

75. Johnson v. City of Opelousas, 658 F.2d 1065 (5th Cir. 1981)
         A parent brought action to challenge the juvenile curfew law
     instituted by the city of Opelousas. The mother and her minor
     son charged that the law was unconstitutional in that it violated
     minors' First Amendment freedoms of speech, association, as-
     sembly, and religion by restricting juveniles' access to these
     functions. The court held that the law was unconstitutionally
     overbroad.

                          b. Banned Materials

76. Pico v. Board of Education, Island Trees Union Free School
     District, 457 U.S. 853 (1982)
         Students sought to prevent the school board from removing
     nine books (Slaughterhouse Five, The Naked Ape, Down These
     Mean Streets, Best Short Stories of Negro Writers, Go Ask Alice,
     Laughing Boy, Black Boy, A Hero Ain't Nothin' But A Sandwich,
     Soul on Ice) on First Amendment grounds. The Supreme Court
     held that, because the removal ensued out of the board's dislike
     for the ideas presented, the students' First Amendment rights
     had been violated. Accordingly, the Court ordered that the
     books be returned to the library.

77. Pratt v. Independent School Dist. No. 831, Forest Lake, Minn.,
     670 F.2d 771 (8th Cir. 1982)
          Junior and senior high school students brought action to
     force the school board to return the film version of the short
     story, "The Lottery," to the curriculum. The Supreme Court
     found the school board guilty of violating the First Amendment
     because the film was removed not for scenes depicting violence,
     but rather because the majority of the board found the film's
     religious and ideological themes offensive. The Court disagreed
     with the board's rationale that removal could be justified as a
     result of the availability of the story in print and audio formats.
     The Court ordered the film returned to the curriculum.

78. Bicknell v. Vergennes Union High School Board of Directors,
     638 F.2d 438 (2d Cir. 1980)
          The plaintiff argued that the school board violated students'
     First Amendment rights by removing two books (Dog Day After-
     noon, The Wanderers) from the library due to vulgarity and in-
     decency of language. The court held that the school board did
     not violate the First Amendment and that the students and li-
     brarian had no right to a hearing prior to removal of the books.
     The court also held that young students have no constitutional
     right of access to material deemed inappropriate for young child-
     ren by the school board.

79. Cary v. Board of Educ. of the Adams-Arapahoe School Dist.
     28-J, Aurora, Colo., 598 F.2d 535 (10th Cir. 1979)
          High school teachers brought action against the school board
     which had banned ten books (A Clockwork Orange, The Exorcist,
     The Reincarnation of Peter Proud, New American Poetry, Start-
     ing From San Francisco, The Yage Letters, Coney Island of the
     Mind, Kaddish and Other Poems, Lunch Poems, Rosemary's Baby)
     from an elective reading list of 1,285 books. The court held
     that since teachers could not show that the board rejected these
     books either to promote a particular religious viewpoint or to
     exclude any particular type of thinking or book, exclusion was
     allowed.

80. Minarcini v. Strongsville City School Dist., 541 F.2d 577 (6th
     Cir. 1976)
          High school students brought a class action suit against their
     school district for refusing to approve certain books as texts
     and ordering that the books in question (Catch 22, by Joseph
     Heller; God Bless You, Mr. Rosewater and Cat's Cradle, by
     Kurt Vonnegut) be removed from the library. The board's ac-
     tions went against the faculty recommendation. The court found
     the school board to be within its rights in not selecting these
     books as texts but that they violated the First Amendment in
     removing them from the library.

81. Salvail v. Nashua Board of Educ., 469 F.Supp. 1269 (D.N.H.
     May 7, 1979)

Action was brought against the school board for removing
Ms. magazine from the high school library. The court held
that the board failed to show sufficient government interest to
warrant removal. The magazine was ordered returned to the
library.

82. Right to Read Defense Comm. of Chelsea v. School Comm. of
the City of Chelsea, 454 F.Supp. 703 (D.Mass. July 5, 1978)
    An injunctive order was sought requiring the school com-
mittee to return an anthology of poetry, Male and Female Under
18, to the library shelves. The court held that removal, prompted
by offensive language in some of the selections, did not serve
substantial governmental interest and was, therefore, an infringement on the First Amendment rights of the students and faculty.
The school committee did not show that the book was obscene,
improperly selected, causing shelf space problems, etc. Accordingly, the court ordered the book returned to the library.

c. Commercial Speech

83. Lamar Outdoor Advertising, Inc. v. Mississippi State Tax Commission, 701 F.2d 314 (5th Cir. 1983)
    Advertisers sought injunction prohibiting the enforcement
of a ban against liquor advertising. The court found that the
First Amendment protected commercial speech. Because Mississippi's ban did not directly promote the health and safety of
state residents, the court ruled that the ban was unconstitutional.

d. Libel

84. Gertz v. Robert Welch, Inc., 418 U.S. 323 (1974)
    Gertz filed a libel suit against the publisher for defamation
of character. The publisher claimed First Amendment protection. The Supreme Court held that since Gertz was not a
public official or a public figure, the publisher was not entitled
to First Amendment protection.

e. Movement

85. Haig v. Agee, 453 U.S. 280 (1981)
    The Secretary of State revoked Agee's passport because his
actions overseas compromised national security and foreign
policy. Agee challenged on First Amendment grounds. The
Supreme Court held that passport revocation did not violate the
First Amendment freedom of movement interpretation if there
existed a significant likelihood for a breach of security.

f. Obscene and Sexually Explicit Material

86. Young v. American Mini Theatres, Inc., 427 U.S. 50 (1976)

"Adult" theater operators challenged the Detroit, Michigan,
ordinance regulating the licensing and location of all forms of
adult entertainment as prior restraint under the First Amendment.   The Supreme Court ruled that the city was justified in
regulating the use of commercial property in that zoning did
not violate free expression; the material in question was still
available.

87.   Paris Adult Theatre I v. Slaton, 413 U.S. 49 (1973)
      "Adult" theater owners sought relief from the injunction pre-
venting them from showing two films.   The state of Georgia
held both films to be hard-core pornography.   The Supreme
Court held that the state had the right to regulate obscene
material shown at adult theaters as long as the statute met First
Amendment standards.

88.   Stanley v. Georgia, 394 U.S. 557 (1969)
      Stanley was convicted of possessing obscene material.   He
claimed that conviction violated his First Amendment rights.
The Supreme Court found that while the First Amendment does
not protect obscenity, it does protect the right of an individual
to possess obscene material for his private use.

89.   A Book Named "John Cleland's Memoirs of a Woman of Pleasure"
      v. Attorney General of the Commonwealth of Massachusetts,
      383 U.S. 413 (1966)
      The case documents the attempt to have the book, better
known as Fanny Hill, declared obscene.   A lower court found
that the book, first published in 1750, was obscene.   The copyright holder appealed the decision.   The Supreme Court ruled
that the book did not meet obscenity standards as set down in
prior cases; therefore, the petition was denied.

90.   Broadway Books, Inc. v. Roberts, 642 F. Supp. 486 (E.D.
      Tenn. June 11, 1986)
      Adult oriented establishments challenged the Chattanooga,
Tennessee, statute regulating their businesses.   The statute
required that there be no booths or closed areas in these outlets; that license applicants disclose names and criminal records;
that applicants have been residents of Chattanooga for thirty
days and be of good moral character.   The court found that
the provision against closed booths was for health matters and
did not violate the First Amendment; disclosure of names and
criminal records likewise did not violate the First Amendment;
residency requirements and the stipulation that applicants be
of good moral character were unconstitutional.   The court ordered
that the statute be altered to omit residency requirements and
the good character stipulation.

91.   Council for Periodical Distributors Association v. Evans, 642
      F.Supp. 552 (M.D.Ala. July 14, 1986)

The publishers charged Montgomery County District Attorney
Evans with prior restraint in violation of the First Amendment
regarding several adult publications, including Playboy and
Penthouse. Evans threatened retailers and distributors of adult
material with criminal prosecution under Alabama's obscenity
statute if they did not stop selling materials. Evans was found
to have sought to ban all such products without first ascertaining whether or not they were indeed obscene under the First
Amendment. The court determined that Evans' actions did indeed constitute prior restraint.

92. Playboy Enterprises, Inc., v. Meese, 639 F.Supp. 581 (D.D.C.
July 3, 1986)
The publisher sought an injunction against Attorney General
Meese in order to prevent his Commission on Obscenity and
Pornography from distributing a "blacklist" or taking other actions to prevent the publication or distribution of magazines
and other publications. The Supreme Court found that the
letter mailed to distributors threatening inclusion on the blacklist amounted to prior restraint under the First Amendment and
ordered the letter retracted.

g. Politics

93. United States v. O'Brien, 391 U.S. 367 (1968)
O'Brien was convicted for burning his draft card. He appealed on the grounds that his action was "symbolic speech"
and, as such, was protected by the First Amendment. The
Supreme Court held that the government's substantial interest
in maintaining adequate reserves of selective service participants
justified the defendant's conviction and did not violate his First
Amendment rights.

94. Michigan State Chamber of Commerce v. Austin, 643 F.Supp.
397 (W.D.Mich. Sept. 3, 1966)
The Chamber of Commerce challenged the Michigan law that
made it illegal for corporations to make independent efforts to
influence political elections on the charge that it violated the
First Amendment. The court found that the law served to aid
the state in preventing secret alliances between politicians and
corporations and was, therefore, constitutional.

h. Publication

95. Abrams v. United States, 250 U.S. 616 (1919)
Abrams was charged with violations of the Espionage Act
of Congress; he published material which was meant to heap
scorn and ridicule on the United States government and sought
to cause slowdowns and stoppages of the production of materials
needed for the war effort. Abrams held that the Espionage Act
was unconstitutional on First Amendment grounds. The Supreme

Court held that the material was not protected under the First
Amendment because it incited people to a violent overthrow of
the United States government.

96. Trachtman v. Anker, 426 F.Supp. 198 (S.D.N.Y. Dec. 15,
    1976), rev'd, and remand 563 F.2d 512 (2d Cir. 1977), cert.
    denied 98 S.Ct. 1491 (1977)
       The student, editor of the high school newspaper, approached
    the principal for permission to distribute a survey on sexuality
    in the school and to publish the results in the school paper.
    Permission was denied. The student then brought suit that
    the school was infringing on his First Amendment rights. The
    District Court held that the school could deny distribution to
    freshman and sophomore students without violating the First
    Amendment but must allow access to junior and senior students.
    The Court of Appeals held that the school was within its rights
    in denying permission to distribute the survey to all students.
    The Supreme Court declined to hear the appeal.

97. Journal Publishing Co. v. Meechem, 801 F.2d 1233 (10th Cir.
    1986)
       The publisher sought dissolution of Meechem's post-trial
    order to jurors in a newsworthy case not to discuss the trial
    with the press. The publisher held that the order violated
    their First Amendment right to gather the news and the jurors'
    First Amendment freedom of expression. The court found that
    the order was overbroad and a violation of the First Amendment.

98. Kuhlmeier v. Hazelwood School Dist., 795 F.2d 1368 (8th Cir.
    1986)
       The student staff of the high school paper accused the
    school district of First Amendment violations when the school
    principal removed two pages from the school paper. The court
    ruled that the paper was a "public forum" and entitled to First
    Amendment protections.

99. Nicholson v. Board of Educ. Torrance Unified School Dist., 682
    F.2d 858 (9th Cir. 1982)
       A high school journalism teacher alleged he was fired due
    to constitutionally protected actions which he took as advisor
    for the school paper. While hearing the case, the judge ruled
    that the school's policy requiring students to submit articles
    on sensitive topics for prepublication review in order to ensure
    accuracy was not a First Amendment violation.

100. Williams v. Spencer, 622 F.2d 1200 (4th Cir. 1980)
        Students were prevented from distributing a non-school
    paper on school grounds because of the ads for drug para-
    phernalia contained within it. The students charged the school
    district with First Amendment violations. The court found the
    school to be within its rights in halting distribution so as to
    protect the health of the students.

101. Gambino v. Fairfax County School Board, 564 F.2d 157 (4th
      Cir. 1977)
            Students sought an injunction on the school board in order
      to allow the publication of an article on contraceptives in the
      school paper. The court found that since the paper was estab-
      lished as a public forum for students and was not part of the
      school curriculum, it was entitled to First Amendment protection.
      The school board was ordered to allow the article to run.

                              i. Religion

102. Wallace v. Jaffree, 105 S.Ct. 2479 (1985)
            A parent filed a complaint that the Alabama statute requir-
      ing one minute of silence for "meditation or voluntary prayer"
      at the beginning of the school day was unconstitutional. The
      Supreme Court held that the law was a violation of the religious
      clause of the First Amendment.

103. Stone v. Graham, 449 U.S. 39 (1980)
            Students filed for an injunction to prevent Kentucky from
      enforcing a statute which required the posting of copies of the
      Ten Commandments in every public school classroom. The Su-
      preme Court found that the statute was unconstitutional under
      the First Amendment.

104. Niemotko v. State of Maryland, 340 U.S. 268 (1951)
            Jehovah's Witnesses were arrested for disorderly conduct
      while attempting to hold Bible classes in a city park. The
      record shows that there was no threat of violence among the
      crowd gathered. The Supreme Court held that the arrest was
      in violation of the First Amendment religious clause and ordered
      the charges dropped.

105. American Civil Liberties Union of Illinois v. City of St. Charles,
      794 F.2d 256 (7th Cir. 1986)
            The ACLU sought an injunction to prevent the city from
      displaying a lighted cross during the Christmas season. The
      ACLU charged that since the cross was prominently displayed
      on the top of a building readily identifiable as city property,
      it violated the First Amendment religious clause. The court
      agreed and granted an injunction.

106. Dettmer v. Landon, 799 F.2d 929 (4th Cir. 1986)
            A prisoner brought suit alleging First Amendment violations
      by the prison officials. Dettmer held that he was a member
      of the Church of Wicca and that witchcraft was his religion.
      He requested certain items (a candle, incense, a hollow statue)
      to be used in his religious ceremonies. Prison officials refused
      on the grounds that the materials requested created a breach
      of security in that institution. The court found that witchcraft
      is a religion entitled to First Amendment protection but that

the prison was within its rights to refuse access to potentially
dangerous materials to the prisoner.

107. Grove v. Mead School Dist. No. 354, 753 F.2d 1528 (9th Cir.
      1985), cert. denied, 106 S.Ct. 85 (1985)
      A student alleged that the use of the book, The Learning
      Tree, as part of the high school curriculum violated the First
      Amendment religious clause and brought action to force the
      school board to remove it from classes. The court held that
      the use of the book did not violate the First Amendment or
      constitute the establishment of a religion. The Supreme Court
      declined to hear the appeal.

108. McLean v. Arkansas Board of Educ., 529 F.Supp. 1255 (E.D.
      Ark. Jan. 5, 1982)
      An injunction was requested in order to keep the school
      board from enforcing a statute requiring the equal treatment
      of creation science and evolution science in classes. The
      court found that the statute violated the First Amendment re-
      ligious clause because it was simply an effort to have the
      biblical version of creation included in the public school cir-
      riculum. The injunction was granted.

109. Palmer v. Board of Educ. of the City of Chicago, 466 F.Supp.
      605 (D.D.C. Feb. 2, 1979), aff'd. 603 F.2d 1271 (7th Cir.
      1979), cert. denied 100 S.Ct. 689 (1979)
      A teacher was discharged for not teaching kindergarten
      students the Pledge of Allegiance, patriotic songs, and for not
      conducting activities surrounding certain national holidays.
      The teacher alleged that, as a Jehovah's witness, these activi-
      ties were against her religious beliefs and her termination was
      a violation of her First Amendment rights. The court held
      that she was constitutionally protected in her right not to re-
      cite the Pledge of Allegiance, but she was not protected against
      refusing to follow the school district's curriculum. The Court
      of Appeals upheld the District Court decision; the Supreme
      Court declined to hear the appeal.

110. Gaines v. Anderson, 421 F.Supp. 337 (D.Mass. Sept. 1, 1976)
      Students challenged the Massachusetts statute requiring a
      period of silence for "meditation or prayer" at the beginning
      of each school day as a violation of the First Amendment re-
      ligious clause. The court held that the statute was not un-
      constitutional because it had not been instituted for the pur-
      pose of sponsoring a religion.

Cases Alleging That a Given Federal
Statute Is Unconstitutional

            a. U.S.C.A. sec. 1461, 1462, 1463, 1464, 1465
      These sections of the United States Code prohibit the

mailing, importation, or transportation of obscene materials
and the broadcast of obscene language.

111. **Federal Communications Commission v. Pacifica Foundation**, 438
      U.S. 726 (1978)
      A radio station broadcast comedian George Carlin's mono-
      logue, "Filthy Words," which satirized indecent language not
      allowed on radio or TV. A father, listening to the broadcast
      with his young son, complained to the FCC. The FCC held
      that the broadcast was prohibited by statute as indecent. The
      Court of Appeals reviewed the case and reversed the FCC de-
      cision. The Supreme Court held that the broadcast was inde-
      cent but not obscene and, as such, was properly prohibited
      by the FCC. The Commission's order did not violate the broad-
      caster's First Amendment rights.

112. **Miller v. California**, 413 U.S. 15 (1973)
      Miller was convicted of mailing obscene material. He ap-
      pealed the conviction. The Supreme Court used this case to
      re-evaluate the constitutional standards regarding obscenity.
      The Court held that to be obscene material must meet three
      guidelines: (1) the average person must find that work,
      taken as whole, appeals to prurient interest; (2) the work
      must portray, in an offensive way, sexual conduct; and (3)
      the work, taken as a whole, must lack serious literary, artis-
      tic, political, or scientific value.

113. **Roth v. United States**, 354 U.S. 476 (1957)
      Roth was prosecuted under the California obscenity statute.
      The Supreme Court held that obscenity is not protected by the
      First Amendment; therefore, the California statute is not un-
      constitutional. This was the first case presented to the Supreme
      Court that challenged obscenity statutes on First Amendment
      grounds.

114. **United States v. Davis**, 353 F.2d 614 (2d Cir. 1965)
      Davis was accused of mailing obscene materials with obscene
      wrappers. He charged that his conviction violated the First
      Amendment and held that the material was not obscene. The
      court found the material to be obscene and, as such, not en-
      titled to First Amendment protection.

                    b. **18 U.S.C.A. sec. 2251 et seq.**
                    (Child Protection Act of 1984)
      These sections of the United States Code prohibit the use
      of minors to produce sexually explicit or other obscene material.
      They also prohibit the importation, transportation, and receipt
      of any child pornography.

115. **New York v. Ferber**, 458 U.S. 747 (1982)
      A bookstore owner charged that the New York statute

prohibiting the promotion of sexual performance by a minor was
unconstitutionally overbroad. The Supreme Court held that
child pornography was not protected by the First Amendment
and that the New York statute was not overbroad.

116. United States v. Andersson, 803 F.2d 903 (7th Cir. 1986)
      Andersson was convicted for mailing child pornography.
He charged that the statute violated his First Amendment rights.
The court held that while Andersson had the constitutional
right to possess pornographic material, that did not confer a
corresponding right to acquire and distribute such material
through the U.S. mails.

117. United States v. Marchant, 803 F.2d 174 (5th Cir. 1986)
      Marchant was convicted of knowingly receiving child porno-
graphy. He contended that the law against receiving child
pornography had been unconstitutionally applied. The court
held that while the First Amendment protects the right to possess obscene material for personal use, it does not protect the
sale and receipt of that material.

          c. 18 U.S.C.A. sec. 2385 (Smith Act)

118. Scales v. United States, 367 U.S. 203 (1961)
      Scales was a member of the Communist Party and was aware
of its intention to attempt an overthrow of the government of
the United States. He was convicted for the violation of the
membership clause of the Smith Act. Scales charged that the
clause violated his First Amendment right of association. The
Supreme Court held that because he was aware of the nature
and purpose of the organization, the conviction did not violate
his First Amendment rights.

          d. 22 U.S.C.A. sec. 611 et seq.
          (Registration of Foreign Propagandists)
      This section of the United State Code requires that all peo-
ple working in this country for a foreign entity must register
themselves and their intentions with the Attorney General's
office. Exemptions are made for (1) other governmental officials; (2) those here for purely religious, scholastic, artistic,
or scientific reasons; and (3) qualified lawyers.

119. Keene v. Meese, 619 F.Supp. 1111 (E.D.Cal. Dept. 12, 1985)
      Keene wanted to show Canadian Films labeled "political
propaganda" by the Foreign Agents Registration Act. The
decision to institute legal proceedings was based upon his contention that the section of the act prohibiting the importation
of "political propaganda" was unconstitutional. The court held
that the "political propaganda" clause of the act violated the
free speech component of the First Amendment.

e. 47 U.S.C.A. Sec. 315
This section of the United States Code provides for the
fair treatment of candidates for public office. It states that
any holder of an FCC license must permit the use of his broadcasting station by any legally qualified candidate. He must
also provide equal opportunities for access to all such qualified
candidates.

120. Columbia Broadcasting System v. Democratic National Committee.
412 U.S. 94 (1973)
Democrats charged that CBS violated their First Amendment
rights by not accepting an editorial announcement. The Supreme Court held that the First Amendment does not require
that a broadcaster accept editorial advertisements.

f. 47 U.S.C.A. sec. 326
This section prohibits the FCC from using any of its regulations to censor broadcasts or interfere with the First Amendment rights of broadcasters.

121. National Association of Independent Television Producers and
Distributors v. Federal Communications Commission, 516 F.2d
526 (2d Cir. 1975)
The TV networks challenged the FCC's prime time access
rule as violating the First Amendment freedom of speech clause.
That rule prevents the networks from broadcasting in all four
of the so-called prime time hours (7 p.m. to 11 p.m.), thereby
allowing local stations access to at least one hour of prime time.
The court held that the FCC rule did not violate the networks'
First Amendment rights.

g. 47 U.S.C.A sec. 398
(Public Broadcasting Act of 1967)
This section of the United States Code prohibits noncommercial, educational stations receiving grants from the Corpora-
tion for Public Broadcasting from editorializing about or supporting or opposing political candidates.

122. Federal Communications Commission v. League of Women Voters
of California, 104 S.Ct. 3106 (1984)
Public stations charged that the section of the Public Broadcasting Act of 1967 which prevented noncommercial stations
from editorializing was unconstitutional. The Supreme Court
held that the statute violated the First Amendment.

h. 47 U.S.C.A. sec. 521 et seq.
(Cable Communications Policy Act of 1984)
This section of the United States Code regulates access to
and the distribution and content of cable transmissions. Section 559 specifically sets forth the punishment for transmitting
obscene material over a cable system.

123. Jones v. Wilkinson, 800 F.2d 989 (10th Cir. 1986)
      Cable operators challenged the Utah Cable Statute as un-
      constitutionally overbroad. The court held that since the law
      could be used to restrict nonobscene language as well as ob-
      scene acts, it violated the First Amendment and was, there-
      fore, void.

124. Marsh Media, Ltd. v. Federal Communications Commission, 798
      F.2d 772 (5th Cir. 1986)
      The television station owner sought a review of FCC regula-
      tions which limited the ownership of TV stations and cable TV
      systems within the same market. The station owner charged
      that the regulations violated his First Amendment rights of ex-
      pression. The court held the FCC's regulations did not violate
      the First Amendment.

                    i. 50 U.S.C.A. sec. 784
                (Subversive Activities Control Act)
      This section of the United States Code prevents any member
      of a Communist-action or Communist-front organization from
      seeking any nonelective office or employment with the United
      States without disclosing membership in said group. It also
      prevents any member of a Communist-action group from being
      employed in any defense facility.

125. United States v. Robel, 389 U.S. 258 (1967)
      Robel questioned the section of the Subversive Activities
      Control Act making it illegal for a member of a Communist-
      action organization to be employed in any defense facility. The
      Supreme Court Ruled that this section violated the First Amend-
      ment in that it banned membership in any group possessed of
      a Communist-action agenda without considering a given indivi-
      dual's degree and quality of membership.

          D. ADDITIONAL CASES RELATING TO CENSORSHIP
                 AND INTELLECTUAL FREEDOM

      Addington v. Texas, 441 U.S. 418

      Adler v. Board of Education, 342 U.S. 485

      Bantam Books, Inc. v. Sullivan, 372 U.S. 58

      Beauharnais v. Illinois, 343 U.S. 250

      Bond v. Floyd, 385 U.S. 116

      Brandenburg v. Ohio, 395 U.S. 444

      Branzburg v. Hayes, 408 U.S. 665

Capitol Broadcasting Co. v. Mitchell, 333 F.Supp. 582

Communist Party v. S.A.C.B., 367 U.S. 1

Dennis v. United States, 341 U.S. 494

Dombrowski v. Pfister, 380 U.S. 479

Friedman v. Rogers, 380 U.S. 479

Ginsburg v. New York, 390 U.S. 629

Hague v. C.I.O., 307 U.S. 496

Int'l. Union of Police Assns., Local 189 v. Barrett, 524 F.Supp.
   760

Kunz v. New York, 340 U.S. 290

Memphis Community School District v. Stachura, 106 S.Ct. 2537

Mishkin v. New York, 383 U.S. 502

Murdock v. Pennsylvania, 319 U.S. 105

Near v. Minnesota, 238 U.S. 697

New York Times Co. v. Sullivan, 376 U.S. 254

New York Times Co. v. United States, 403 U.S. 713

Pell v. Procunier, 417 U.S. 817

Red Lion Broadcasting Co. v. FCC, 395 U.S. 367

Saia v. New York, 334 U.S. 558

Shelton v. Tucker, 364 U.S. 479

Smith v. Daily Mail Publishing Co., 443 U.S. 97

Thornhill v. Alabama, 310 U.S. 88

Valentine v. Chrestensen, 316 U.S. 52

West Virginia State Board of Education v. Barnette, 319 U.S.
   624

PART III:

PROFESSIONS CONCERNED WITH INTELLECTUAL FREEDOM

In view of the fact that censorship is a phenomenon pervading the entire fabric of society, it may appear to be a somewhat limiting proposition to have selected only four professions--education, journalism, librarianship, and politics and government service--for coverage in this chapter. However, it could easily be argued that education, journalism, and librarianship are the occupations most vitally concerned with protection of First Amendment rights. On the other hand, the federal government--while responsible for the institution of the Bill of Rights and the protection of many human rights--has been perhaps the most efficient and far-reaching censor within the domestic scene. In short, education, library service, and journalism represent ideal choices for study in consideration of the following factors: (1) the frequency with which censorship occurs in these fields; (2) their potential vulnerability to censorship from both within without; (3) the myriad forms of suppression experienced by professionals in these fields; and (4) their pivotal role in protecting, to some degree, the First Amendment rights of every American citizen.

A perusal of the anti-censorship organizations in Chapter IV underscores the fact that each of these professions has evolved a sophisticated infrastructure for combating inroads against intellectual freedom. The developments taking place within librarianship over the past half century serve as a case in point for all professions concerned with the flow of information. [1] During the thirties, the confluence of an extraordinarily high number of censoring activities and the growing maturity of the profession's prime unifying force, the American Library Association, led to the institution of the Intellectual Freedom Committee in 1940. The ALA body has been responsible for the development of policy statements as the need arises, most notably further interpretations of the Library Bill of Rights. These include Free Access to Libraries for Minors (1972); Administrative Policies and Procedures Affecting Access to Library Resources and Services (1982); Statement on Labeling (1951); Expurgation of Library Materials (1973); Diversity in Collection Development (1982); Evaluating Library Collections (1973); Challenged Materials (1971); Restricted Access to Library Materials (1973); Exhibit Spaces and

and Meeting Rooms (1981); Library-Initiated Programs as a Resource
(1982). Additional promulgations include the Policy on Governmental
Intimidation (1973) and the Policy on Confidentiality of Library Records (1971).

The responsibilities of educating librarians and the general
public on the importance of intellectual freedom and implementing
ALA policies in this area were transferred to the newly-established
Office for Intellectual Freedom in 1967. The OIF's programs include
publishing; the maintenance of exhibits at conferences, workshops,
etc.; consulting; and the coordination of ALA's intellectual freedom
activities with other agencies having similar concerns; e.g., state
library association intellectual freedom committees, the Association of
American Publishers, the American Civil Liberties Union, the National
Education Association, and others.

In addition, ALA has created the following subgroups to assist
in coordinating various policies relating to intellectual freedom: (1)
the Intellectual Freedom Round Table (1973), which offers opportunities for ALA members to become active in the Association's intellectual freedom activities; (2) the Staff Committee on Mediation,
Arbitration, and Inquiry (1971), which serves a quasi-judicial function in handling cases involving violations of the spirit of the Library
Bill of Rights, tenure, professional status, fair employment practices, ethical practices, due process, etc.; and (3) the Freedom to
Read Foundation (1969), which provides defense machinery (i.e.,
financial and legal assistance) enabling librarians to protect their
jobs while in support of intellectual freedom as well as a device for
concerned individuals and groups to set legal precedents for the
freedom to read.

This chapter includes materials which illustrate the problems
faced by the aforementioned professions with respect to attacks on
intellectual freedom as well as the methods employed by each in combating censorship. The delineation of government-inspired censorship in the final section provides a bridge to the coverage of individual and group censors which commences Chapter IV.

NOTE

1.   The points about ALA which follow have been based largely upon
     Judith F. Krug and James A. Harvey's "ALA and Intellectual
     Freedom: A Historical Overview," In: Intellectual Freedom
     Manual, compiled by the Office for Intellectual Freedom of the
     American Library Association. 2d ed. Chicago: American Li-
     brary Association, 1983. pp. x-xxx.

EDUCATION

A. TRENDS IN SCHOOL CENSORSHIP

126. Bean, Joseph P. Public Education: River of Pollution. Ful-
lerton, CA.: Educator Publications, n.d.
    The monograph explores the problems associated with public
education, many of which relate to basic First Amendment issues. Bean provides strategems for wresting control of the
educational process from the schools.

127. Donelson, Kenneth L. "Obscenity and the Chill Factor: Court
Decisions and Their Relationships to School Censorship," In:
Dealing With Censorship, edited by James E. Davis. Urbana,
Ill.: National Council of Teachers of English, 1979. pp. 63-
75.
    Donelson surveys the meanings and tests of obscenity evolved
through more than two hundred years of court decisions and
the influences these decisions have had and may have on censorship problems in the schools.

128. Glatthorn, Allan. "Censorship and the Classroom Teacher,"
In: Dealing With Censorship, edited by James E. Davis. Urbana, Ill.: National Council of Teachers of English, 1979.
pp. 48-53.
    Glatthorn notes that schools are in the midst of a wave of
censorship that has not yet crested. He posits that the rash
of attacks suggests that some changes are needed; e.g., English teachers need to show more acceptance and respect for
values other than their own; a new respect for the privacy of
the young.

129. Hogan, Robert F. "Some Thoughts on Censorship in the School,"
In: Dealing With Censorship, edited by James E. Davis. Urbana, Ill.: National Council of Teachers of English, 1979.
pp. 86-95.
    Hogan discusses the forces behind the rising frequency and
intensity of censorship in the school. In addition to external
forces, some of the blame comes from within: (1) the collec-
tivization of parents; (2) English teachers have asserted their
"rights" faster and further than they have prepared the rest

of the community to accept; (3) teachers have failed to take
into responsible account the rest of the media.

130. Jenkinson, Edward B. "Dirty Dictionaries, Obscene Nursery
      Rhymes and Burned Books," In: Dealing With Censorship,
      edited by James E. Davis. Urbana, Ill.: National Council of
      Teachers of English, 1979. pp. 2-13.
          Jenkinson surveys current trends in school censorship.
      Topics include: Why Is Censorship Activity on the Rise?;
      What Is Being Censored?; What Are the Results of Attempts
      to Censor Books or Other Teaching Materials?

131. "Parental Control of Public School Curriculum," Catholic Lawyer.
      21 (1975) 197-210.
          An analysis of states' rights to administer public education
      as it conflicts with parents' rights to guide the development of
      their offspring. Parents are likely to be successful in court
      when their arguments are concerned with the right to free
      exercise of religion.

132. Small, Robert C., Jr. "Censorship and English: Some Things
      We Don't Seem to Think About Very Often (But Should)," In:
      Dealing With Censorship, edited by James E. Davis. Urbana,
      Ill.: National Council of Teachers of English, 1979. pp. 54-
      62.
          Small notes that while three dimensions of censorship--i.e.,
      the details of specific cases, arguments against censorship,
      and advice about how to prepare for censorship attacks--have
      been explored thoroughly, three others of equal worth are
      rarely considered: the historical and social, the educational,
      and the human.

133. Wellborn, Stanley N. "Drive to Ban Books Spreads in U.S.,"
      In: The First Freedom Today, edited by Robert B. Downs and
      Ralph E. McCoy. Chicago: American Library Association,
      1984. pp. 53-54. Reprinted in: U.S. News and World Report.
      29:9 (March 8, 1982) 66.
          Wellborn surveys attempts to censor books, plays, and mu-
      sical productions in schools during the early eighties. He
      notes the arguments used by both censors and advocates of
      freedom of expression.

B. SELF-CENSORSHIP IN THE SCHOOLS

134. Bane, David. "We Are All Censors," Minnesota English Jour-
      nal. 12:1 (Winter 1976) 34-37.
          In the process of assisting students to develop value-skills,
      teachers are practicing censorship via the exclusion of certain
      choices from the learning environment.

135.   "Banning Books: An Ancient Sport Makes A Rowdy Comeback
       Among School Boards," American School Board Journal.   160
       (May 1973) 25-44.
           A series of articles focusing on the role of the school board
       with respect to censorship.   Topics covered include textbooks,
       student publications, and the library.

136.   Glenn, Charles.   "Why Public Schools Don't Listen," Christianity
       Today, 29:13 (September 20, 1985)
           Glenn focuses upon the dilemma facing educators when con-
       fronted with the concern of parents about public schools' treat-
       ment of religion and values.   He notes that the former go to
       great lengths to assure fairness and to avoid controversial
       materials, such as religion, not realizing that to avoid some-
       thing gives some students the message that it is unimportant.

                C.   THE MIND OF THE SCHOOL CENSOR

137.   Donlan, Dan.   "Parent versus Teacher: The Dirty Word,"
       In: Diversity in Mature Reading: Theory and Research,
       edited by Phil L. Nacke.   22nd Yearbook.   Volume 1.   Boone,
       N.C.:   National Reading Conference, 1973.   pp. 224-231.
           Donlan delineates the forces at the core of parental censor-
       ship of school reading materials.

138.   Jenkinson, Edward B.   Censors in the Classroom; The Mind
       Benders.   Carbondale: Southern Illinois University Press,
       1979; New York: Avon, 1982.
           The survey focuses upon the motivations and implications
       of this practice.   Numerous case studies have been integrated
       into the narrative.   The author also provides tips on how to
       deal with the censor.

                D.   PREPARATIONS FOR DEALING WITH
                     THE SCHOOL CENSOR

139.   Ashley, Benedict M.   "Ethical Pluralism in Our Schools,"   Iowa
       English Bulletin Yearbook, 25 (November 1975) 34-40.
           Ashley argues that progress in fighting censorship can only
       be made when schools develop constructive approaches which
       encompass an acceptance of pluralistic values.

140.   Ball, Revonda J.   An Examination of the Current Threat of
       Dismissal of Public High School Teachers Because of Contro-
       versy about Selected Reading Materials and Suggested Activities

for Teachers. Durham, N.C.: Duke University, 1973. Ph.D. dissertation, available from University Microfilms, no. 74-1121.

The study focuses on the legal, professional, and community perspectives concerning the utilization of controversial materials. Recommendations are given for programs which will enable English teachers to provide quality learning opportunities while simultaneously avoiding dismissal.

141. Bauer, Marion Dane. "The Censor Within," In: Celebrating Censored Books, edited by Nicholas J. Karolides and Lee Burress. Racine, Wisc.: Wisconsin Council of Teachers of English, 1985. pp. 118-120. Reprinted in: Top of the News. V. 41 (Fall 1984) 67-71.

Bauer argues that fiction must be judged according to its literary integrity, not by its moral "rightness," by whatever set of values that rightness is perceived.

142. Berkley, June. "Teach the Parents Well: An Anti-Censorship Experiment in Adult Education," In: Dealing With Censorship, edited by James E. Davis. Urbana, Ill.: National Council of Teachers of English, 1979. pp. 180-186.

Berkley offers a constructive approach to minimizing attempts at censorship on behalf of parents; i.e., teaching them the more controversial books in adult education classes.

143. Donelson, Kenneth L. "Censorship and the Teaching of English: A Few Problems and Fewer Solutions," Journal of the Colorado Language Arts Society. 4:1 (October 1968) 5-15, 18-20.

Donelson notes that ultimate judgment in book selection for classroom use must rest with the teacher, who should be able to defend all choices via literary and moral considerations. Censorship occurs whenever such choices are thwarted by the community. Donelson delineates what the English teacher should know in order to effectively counteract censorship: (1) rational men throughout history have defended censorship on moral, political, and philosophical grounds; (2) while many censors defend their own judgments emotionally, other censors are philosophical and rational; (3) censorship is objectionable and the necessity for it unconfirmed; (4) goals in teaching literature are enjoyment, understanding, knowledge about contrasting values, and appreciation of art. Practical recommendations include the establishment of book selection committees, insistence upon professionalism from all faculty, informing the public about policies, devising a procedure for handling censorship cases, and remaining calm in the face of censoring activities.

144. Donelson, Kenneth L. "A Few Safe Assumptions About Censorship and the Censor," Peabody Journal of Education. 50 (April 1973) 235-244. Reprinted in: Education Digest. xxxix (September 1973) 54-56.

Donelson provides seven points which will enable educators
to deal more constructively with censorship: (1) any books
or ideas or teaching methods are potentially censorable: (2) new
books or ideas or teaching methods are more likely to come
under attack than established ones; (3) censorship is capricious
and arbitrary; (4) censorship comes from within the school
system as well as from outside; (5) most people are not willing
to consider ideas about sex or sexually-oriented literature when
they conflict with folk wisdom; (6) censorship is a real threat
that can happen to you; (7) censorship usually strikes unex-
pectedly, and schools experiencing censorship often become
fearful of trying anything new or different.

145.   Escott, Richard H.   "Intellectual Freedom and the School Ad-
       ministrator," School Media Quarterly.   2 (Winter 1973) 118-121.
       Escott focuses on the problematical considerations defining
the school administrator's perspective in instances of censorship.

146.   Frank, John P., and Robert F. Hogan.   Obscenity, the Law,
       and the English Teacher.   Champaign, Ill.:   National Council
       of Teachers of English, 1966.
       The nature of obscenity is explored in the work.   Essen-
tially a primer for English teachers confronted with the specter
of censorship.

147.   Gaines, Ervin J.   "Censorship and What To Do About It,"
       Minnesota English Journal.   5:1 (Winter 1969) 5-8.
       Gaines discusses the legal ramifications of employing litera-
ture concerned with sex in the school.

148.   Hove, John, ed.   Meeting Censorship in the School: A Series
       of Case Studies.   Champaign, Ill.:   National Council of Teachers
       of English, 1967.
       The case studies serve a two-fold purpose: (1) to illustrate
the varied threats to intellectual freedom in the school, and
(2) to provide a constructive framework for combating censorship.

149.   Shugert, Diane P.   "How to Write a Rationale in Defense of a
       Book," In: Dealing With Censorship, edited by James E. Davis.
       Urbana, Ill.:   National Council of Teachers of English, 1979.
       pp. 187-201.
       Shugert argues that one of the most effective ways of deal-
ing with censorship is to have ready, prepared in advance,
written justifications for teaching the books you are teaching.
She provides suggestions for writing rationales along with
several examples of format.

150.   "Try Out This Model School District Policy on Censorship,"
       American School Board Journal.   60 (May 1973) 44.

The article offers concise guidelines for dealing with censorship.

151. Woodworth, Mary L. <u>Intellectual Freedom, the Young Adult,</u>
      <u>and Schools; A Wisconsin Study</u>. rev. ed. Madison: Univer-
      sity of Wisconsin-Extension, 1976.
      Woodworth explores the forces at work in typical censorship
      cases which, while derived from observations within the state
      of Wisconsin, are representative of the nation as a whole. Her
      study provides insights on how to deal with the censor on a
      constructive basis.

               E. RESEARCH AND SCHOOL CENSORSHIP

152. Association of American Publishers, American Library Associa-
      tion, and Association for Supervision and Curriculum Develop-
      ment. "Limiting What Students May Read," "<u>Book and Ma-</u>
      <u>terials Selection for School Libraries and Classrooms: Pro-</u>
      <u>cedures, Challenges, and Responses</u>. 1981. Reprinted in:
      <u>The First Freedom Today</u>, edited by Robert B. Downs and
      Ralph E. McCoy. Chicago: American Library Association,
      1984. pp. 97-100.
      An abridged report on a survey of 1,891 public elementary
      and secondary school adminstrators and librarians concerning
      the selection practices and censorship pressures in public
      schools. Covers the reasons for initiating the study, a sum-
      mary of the findings, and recommendations on how to deal with
      censorship.

153. Burress, Lee. "A Brief Report of the 1977 NCTE Censorship
      Survey," In: <u>Dealing With Censorship</u>, edited by James E.
      Davis. Urbana, Ill.: NCTE, 1979. pp. 14-47.
      Burress reports the finding of a February 1977 survey con-
      cerned with censorship in the nation's secondary schools. Data
      have been provided for the following topics: (1) Source of
      Objections; (2) List of Books Objected To (including objectors
      and type of objections to these titles); (3) Results of the Cen-
      sorship Events; (4) List of All Periodicals Objected To; (5)
      Disposition of Objections to Periodicals; (6) List of AV Ma-
      terials Objected To; (7) Type of Objector in Attempted Film
      and AV Censorship events; (8) Reasons for Objections to AV
      Materials; (9) Results of Objections to Films and AF; (10)
      Sources of Objections to School Publications; (11) Reasons for
      Objections to School Publications; (12) Results of Objections to
      School Publications. Burress concludes that censorship pres-
      sure is a prominent and growing part of school life. A copy
      of the questionnaire has been included.

154.   LaConte, Ronald T.   "The Relationship Between Book Selection
       Practices and Certain Controversial Elements of Literature in
       Bergen County, New Jersey Public Senior High School English
       Departments," Rutgers the State University of New Jersey,
       January 1967, Thesis, available from University Microfilms, Ann
       Arbor, Michigan.
          This study of book selection practices and certain elements
       of books which at some time had been attacked as unsuitable
       for high school students involved the English Department chair-
       men of 34 public high schools in Bergen County, New Jersey.
       Data from questionnaires and interviews were tabulated and
       statistically analyzed.   In addition to substantiating the exis-
       tence of a relationship between controversial elements and
       selection practices, the following were among the conclusions
       supported by data found to be significant at the .05 level:
       (1) controversial political and religious views are not likely to
       cause department chairmen to reject a book; (2) department
       chairmen involved in prior censorship incidents tend to restrict
       or reject fewer books than those who had not been involved
       in incidents; (3) department chairmen from schools having a
       written policy for handling objections to books restricted or
       rejected fewer controversial books than those from schools with-
       out a policy.

155.   Scales, Peter.   The Front Lines of Sexuality Education: A
       Guide to Building and Maintaining Community Support.   Net-
       work Publications, 1984.
          A study of the politics of sexuality education in twenty-
       three communities, conducted by the author for the U.S. Cen-
       ters for Disease Control in 1979-1981, provided the impetus
       for this work.   In addition to a description of that study,
       Scales presents guidelines for successful approaches and train-
       ing exercises for managing controversy and building community
       support.

                      F.   CENSORSHIP OF SCHOOL MATERIALS

Textbook Censorship

156.   Baxter, James E.   Selection and Censorship of Public School
       Textbooks.   Hattiesburg: University of Southern Mississippi,
       1964.   Ph.D. dissertation, available from University Microfilms,
       no. 65-760.
          Baxter concludes that textbook selection constitutes a pro-
       fessional responsibility; lay or political input pose potentially
       substantitive threats to intellectual freedom.

157.   Bradford, Kenneth.   "Report to the Virginia Board of Education

on Changes in Works Contained in Secondary Literature Textbooks," Newsletter on Intellectual Freedom. 34:3 (May 1985)
67, 93-95.
     Virginia Board of Education member Bradford attempts to
justify that body's acceptance of literary classics as modified
by textbook publications. His arguments include (1) the dic-
tates of powerful states such as Texas and California, (2) differing attitudes with a heterogenous society, (3) aesthetic in-
sensitivity on the part of publishers, and (4) purely business
considerations.

158. Del Frattore, Joan. "Contemporary Censorship Pressures and
      Their Effect on Literature Textbooks," Association of Depart-
      ments of English Bulletin. (Spring 1986) 35-40.
           The author sees a substantive drop in the quality of in-
      structional materials as a result of censoring threats.

159. "Global ed under Fire," Newsletter on Intellectual Freedom.
      35:4 (July 1986) 115-116.
           Report on incidents in several Colorado school districts in
      which parents have raised a storm of protest over social studies
      materials believed to belittle American values. Targeted are
      "global education" materials produced by the University of
      Denver's Center for Teaching International Relations, which
      have been termed "pacifistic," "capitulationist," and "biased
      toward radical political change" by U.S. Department of Educa-
      tion staffer Gregg Cunningham.

160. Haymes, Don. "Religious Freedom and the Public Schools,"
      The Christian Century. 103:36 (November 26, 1986) 1060-1061.
           In light of recent textbook controversies in Tennessee and
      Alabama, Haymes feels it is unlikely that public schools will
      ever again reflect a Christian consensus. This situation is,
      in his opinion, a great gift because it requires Christians to
      firmly commit themselves to "whom they will serve."

161. Hentoff, Nat. "The Dumbing of America," The Progressive.
      48 (February 1984) 29-31.
           Hentoff condemns the practice of textbook censorship.

162. Jenkinson, Edward B. The Schoolbook Protest Movement.
      Bloomington, Ind.: Phi Delta Kappa Educational Foundation,
      1986.
           An in-depth study of the forces coalescing into the current
      climate for schoolbook censorship.

163. Suhor, Charles. "Basic Training and Combat Duty--Preventive
      and Reactive Action," In: Dealing With Censorship, edited by
      James E. Davis. Urbana, Ill.: National Council of Teachers
      of English, 1979. pp. 168-179.
           Suhor provides a case study delineating the censoring of a

textbook at a high school in East Baton Rouge Parish, Louisi-
ana. He makes suggestions about how to change the climate
by adopting an activist state of mind.

164.   "University Professors Warn Against School Censorship," Newsletter on Intellectual Freedom.   36:1 (January 1987) 7, 35.
A condensation of the key points from an eighteen-page
report, Liberty and Learning in the Schools: Higher Education's Concerns, produced by the AAUP's Commission on Academic Freedom and Pre-College Education (Washington, D.C.:
Am. Assoc. of University Professors, 1986). In the report,
the commission warns that the increasing incidence of textbook censorship is producing some students who are unprepared for college and teaching youngsters that suppression of
controversial ideas is acceptable.

165.   Vitz, Paul C. Censorship: Evidence of Bias in Our Children's
Textbooks. Ann Arbor, Mich.:   Servant, 1986.
A study of missing elements in public education's treatment
of American life and history with the ultimate aim of developing a curriculum sensitive to the convictions of devoutly Christian parents. Vitz finds that the role of religion in past and
present society has been seriously neglected. In addition,
there exists a distorted portrayal of family life that doesn't
stress commitment to marriage as the societal norm or the vo-
cation of full-time parenting. There is a similar neglect of
patriotism, business, labor, and altruism. Prominent contemporary political figures profiled are usually "liberal." The
conclusion is essentially a pessimistic one; that public schools
and the textbook industry cannot be reformed, and that the
only solution is tax support for religious schools.

166.   Vitz, Paul C. "Religion and Traditional Values in Public School
Textbooks," The Public Interest. (Summer 1986) 79-90.
A condensed summation of the author's research on textbooks and basal readers used in schools. He finds a pattern
of censorship by the publishers and purchasers of these materials that is far more threatening than that represented by
groups of parents.

a.   The Island Trees Case

167.   "Appeals Court Orders Retrial of Island Trees School Case,"
Publishers Weekly. 218:16 (October 17, 1980) 12, 26.
Because the constitutional rights of students were apparently
violated by the "erratic, arbitrary and freewheeling manner"
in which the school board in 1976 removed ten books from the
libraries and curriculum of the Island Trees Union Free School
District, the U.S. Court of Appeals for the Second Circuit
has sent the case back to a lower court for trial. The developments surrounding this decision are documented in detail.

168. Hentoff, Nat. "Island Trees v. Pico: The Battle Ahead,"
      Collection Building. 5:1 (Spring 1983) 9-12.
            An eloquent apology for intellectual freedom. Hentoff notes
      that the Pico ruling fails to address the issue of preselection
      censorship; herein may lie a major battleground for future
      altercations between the forces for and against censorship.

169. Rich, R. Bruce. "The Supreme Court's Decision in Island
      Trees," Newsletter on Intellectual Freedom. 31:5 (September
      1982) 149, 173-181. Reprinted in: The First Freedom Today,
      edited by Robert B. Downs and Ralph E. McCoy. Chicago:
      American Library Association, 1984. pp. 74-83
            An analysis of the decision, with a large portion of the es-
      say given over to excerpts from the opinions.

170. "School Censorship Cases: Island Trees," In: The First Free-
      dom Today, edited by Robert B. Downs and Ralph E. McCoy.
            A summary of the events taking place between November
      1975 and June 25, 1982, when a deeply divided Supreme Court
      ruled on the case.

171. Stone, Robert D. "Island Trees v. Pico: The Legal Implica-
      tions," Collection Building. 5:1 (Spring 1983) 3-8.
            An analysis of the June 25, 1982, decision of the Supreme
      Court in the Island Trees trial. Stone concludes the Court
      has failed to resolve the case; therefore, the issue of the re-
      moval of books from school libraries will be back before that
      body. While the author does not profess to know how the
      Court will rule the next time, he feels that it is fair to predict
      that any future constraint on the authority of school boards
      with respect to library books will be narrower in scope and
      clearer in application than the decision in Island Trees.

172. "Two Federal Judges Uphold Library Censorship," Newsletter
      on Intellectual Freedom. 28:6 (November 1979) 129, 141-145.
            The article consists of substantial excerpts from two federal
      court decisions handed down in August 1979--Pico v. Board of
      Education and Bicknell v. Vergenness Union High School Board
      --which represented at least temporary victories for school
      library censors.

                  b. The Kanawha County (West Virginia) Case

173. Faigley, Lester. "What Happened in Kanawha County," English
      Journal. 64 (May 1975) 7-9.
            Faigley summarizes the developments surrounding the cen-
      sorship of school materials in Kanawha County. He attempts
      to ascertain the broader implications of this case.

174. Jenkinson, Edward B. "The Textbook War in Kanawha County,"
      In: Censors in the Classroom; The Mind Benders. Carbondale:
      Southern Illinois University Press, 1979. pp. 17-27.

Chronology of the 1974 textbook controversy. Jenkinson
discusses at length the immediate and probable long-term implications of the case.

175.   "School Censorship Cases: Kanawha County," In: The First
Freedom Today, edited by Robert B. Downs and Ralph E. Mc-
Coy. Chicago: American Library Association, 1984. pp. 71-
72.
A concise synopsis of the 1974 altercation. Includes the
guidelines for textbook selection adopted by the Kanawha County
Board of Education.

176.   Zuidema, Henry P. "Why Parent 'Minutemen' Are Taking Up
Arms in Defense of Their Children," Liberty. 71 (January/
February 1976) 10-13.
Zuidema defends the cause of the censors in the Kanawha
County controversy. He posits that the central issue involved
the presence of values in textbooks which conflicted with local
mores. These values ensued out of multicultural and multi-
ethnic perspectives incorporated as a result of legal and professional pressures.

Censorship of Nonprint Media

177.   Donelson, Kenneth L. "The Censorship of Non-Print Media
Comes to the English Classroom," English Journal. 62 (December 1973) 1226-1227.
Donelson states that "censorship of non-print media threatens
to become as big a problem for English teachers as censorship
of printed matter." He lists titles of short films which have
been singled out for attack.

178.   Donelson, Kenneth L. "Gore, Filth, and Communism: Censorship Comes to Non-Print Media," Kentucky English Bulletin.
24:2 (Winter 1974/75) 5-10.
Donelson feels that the censorship of audio-visual materials
will increase as more teachers develop an awareness of their
utility in the classroom.

Creation-Science/Evolution-Science Controversy

179.   Edwords, Frederick. "Textbook Censorship," The Humanist.
43 (July/August 1983) 35.
Edwords delineates the nature of the controversy between
the two camps.

180.   "Freedom of Religion and Science Instruction in Public Schools,"
Yale Library Journal. 87 (1978) 515-570.
The article raises the following questions: (1) whether the

exclusive presentation of the general theory of evolution in
the public schools acts as a burden on the free exercise of
religion; (2) whether the compulsory characteristics of public
schooling renders this burden substantial; (3) whether the
government interest in the general theory is so compelling as
to justify a restraint on religious freedom. In concluding that
the general theory abridges the free exercise clause of the
First Amendment, it is urged that high school instruction be
neutralized or allow for the exemption of students from particular courses.

181. Nelkin, Dorothy. "The Science-Textbook Controversies,"
      Scientific American. V. 234 (April 1976) 33-39. Reprinted in:
      The First Freedom Today, edited by Robert B. Downs and
      Ralph E. McCoy. Chicago: American Library Association,
      1984. pp. 137-146.
         Nelkin delineates the clash between creationists and adherents
      to the theory of evolution. She offers the following assessment
      of the implications of this conflict: "As questions that are
      normally resolved by professional consensus are brought into
      the political arena, and as democratic values such as freedom
      of choice, equality and fairness enter into science policy, the
      consequences of such resistance to science may be painful."

182. O'Neil, Robert M. "Creationism, Curriculum, and the Constitu-
      tion," Academe. 68:2 (March/April 1982) 21-26. Reprinted
      in: The First Freedom Today, edited by Robert B. Downs
      and Ralph E. McCoy. Chicago: American Library Association,
      1984. pp. 171-177.
         O'Neil discusses the threat posed to educators by the cre-
      ationist controversy.

                   a. The Little Rock (Arkansas) Case

183. "ACLU Challenges Arkansas Act on 'Creationism' in Schools,"
      Publishers Weekly. 219:24 (June 12, 1981) 16.
         A detailed account of the events leading up to the ACLU's
      federal lawsuit aimed at preventing Arkansas from enforcing a
      law that would, in its words, "require balanced treatment of
      creation-science and evolution-science in public schools."

184. Lyons, Gene. "Repealing the Enlightenment," Harper's Maga-
      zine. 264:1582 (April 1982) 38-78. Reprinted in: The First
      Freedom Today, edited by Robert B. Downs and Ralph E. Mc-
      Coy. Chicago: American Library Association, 1984. pp. 146-
      156.
         Lyons covers the Little Rock trial resulting from the ACLU
      challenge of the 1981 Arkansas statute, "Balanced Treatment
      of Creation Science and Evolution Science Act," which mandated
      that public schools would provide balanced treatment of the two
      theories.

185.   Overton, William R.   "Creationism in Schools: The Decision in
       McLean v. the Arkansas Board of Education," In: The First
       Freedom Today, edited by Robert B. Downs and Ralph E. Mc-
       Coy.   Chicago: American Library Association, 1984.   pp. 157-
       164.
           Excerpts of Judge Overton's opinion in McLean v. The Ar-
       kansas Board of Education which enjoined the board from im-
       plementing the "Balanced Treatment for Creation Science and
       Evolution Science Act" passed by the state legislature.

                        b.   The Scopes Case

186.   Emerson, Thomas I., and David Haber.   "The Scopes Case in
       Modern Dress," University of Chicago Law Review.   27 (1960)
       522-528.
           The authors argue that present interpretations of free ex-
       pression would render the Tennessee anti-evolution act uncon-
       stitutional.

The Secular Humanism Controversy

187.   Kleinman, Dana.   "Parents' Groups Purging Schools of 'Humanist'
       Books and Classes," The New York Times.   V. 130 (May 17,
       1981), 1.   Reprinted in: The First Freedom Today, edited by
       Robert B. Downs and Ralph E. McCoy.   Chicago: American
       Library Association, 1984.   pp. 182-186.
           Kleinman depicts the effect of the crusade against humanism
       on libraries and education.

188.   LaHaye, Tim.   The Battle for the Mind.   Old Tappan, N.J.:
       Fleming H. Revell, 1980.
           The work warns against the onslaught of secular humanism.
       LaHaye maps out specific strategies for dealing with this
       problem.

189.   Rhode, Robert T.   "Is Secular Humanism the Religion of the
       Public Schools?" In: Dealing With Censorship, edited by
       James E. Davis.   Urbana, Ill.:   National Council of Teachers
       of English, 1979.   pp. 117-124.
           Rhode delineates the phenomenon of secular humanism.   He
       concludes that, "It is time for teachers, administrators, librar-
       ians, and publishers to become fully informed of the threat
       of being labeled secular humanists.   Also, it is time for schools
       to improve their communication with local communities.   Again,
       it is time for schools to develop effective communication and
       written rationales, the schools should be better able to defend
       against the attacks that are to come."

190.   Woodward, Kenneth L., and Eloise Salholz.   "The Right's New
       Bogyman," In: The First Freedom Today, edited by Robert B.

Downs and Ralph E. McCoy. Chicago: American Library Association, 1984. pp. 179-182.

The authors survey the rise of the secular humanism controversy. They cite the words of philosopher Jacques Maritain that "humanism is inseparable from civilization or culture." By rejecting humanism, fundamentalists are, in a sense, rejecting the entire Western tradition.

a. The Alabama Textbook Case

191. Bowen, Ezra, and Joseph J. Kane. "A Courtroom Clash Over Textbooks; Evangelicals Attack Secular Humanism in Alabama Schools," Time. (October 27, 1986) 94.

The article documents the events leading up to the impending federal court case between 624 Christian Evangelicals, supported by Pat Robertson's National Legal Foundation, and the Alabama State Board of Education, backed by People for the American Way. According to the PAW, the issue--whether some 45 texts used in Alabama schoolrooms illegally espouse a religion called secular humanism--is likely to spread throughout the nation.

192. Vobejda, Barbara. "Judge Bans 'Humanist' Textbooks; Ruling a Victory For Fundamentalists," Washington Post. 110:90 (March 5, 1987) A1, A21.

In Mobile, Alabama, U.S. District Court Judge W. Brevard Hand ruled that more than 40 textbooks in the fields of social studies, history, and home economics must be stricken from the state's list of acceptable readings because they promote the "religion" of "secular humanism." A spokesman for People for the American Way termed the March 4 decision "nothing less than government censorship of the school curriculum and a dangerous attempt to set up the sectarian belief of one group as a measure of what may be taught."

b. The "Scopes II" Case

193. Flygare, Thomas J. "Some Thoughts on the Tennessee Textbook Case," Phi Delta Kappan. 68:6 (February 1987) 474-475.

Flygare summarizes the decision and offers his impressions on the case: "Judge Hull found that the constitutional rights of the plaintiffs had been violated. But he stopped short of requiring the school system to provide alternative textbooks for use inside the school. Rather, he ordered school officials to allow students whose religious beliefs are offended by the Holt series to 'opt out' of reading instruction only ... It is not difficult to understand how Judge Hull reached his conclusion. Perhaps some of the criticism that has been leveled at him might be more appropriately directed at the school officials who created and enforced the compulsory textbook policy. Their objectives may have been worthy, but they failed to

foresee the full consequences of the way in which their policy
was adopted and administered."

194.   Glenn, Charles L.   "Textbook Controversies: A 'Disaster for
Public Schools'?"   Phi Delta Kappan.   68:6 (February 1987)
451-455.
       Glenn discusses how educators should react to Mozert v.
Hawkins County. He argues for "a little common sense and
flexibility--not panic, not a retreat from what we believe to
be essential to education, not rigidity about our present procedures and requirements--would enable those of us who work
in public education to respond positively to this new challenge,
as we have to so many others."

195.   Jenkinson, Edward B.   "The Significance of the Decision in
'Scopes II,'" Phi Delta Kappan.   68:6 (February 1987) 445-450.
       Jenkinson analyzes the controversial decision in Mozert v.
Hawkins County. He notes that for now the case "is only as
significant as educators allow it to be. It has no impact outside the eastern district of Tennessee, and Judge Hull has
tried to limit even that impact to the plaintiff-students
and to the Holt reading series only."

196.   Lee, Robert W.   "Humanism and the Tennessee Textbooks,"
Conservative Digest.   13:2 (February 1987) 81-88.
       Lee chronicles the events leading up to and surrounding
the Mozert, et al v. Hawkins County Public Schools federal
court case. The key issues of the case--humanism as religion,
governmental indoctrination in education, etc.--are presented
and argued from a distinctly reactionary perspective. Lee
argues that he has delineated the case without the distortions
set forth by allegedly irresponsible journalists who made it
appear that the plaintiffs were "a bunch of ignorant clods bent
on censoring The Diary of Anne Frank, 'The Three Little Pigs,'
'Goldilocks and the Three Bears,' and even The Wizard of Oz."

197.   "A Reprise of Scopes," Newsweek.   (July 28, 1986) 18-20.
       The article reports on the circumstances at the core of the
case.

G.   THE FIRST AMENDMENT IN THE SCHOOLS

198.   Alexander, M. David.   "First Amendment: Curriculum, Libraries,
and Textbooks," In: School Law in Contemporary Society,
edited by M.A. McGhehy. Topeka, Kansas: National Organization on Legal Problems of Education, 1980. pp. 154-162.
       Alexander discusses the extent to which First Amendment
rights have utility within a school setting.

199. Bryson, Joseph E., and Elizabeth W. Detty. <u>The Legal Aspects</u>
      <u>of Censorship of Public School Library & Instructional Materials</u>.
      Michie, 1982.
          The authors delineate the tension between censorship and
      First Amendment rights in the schools.

200. Mott, Kenneth, and Stephen Edelstein. "Church, State, and
      Education: the Supreme Court and Its Critics," <u>Journal of</u>
      <u>Law and Education</u>. 2 (1973) 531-591.
          The authors address the problems inherent in achieving a
      consistent, workable, and fair-minded theory of the First
      Amendment in a pluralistic society.

201. Remes, David H. "Wrong in Every Respect," <u>Education Week</u>.
      3 (December 1986) 19-24.
          Remes, a lawyer specializing in First Amendment cases, has
      the following message with respect to public education: "Public
      education is not 'public' just because it is free. It is 'public'
      because it is a kind of education--an education that instructs
      children, as Justice William J. Brennan has put it, in 'a heri-
      tage common to all American groups and religions.' That heri-
      tage is one that includes <u>The Diary of Anne Frank</u> and <u>Huckle-</u>
      <u>berry Finn</u>. It is a heritage of tolerance and diversity. Public
      education is not and cannot be an education that instructs
      children in the orthodoxies of their parents."

202. Yudof, Mark G. "The State as Editor or Censor: Book Selec-
      tion and the Public Schools," In: <u>The First Freedom Today</u>,
      edited by Robert B. Downs and Ralph E. McCoy. Chicago:
      American Library Association, 1984. pp. 57-70.
          Yudof analyzes recent court decisions in the light of the
      role of public schools in the process of socialization. He con-
      cludes that the protection of First Amendment rights depends
      on "revitalizing our traditions of local control of education and
      on keeping state and federal governments as far removed as
      possible from school book decisions. In the last analysis, peo-
      ple will have the kind of schools that they want and deserve."

Faculty Rights

203. <u>Bill of Rights Newsletter</u>. Los Angeles: Constitutional Rights
      Foundation, 1967-present. Biennial.
          The serial's primary aim is to optimize the effectiveness of
      California social studies teachers with respect to the Constitu-
      tion. Past issues have covered fair trial and free press (April
      1967), academic freedom in public schools (Spring 1968), and
      a school textbook controversy (Fall 1975).

204. Clay, Richard H. C. "The Dismissal of Public School Teachers
      for Aberrant Behavior," <u>Kentucky Law Journal</u>. 64 (1976) 911-
      936.

Based upon the proposition that teachers influence their students to a significant degree, the article posits that school authorities should exercise great discretion in ascertaining what conduct leads to dismissal.   Clay also feels that the privacy rights of teachers should be severely limited.

205.   Drinkwater, W. Wayne, and Charles Claiborne Barksdale.   "Cook v. Hudson: The State's Interest in Integration Versus the First Amendment Rights of the Public School Teacher," Mississippi Law Journal.   45 (1974) 935-1002.
An analysis of a case concerned with three public school teachers who enrolled their children in private, all-white schools, thereby violating school board regulations.   The authors posit that the school board policy suffers from overbreadth.

206.   Flygare, Thomas J.   "Teacher Loyalty Oaths After Cole v. Richardson: Muddy Waters?" Journal of Law and Education. 2 (1973) 193-213.
Flygare asserts that the dismissal of teachers without notice on grounds of refusing to sign a loyalty oath constitutes an infringement of due process rights.   He sets forth three approaches for keeping within the limits established in the Cole case.

207.   Goldstein, Stephen R.   "The Asserted Constitutional Right of Public School Teachers to Determine What They Teach," Pennsylvania Law Review.   124 (1976) 1293-1357.
Goldstein argues that the right of teachers to override their superiors in the determination of course content lacks a constitutional basis.   He concludes that this represents a desirable state of affairs as parental control--via the school board-- should be ultimately responsible for inculcating social values.

208.   Johanns, Michael.   "Maryland Federal District Court Upholds Transfer and Dismissal of Teacher Because of 'Repeated' and 'Unnecessary' Public Appearances Made to Explain His Plight as a Homosexual Teacher," Creighton Law Review.   7 (1973) 92- 104.
An analysis of Acanfora v. Board of Education; Acanfora's dismissal was deemed justifiable in view of the fact that his lack of decorum outside the classroom disrupted the educational process.

209.   Johnson, Gregg D.   "Intellectual Freedom in Schools: A Bibliography," Newsletter on Intellectual Freedom.   28:5 (September 1979) 102, 120-123.
An annotated listing of law journal articles published between 1968-1979 which address the First Amendment rights of teachers, librarians, and students in public schools and universities.

56 Intellectual Freedom and Censorship

210. Keith, Bradley J. "Academic Freedom: Some Tentative Guidelines," Marquette Law Review. 55 (1972) 379-387.
Keith surveys recent academic freedom cases. He posits that free expression in teaching may be limited by its relevance to course concerns.

211. Miller, Norman R. "Teachers' Freedom of Expression within the Classroom: a Search for Standards," Georgia Law Review. 8 (1974) 837-897.
Miller argues that while freedom of expression is greatest when concerned with public issues, foremost constitutional protection should be afforded teaching methods.

212. Morris, Arval A. "Academic Freedom and Loyalty Oaths," Law and Contemporary Problems. 28 (1963) 487-514.
Morris advocates the termination of loyalty oaths, his rationale being that they are incompatible with critical and independent thinking.

213. Moskowitz, Ivor R., and Richard E. Casagrande. "Teachers and the First Amendment: Academic Freedom and Exhaustion of Administrative Remedies Under 41 U.S.C. Section 1983," Albany Law Review. 39 (1975) 661-705.
The authors analyze the federal statute relevant to the majority of First Amendment cases involving teachers.

214. Nahmod, Sheldon H. "Controversy in the Classroom: the High School Teacher and Freedom of Expression," George Washington Law Review. 39 (1971) 1032-1063.
The article focuses on court cases which have played a role in defining the extent of a teacher's First Amendment protection in the classroom.

215. Rubin, David. The Rights of Teachers; American Civil Liberties Union Handbook. New York: Avon, 1972.
A primer on the First Amendment rights of educators.

The Rights of Students and Parents

216. Banta, Robert Edward. "School Authorities May Prohibit Sex Questionnaire to Prevent Possible Psychological Harm to Other Students," Vanderbilt Law Review. 31 (1978) 173-183.
A study of Trachtman vs. Anker, in which the U.S. Court of Appeals for the Second Circuit held that the distribution of a sex questionnaire could be constitutionally prohibited due to possible psychological harm to high school students. Banta notes in some detail the flaws in the decision; he concludes that the case enables school officials to circumvent the guidelines previously established in the Tinker case.

217.   "Behind the Schoolhouse Gate: Sex and the Student Pollster,"
       New York University Law Review.   54 (1979) 161-203.
           In addition to criticizing the Trachtman vs. Anker case,
       adjudicative models for deciding student speech controversies
       are provided.

218.   Boaz, Martha.   "The Student Does Have the Right to Read,"
       California School Libraries.   41 (January 1970) 63-67.
           Boaz argues that the student has a right to search for truth
       wherever it may be found.

219.   "Education and the Law: State Interests and Individual Rights,"
       Michigan Law Review.   74 (1976) 1373-1502.
           This essay argues that the role of education is to inculcate
       social values and a modicum of scholastic ability; however, this
       process does not have to infringe on the autonomy interests
       of the individual.

220.   Flygare, Thomas J.   "Is Tinker Dead?"   Phi Delta Kappan.
       68:2 (October 1986) 165-166.
           Flygare discusses whether the decision in Bethel School
       District No. 403 v. Fraser, rendered on July 7, 1986, by the
       Supreme Court, will ultimately overrule the landmark student
       free speech decision in Tinker v. Des Moines Independent Com-
       munity School District (1969).   He argues, "If, under Fraser,
       school officials are permitted to bar all forms of political speech
       from the schools, however, Fraser is construed to allow punish-
       ment of only those students who engage in profanity and sexual
       innuendo, then the right to engage in nondistruptive political
       speech as outlined by Tinker may be preserved."

221.   Glasser, Ira, and Alan H. Levine.   "Bringing Student Rights
       to New York City's School System," Journal of Law and Educa-
       tion.   1 (1972) 213-229.
           The article focuses on the publication and circulation of
       200,000 student rights handbooks on the part of the Board of
       Education for the New York City public school system.   Placed
       within the context of past developments concerning student
       rights, the authors argue that this move was of dubious prac-
       tical value.

222.   Goldstein, Stephen R.   "Reflections on Developing Trends in
       the Law of Student Rights," Pennsylvania Law Review.   118
       (1970) 612-620.
           Goldstein notes recent trends in the evolution of student
       rights cases, including recognition of privacy rights and the
       growing judicial demand that school regulations be nationally
       suited to legitimate ends.

223.   Hirschoff, Mary-Michelle Upson.   "Parents and the Public
       School Curriculum: Is There a Right to Have One's Child

Excused from Objectionable Instruction?" <u>Southern California Law Review</u>. 50 (1977) 871-959.
Hirschoff advocates legislation enabling parents to have offspring excused from objectionable instruction.

224. Kane, Peter E. "Freedom of Speech for Public School Students," <u>Speech Teacher</u>. 20 (January 1971) 21-28.
Kane surveys the First Amendment rights of students that have been reinforced in the courts.

225. Levine, Alan H., and Eve Cary, compilers. <u>The Rights of Students; An ACLU Handbook</u>. New York: Discus/Avon, 1977.
An exposition of student rights based upon a straightforward interpretation of the Constitution and relevant court decisions.

226. Van Doren, Keith W. "Constitutional Rights of High School Students," <u>Drake Law Review</u>. 23 (1974) 403-422.
An introductory survey to the First and Fourteenth Amendment rights of high school students.

The Rights of the Student Press

227. Abbott, C. Michael. "The Student Press: Some First Impressions," <u>Wayne Law Review</u>. 16 (Winter 1969) 1-36.
Abbott examines the extent of the protection afforded by the First and Fourteenth Amendments with respect to dissidence in student publications.

228. Abbott, C. Michael. "The Student Press: Some Second Thoughts," <u>Wayne Law Review</u>. 16 (Summer 1970) 989-1004.
Abbott discusses court decisions concerning the First Amendment rights of the student press which have been handed down since the appearance of his Winter 1969 article in the <u>Wayne Law Review</u> (see item 227). He detects that recent cases have been inconsistent in their interpretation of these rights.

229. "Board of Education Rule Requiring Prior Submission of Private Student Newspaper Is Unconstitutionally Vague and Overbroad--Nitzberg v. Parks," <u>Maryland Law Review</u>. 35 (1976) 512-522.
An analysis of the decision of the U.S. Court of Appeals for the Fourth Circuit which held that a school board order proscribing publication of two student newspapers suffered from overbreadth and lacked necessary procedural safeguards. Its significance in light of the <u>Tinker</u> case is given particular attention.

230. Estrin, Herman A., and Arthur M. Sanderson, editors. <u>Freedom and Censorship of the College Press</u>. Dubuque, Iowa: W.C. Brown, 1966.

A collection of essays and documents concerned with the
student press, its responsibilities, First Amendment rights,
and relationship to censorship.

231. Flygare, Thomas J. "School-Sponsored Student Newspapers
      Are Entitled to First Amendment Protection," Phi Delta Kappan.
      58 (June 1977) 768-769.
         Flygare provides a rationale for his stance that First Amend-
      ment rights should be extended to student publications.

232. Huffman, John L., and Denise M. Trauth. "Freedom of Expres-
      sion in Public High Schools Since 'Ginsberg' & 'Tinker.'" Paper
      presented at the Annual Meeting of the Association for Educa-
      tion in Journalism, Boston, August 9-13, 1980. Available from
      ERIC, ED 188220.
         A review of the related cases that have been adjudicated
      in the United States Circuit Courts of Appeals in the decade
      since Ginsberg v. New York and Tinker v. Des Moines Indepen-
      dent School District reveals that the courts are not in agreement
      in delineating the First Amendment publication rights of high
      school students. Huffman notes that circuit courts are moving
      in different judicial directions, each relying on its own inter-
      pretation of the standards proposed by the United States Su-
      preme Court in Ginsberg and Tinker. As a result, there
      exists a wide spectrum of constitutional interpretation in this
      area, ranging from sharply limited rights to virtually full First
      Amendment rights for students. He concludes that until the
      Supreme Court sees fit to clarify its stand and explicate the
      area of students' First Amendment rights, the power of school
      authorities with respect to the rights of students will depend
      largely on the developed law in each individual court.

233. Manual for Student Expression: The First Amendment Rights
      of the High School Press. Washington, D.C.: The Student
      Press Law Center, 1976.
         An indispensible reference tool for all concerned with stu-
      dent rights in general as well as the more narrow area of
      journalistic endeavor.

                    H. HIGHER EDUCATION

234. Commager, Henry Steele. "The Nature of Academic Freedom,"
      Saturday Review. 49 (August 27, 1966) 13-15ff.
         An uncompromising apology for academic freedom. Commager
      notes that "those who today assure us that academic freedom is
      all right in ordinary times, but that in time of crisis it must
      give way to importunate demands of national unity, those who
      argue that academic freedom is all very well in time of peace

but a pernicious indulgence in time of war, are like the Southern slaveocracy and the Nazis and the white supremacists of
South Africa, if not in conduct, then in principle.

235. "Development in the Law--Academic Freedom," Harvard Law
      Review. 81 (1968) 1045-1159.
            A landmark article in the field. Covers collective bargain-
      ing, the advancement of student rights within a system of
      private ordering, and the theoretical foundations of academic
      freedom.

236. Gallagher, Margaret Anne. "A Tyranny of Pity," National Re-
      view. 38:8 (September 26, 1986) 28-32.
            Gallacher's premise is that liberal arts colleges are sup-
      pressing intellectual dissent in the name of protecting racial
      and sexual minorities. The article includes a special section
      entitled, "Silencing the Right," a condensation of an Accuracy
      in Academia pamphlet which lists documented cases of efforts
      to silence speakers espousing rightist views on college campuses.

Faculty Rights

237. Adams, Kathleen W. "Personality Control and Academic Free-
      dom--Rampey v. Allen," Utah Law Review. 27 (1975) 234-
      245.
            An analysis of the decision of the U.S. Court of Appeals
      for the Tenth Circuit that a college president's dismissal of
      several faculty members and administrators violated their First
      Amendment rights.

238. Brown, Ronald C. "Tenure Rights in Contractual and Constitu-
      tional Context," Journal of Law and Education. 6 (1977) 279-
      318.
            Brown explores the probable outcome of enforceable tenure
      rights within the context of contemporary Virginia law, a state
      devoid of any tenure statute.

239. Kutner, Luis. "The Freedom of Academic Freedom: A Legal
      Dilemma," Chi-Kent Law Review. 48 (1971) 168-169.
            Acknowledging the impact of tenure on academic freedom,
      Kutner posits that members of the academic community are most
      responsible for the protection of academic freedom.

Student Rights

240. Barrier, Mary L. "Restriction of the First Amendment in an
      Academic Environment," University of Kansas Law Review. 22
      (Summer 1974) 597-605.
            An analysis of Papish v. Board of Curators (1973), in which

the Supreme Court ruled against the University of Missouri's
expulsion of a journalism student for distributing an allegedly
obscene counterculture newspaper.

241. Bogoty, Lewis. "Beyond Tinker and Healy: Applying the
First Amendment to Student Activities," Columbia Law Review.
78 (1978) 1700-1713.
      Focusing on group activities at college campuses, Bogoty
posits that universities may now deny recognition of student
groups only when the Brandenburg guidelines are met or the
group refuses to follow reasonable regulations. He adds that
universities are not required to provide all groups with financial aid.

242. Ladd, Edward T. "Civil Liberties for Students--At What Age?"
Journal of Law and Education. 3 (1974) 251-262.
      An indictment of the "off-on" rights status of the student
who reaches adulthood at the age of eighteen. Ladd argues
that schools could assist in making the transition educationally
productive.

JOURNALISM

A. THE ROLE OF THE PRESS IN AMERICAN SOCIETY

243. Abrams, Floyd. "Judges and Journalists: Who Decides What?"
      Nieman Reports. 28:4 (Winter 1974) 34-41.
          Abrams--a lawyer well-versed in defending the press in
      libel cases--argues that journalists and publishers must be un-
      flagging in the advocacy of their right to decide what to print.

244. American Society of Newspaper Editors. "Code of Ethics or
      Canons of Journalism," Editor and Publisher. 109:11 (March
      1975) 13, 15.
          The article presents a revision of the 1923 Code; areas
      covered include responsibility, freedom of the press, independ-
      ence, truth and accuracy, and impartiality and fair play.

245. Bagdikian, Ben H. "Considerations on the Future of American
      Journalism," In: Liberating the Media; the New Journalism,
      edited by Charles C. Flippen. Washington, D.C.: Acropolis,
      1973. pp. 192-202.
          Bagdikian posits that the future of the profession will be
      determined by politicians and court cases. He adds that jour-
      nalists must fight to retain their First Amendment rights in
      the best interests of a democratic society.

246. Bagdikian, Ben H. The Effete Conspiracy and Other Crimes
      of the Press. New York: Harper & Row, 1972.
          This collection of essays enumerates such press "crimes"
      as its conservative bent; its inability to confront the political,
      financial, and religious concerns of the ownership; its sup-
      pression of important news; etc.

247. Berns, Walter. "The Constitution and a Responsible Press,"
      In: The Mass Media and Modern Democracy, edited by Harry
      M. Clor. Chicago: Rand McNally, 1974. pp. 113-135.
          Berns argues that First Amendment rights have taken prece-
      dence over laws enacted to ensure a responsible press in re-
      cent years. He feels that the latter are "not incompatible with
      free government; they may be a necessary condition of it."

248.   Wicker, Tom. "Our All-Too-Timid Press," In: The First Free-
       dom Today, edited by Robert B. Downs and Ralph E. McCoy.
       Chicago: American Library Association, 1984. pp. 273-277.
           Wicker states that a case can be made for tolerance of ir-
       responsibility on the part of the press because freedom con-
       tains within itself the possibility of irresponsibility. He con-
       cludes, "my life in journalism has persuaded me that the press
       too often tries to guard its freedom by shirking its responsi-
       bility and that this leads to default on both. What the press
       in America needs is less inhibition, not more restraint."

249.   Wolfson, Lewis W. "Whose First Amendment?" The Progressive.
       39:1 (January 1975) 42-46.
           Wolfson notes that while the press has been vindicated in
       its First Amendment rights by Watergate, the Pentagon Papers,
       etc., it still must deal with a crisis in public confidence. He
       offers the following prescription for this dilemma: "[Journalists]
       can show that their First Amendment freedom is everybody's free-
       dom by spurring debate on their pages by all voices, and by
       leveling with the people about their own shortcomings."

                    B.   HISTORY OF THE PRESS

250.   Barnett, Lincoln. "The Case of John Peter Zenger," American
       Heritage. 23:1 (December 1971) 33-41, 103-105.
           This account of the landmark libel case focuses upon its
       legacy; i.e., its establishment of (1) the validity of truth as
       a defense of libel, and (2) the right of the jury to decide
       libelousness.

251.   Levy, Leonard W. Emergence of a Free Press. New York:
       Oxford University Press, 1985.
           A substantially expanded and revised version of the author's
       landmark 1960 work, Legacy of Suppression. While retaining
       his prior thesis that the First Amendment--as originally con-
       ceived--was not the bulwark of the free press that many
       thought it to be, Levy now argues that the early press was in
       practice far more robust in its criticisms of public affairs than
       existing laws and theoretical tradition would seem to have al-
       lowed.

252.   Levy, Leonard W., ed. Freedom of the Press from Zenger to
       Jefferson; Early American Libertarian Theories. Indianapolis:
       Bobbs-Merrill, 1966.
           An anthology incorporating original documents, writings,
       and other records concerned with freedom of the press between
       1735-1804. The work is comprised of six parts: (I) The Form-
       ative Period: "Cato" and Zenger; (II) The Revolutionary

Period: Patriots and Blackstonians; (III) The Constitutional
Period: Neo-Blackstonians; (IV) The New Libertarianism; (V)
The Special Case of Thomas Jefferson; (VI) Epilogue: Zenger
Revivivus.

253.   "The Zenger Case: 250 Years Later," Newsletter on Intellectual
       Freedom.   34:6 (November 1985) 185, 205-215.
           The edited transcription of "Today's Implications of the
       Trial of John Peter Zenger," a program held at The American
       Library Association's 1985 annual conference, featuring Burton
       Joseph, prominent First Amendment attorney; Heather Florence,
       general counsel to Bantam Books, Inc.; R. Bruce Rich, general
       counsel to the Association of American Publishers Freedom to
       Read Committee; and Franklyn Haiman, Professor of Communica-
       tion Studies at Northwestern University.   Zenger, owner of
       the newspaper, The New York Weekly, was charged with sedi-
       tious libel in 1735; his case has come down as a symbol that
       free expression cannot be at the pleasure of the government
       and the government is incapable of deciding what is truthful
       and what expression has merit to be allowed to be exchanged
       in the marketplace of political controversy.

            C.   NOTABLE JOURNALISTIC ISSUES RELATED
                     TO THE FIRST AMENDMENT

Free Press vs. Fair Trial/Gag Orders

254.   American Civil Liberties Union.   "Prejudicial Pre-Trial Publi-
       city," In: The First Freedom Today, edited by Robert B.
       Downs and Ralph E. McCoy.   Chicago: American Library As-
       sociation, 1984.   pp. 300-302.
           A policy statement by the Board of Directors of the ACLU
       which illustrates that body's dilemma over two conflicting civil
       rights values: First Amendment freedom, and the need to
       maintain rigouous standards of due process in criminal proceed-
       ings.   The document seeks greater cooperation between press,
       bar, and bench.

255.   Daniel, Clifton.   "Fair Trial and Freedom of the Press," Case
       and Comment.   (September/October 1960).   Reprinted in:
       The First Freedom Today, edited by Robert B. Downs and
       Ralph E. McCoy.   Chicago: American Library Association,
       1984.   pp. 311-315.
           While acknowledging the abuses of the press in covering
       trials and applauding the efforts of the legal profession to dis-
       cipline its members to ensure a fair trial, Daniel itemizes what
       the press will not do to endanger its freedom to publish: (1)
       submit to censorship; (2) surrender the freedom to publish

anything that is said or done in public, within the bounds of
libel and good taste; (3) yield up the privilege of publishing
anything said in open court; (4) surrender the power to ex-
pose and criticize the acts of public officials; (5) do some of
the ridiculous things that lawyers suggest be done; (6) submit
to legislation that clearly abridges the constitutional guarantee
of a free press; (7) accept any compulsory code of conduct.

256. Friendly, Alfred, and Ronald L. Goldfarb. Crime and Publicity; The Impact of News on the Administration of Justice.
New York: Twentieth Century Fund, 1967.
       The authors--one a newspaper executive, the other a prac-
ticing trial lawyer--delineate the free press-fair trial problem:
"On the one hand is the contention that the public interest in
news is justifiable and irresistible, at least in a democracy,
and to the extent information about crime is denied the public,
or minimized or even delayed, to that extent injury is done to
the public; on the other hand is the assertion that the public
interest can itself contaminate certain of those procedures of
the court, specifically the objectivity of the jurors, that assure a defendant a fair trial."

257. Lewis, Anthony. "Press Power and the First Amendment,"
Civil Liberties Review. 1 (Fall 1973) 183-185. Reprinted in:
The First Freedom Today, edited by Robert B. Downs and
Ralph E. McCoy. Chicago: American Library Association,
1984. pp. 315-317.
       Lewis argues against a specific journalist's privilege to pro-
tect news sources.

258. Nizer, Louis. "Trial By Headline," McCalls. v. 94 (February
1967) 93, 182-184. Reprinted In: The First Freedom Today,
edited by Robert B. Downs and Ralph E. McCoy. Chicago:
American Library Association, 1984. pp. 305-310.
       Nizer argues for limiting press coverage of criminal trials.

259. Pfaff, Ellen O. "Gag Orders on Criminal Defendants," Hast-
ings Law Journal. 27 (July 1976) 369-399.
       Pfaff argues that legal justification does not exist for limit-
ing the defendant's First Amendment right to speak freely on
any issue.

260. Schmidt, Richard M., Jr. "First and Sixth: Sibling Rivalry,"
The Quill. (September 1976) 25-27. Reprinted in: The First
Freedom Today, edited by Robert B. Downs and Ralph E. McCoy.
Chicago: American Library Association, 1984. pp. 296-300.
       Schmidt delineates the relationship between the two amend-
ments.

261. State Bar of California. "Joint Declaration Regarding News
Coverage of Criminal Proceedings in California," Journal of the

State Bar of California. (March/April 1970). Reprinted in:
The First Freedom Today, edited by Robert B. Downs and
Ralph E. McCoy. Chicago: American Library Association,
1984. pp. 303-305.
     A model statement of principles which reflect a willingness
on the part of the press, the bar, and the bench to draft
mutually acceptable and voluntary guidelines that recognize the
two basic constitutional rights.

Libel/Invasion of Privacy

262. Anderson, David A. "A Response to Professor Robertson:
      The Issue Control of Press Power," Texas Law Review. 54
      (January 1976) 271-184.
           Gertz v. Robert Welch, Inc. (1974) represented a reversal
      of the Supreme Court's prior protection of the press from libel
      judgments. This article responds to David Robertson's defense
      of that decision which appears in the same issue (pp. 199-284).

263. Anderson, David A. "The Selective Impact of Libel Law,"
      Columbia Journalism Review. 14:1 (May/June 1975) 38-40, 42.
           Citing recent Supreme Court cases, Anderson notes that
      "the legal system as it now operates in matters of libel, favors
      the established media outlets over the newer ones, rich news
      subjects over poorer ones, and 'professional' reporting over
      advocacy." He advocates a sound insurance system as a means
      of placing all journalists on an equal footing.

264. Brennan, William J., Jr. "Uninhibited, Robust, and Wide-
      Open," In: The First Freedom Today, edited by Robert B.
      Downs and Ralph E. McCoy. Chicago: American Library As-
      sociation, 1984. pp. 287-291.
           Reprint of the majority opinion delivered by Justice Brennan
      in New York Times v. Sullivan. The Supreme Court reversed
      the Supreme Court of Alabama's decision that L. B. Sullivan,
      a Commissioner of Montgomery, had been libeled by statements
      in a full-page ad carried in the March 29, 1960 issue of The
      New York Times.

265. Miller, Arthur B. "Overzealous Reporters Vs. the Right to
      Privacy," Los Angeles Times. (April 16, 1978). Reprinted
      in: The First Freedom Today, edited by Robert B. Downs
      and Ralph E. McCoy. Chicago: American Library Association,
      1984. pp. 284-287.
           Miller argues that the public's right to privacy needs in-
      creased protection against the press.

266. Picard, Robert G. "Self-Censorship Threatens U.S. Press
      Freedom," Index on Censorship. 2:3 (June 1982) 15-17. Re-
      printed in: The First Freedom Today, edited by Robert B.

Downs and Ralph E. McCoy.   Chicago: American Library Association, 1984. pp. 291-295.
    Picard argues that publishers and broadcasters are increas-
ingly exercising self-censorship in order to avoid costly litigation.

267.   Robertson, David W.   "Defamation and the First Amendment:
In Praise of Gertz v. Robert Welch, Inc.," Texas Law Review.
54 (January 1976) 199-270.
    Robertson applauds the Supreme Court's decision in that it
rejects the knowing or reckless falsity requirement for cases
concerned with defamation of character in favor of liability
based on fault.

268.   Schwartz, Alan U.   "Using the Courts to Muzzle the Press,"
The Atlantic.   239:2 (February 1977) 29-34.   Reprinted in:
The First Freedom Today, edited by Robert B. Downs and
Ralph E. McCoy.   Chicago: American Library Association,
1984.   pp. 278-284.
    Schwartz expresses concern that Supreme Court decisions
between 1964 and 1976 concerned with libel and privacy may
facilitate excessive self-censorship by reporters.

Right of Access to Information and the Media

269.   Barron, Jerome A.   "Access to the Press--A New First Amendment Right," Harvard Law Review.   80:8 (June 1967) 1641-
1677.   Reprinted in: Mass Communication Law, by Donald M.
Gillmor and Jerome A. Barron, St. Paul, Minn.:   West, 1969
(2nd ed., pp. 553-572); Readings in Mass Communications,
edited by Michael C. Emery and Ted C. Smythe, Dubuque,
Iowa: W. C. Brown, 1980 (pp. 16-22); and Mass Media and
the Law, edited by David G. Clark and Earl R. Hutchison
N.Y.:   Wiley-Interscience, 1970 (pp. 421-461).
    A seminal article concerned with the issue of "right of ac-
cess."   Barron argues that a twentieth-century interpretation
of the First Amendment--which would require corporate-owned
newspapers to champion new ideas and old grievances--is needed
in order to restore credibility to the press.

270.   Barron, Jerome A.   Freedom of the Press for Whom?   The Right
of Access to Mass Media.   Bloomington, Ind.:   Indiana University Press, 1973.
    Barron states that "freedom of expression is meaningless if
all the important means of expression--press, television, radio--
are closed.   In the past, freedom of the press was achieved
by forbidding government.   Now the communications industry
itself is the major censor."   He goes on to analyze how the
media presently function and provides suggestions for democra-
tizing them.

271. Commission on Freedom and Equality of Access to Information,
     American Library Association. Freedom and Equality of Access
     to Information: A Report to the American Library Association.
     Dan M. Lacy, chair. Chicago: American Library Association,
     1986.
        The study attempts to (1) define and find synthesis in is-
     sues (social, economic, political, and technological) arising from
     the ability of modern technologies to enhance and extend the
     production and dissemination of information, and (2) identify
     those particular issues in which decisions as to public or pri-
     vate sector policy may be needed to assure the level of access
     to information required for economic growth, for effective citizen
     participation in public affairs, and for individual self-fulfillment.
     the Commission offers twenty-four recommendations spanning
     telecommunications, electronically stored information, govern-
     ment information, censorship, copyright, libel, and libraries
     and access to information.

272. Freedman, Janet. "Privileged Access: Who Shall Know." So-
     cial Policy. 8:5 (March/April 1978) 44-46.
        Freedman analyzes the implications of the implementation of
     computerized databases in libraries. She posits that these
     sources may result in limiting access to information by economi-
     cally-disadvantaged individuals.

273. "Less Access to Less Information By and About the U.S. Govern-
     ment: a 1986 Chronology (January-June)," Newsletter on In-
     tellectual Freedom. 35:6 (November 1986) 204-205, 234-235.
        A collection of news briefs, drawn from leading newspapers,
     journals, and government documents, which highlight develop-
     ments resulting in inroads to public access to information pro-
     duced by and disseminated within the federal government. This
     installment represents a continuation of four previous articles
     appearing in the Newsletter on Intellectual Freedom covering
     the period from April 1981 to the present compilation, includ-
     ing the November 1985 and March 1986 issues.

274. Rettig, James. "Rights, Resolutions, Fees, and Reality,"
     Library Journal. 106:3 (February 2, 1981) 301-304.
        Contrary to the recommendations of professional associations
     such as the American Library Association, the author feels
     that the economic climate necessitates that many libraries either
     charge fees for information services or eliminate them altogether.
     He advises that fees be charged to all users; exceptions should
     be based on uniform criteria such as ability to pay, rather
     than group status.

275. Schmidt, Benno, Jr. Freedom of the Press vs. Public Access.
     New York: Praeger, 1976.
        Schmidt surveys broadcast regulations and print-media
     problems relating to access. He examines whether or not

access obligations sustained for the electronic media are constitutionally barred for the print media.

276.   Tauer, Carol A.   "Information as a Human Right," Minnesota
       Libraries.   (Winter 1984-85) 332-334.
       Tauer provides a rationale for right of access.

The Right to Know

277.   Alt, James D.   "The Right to Record and Broadcast Public
       Legislative Proceedings," University of Chicago Law Review.
       42 (Winter 1975) 336-361.
       Alt agrees that the First Amendment protects the right of
       journalists to record and broadcast public legislative proceed-
       ings.

278.   Anderson, Jack.   "Why I Blew the Whistle," Parade.   (February
       13, 1972) 6, 8.
       Anderson provides a rationale for citizens' right to know.

279.   Anderson, Jack, with George Clifford.   The Anderson Papers.
       New York: Random House, 1973.
       This landmark of investigative reporting underscores the
       importance of providing public access to government information.

280.   Bennis, Warren.   "Have We Gone Overboard on 'The Right to
       Know'?"   Saturday Review.   3:11 (March 6, 1976) 18-21.
       Bennis argues that "disclosure mania" inhibits the operation
       of government.   He considers the key to effective government
       to be the selection of honest--and qualified--public officials.

281.   Emerson, Thomas I.   "The Danger of State Secrecy," The Na-
       tion.   (March 30, 1974) Reprinted in The First Freedom Today,
       edited by Robert B. Downs and Ralph E. McCoy.   Chicago:
       American Library Association, 1984.   pp. 257-263.
       Emerson argues that secrecy in a democratic society is a
       source of illegitimate power.   He provides recommendations
       which might facilitate the kind of legal structure that is neces-
       sary to maintain an effective system of open government.

282.   Gordon, Andrew C., and John P. Heinz, editors.   Public Ac-
       cess to Information.   New Brunswick, N.J.:   Transaction Books,
       1979.
       The compilation spans the various issues concerned with the
       public's right to know.

283.   Levin, Marc A.   "Access and Dissemination Issues Concerning
       Federal Government Information," Special Libraries.   74:2
       (April 1983) 127-137.   Reprinted in: Library Lit. 14--The
       Best of 1983, edited by Bill Katz.   Metuchen, N.J.:   Scare-
       crow, 1984.   pp. 275-288.

Levin states that the traditional presumption underlying
U.S. information policy has been the open availability of and
ease of access to information relevant to the needs or desires
of American citizens in keeping with the principles enunciated
in the First Amendment. He adds that historically, however,
there has been no comprehensive national information policy
and no consensus about instituting one from within the government. He illustrates how this lack of centralization has led to
a mosaic of public and administrative laws and varying policy
interpretations within the government.

284. Minor, Dale. The Information War. New York: Hawthorne
      Books, 1970.
          Minor examines the nature of government censorship, the
      press' interpretation of the news, and factors determining what
      information reaches the public.

285. O'Brien, David M. The Public Right to Know: The Supreme
      Court and the First Amendment. New York: Praeger, 1981.
          O'Brien posits that the "right to know" is not explicitly
      guaranteed in the Constitution; however, the Supreme Court
      has interpreted the First Amendment "as securing the conditions
      for an informed public."

286. Schiller, Anita R., and Herbert I. Schiller. "The Privatizing
      of Information: Who Can Own What America Knows?" The
      Nation. 234:15 (April 17, 1982) 461-463.
          The authors delineate the inherent clash between govern-
      ment interests and the rights of private citizens. More specifi-
      cally, they discuss the inclination of the Reagan Administration
      and the Information Industry Association to shift control of
      the national information base from public to private hands.
      They feel that if information is viewed only as a commodity,
      much socially-needed information won't ever be collected or
      disseminated. The implications for a democracy which requires
      an informed electorate could be devastating.

287. Varlejs, Jana, editor. The Right to Information; Legal Ques-
      tions and Policy Issues. Jefferson, N.C.: McFarland, 1984.
          The monograph is comprised of speeches given at the twenty-
      first annual Rutgers GSLIS Alumni-Faculty Symposium. The
      programs considered the following: (1) components of informa-
      tion policy (laws, regulations, agencies, public- and private-
      sector participants); (2) information rights (property, privacy,
      First Amendment); (3) equity for producers, users, and inter-
      mediaries (what kinds of policies and mechanisms are needed);
      (4) action agenda for the library/information profession (build-
      ing consensus and alliances, user interest advocacy). Presen-
      tations included: "The Right to Privacy vs. the Right to
      Know," by Edward J. Bloustein; "Librarians, Publishers and
      the New Information Environment," by Irving Louis Horowitz;

"The New Information Agenda in Washington: Some Case Stud-
ies from the Private Sector Viewpoint," by Paul Zurkowski;
"The Right to Know: The Librarian's Responsibilities," by
Shirley Echelman.

288.   Wessel, Andrew E.   The Social Use of Information: Ownership
and Access.   New York: John Wiley and Sons, 1976.
      Wessel provides a framework for instituting equitable access
to automated information systems.

      a.   The Freedom of Information Act (F.O.I.A.)

289.   Archibald, Samuel J.   "Whose FOI Law?"   Bulletin of the American Society of Newspaper Editors.   536 (December 1969) 10-12.
      Archibald cites the value of the act to the press.   He also
advocates the use of the University of Missouri Freedom of Information Center by journalists.

290.   Havemann, Joel, and Sarah E. Warren.   "The Legal Twists and
Twirls of the Freedom of Information Act," National Journal:
The Weekly on Politics and Government.   10:24 (June 17, 1978)
968-971.
      The article assesses the impact of the 1974 amendments to
the Freedom of Information Act.

291.   Landau, Jack C.   "President Reagan and the Press," The News
Media & the Law.   (February/March 1982). Reprinted in: The
First Freedom Today, edited by Robert B. Downs and Ralph
E. McCoy.   Chicago: American Library Association, 1984.   pp.
271-272.
      Landau asserts that the presidential order issued in October
1981--whereby government officials may classify information
even if they are uncertain whether secrecy is needed to protect
national security--is saying: "We are not accountable to 'you'
(the public), we are only accountable to 'us' (the government)."

292.   Miller, Nancy.   "Public Access to Public Records: Some
Threatening Reforms," Wilson Library Bulletin.   56:2 (October 1981) 95-99.
      Miller provides historical background relating to govern-
ment policies on access to government information prior to the
enactment of the Freedom of Information Act.   She analyzes
the act and the degree to which presidential administrations
have complied with it.

293.   Relyea, Harold C.   "The Rise and Pause of the U.S. Freedom
of Information Act," Government Publications Review.   10
(January/February 1983) 19-33.   Reprinted in: Library Lit.
14--The Best of 1983, edited by Bill Katz.   Metuchen, N.J.:
Scarecrow, 1984.   pp. 305-325.
      Relyea provides a concise history of the act, including the

forces leading to its enactment in 1966 and later attempts to
modify its provisions.

b.   The "Pentagon Papers"

294. Bagdikian, Ben H.   "The First Amendment on Trial: What
      Did We Learn?" Columbia Journalism Review.   10:3 (September/
      October 1971) 45-50.   Reprinted in: The First Freedom To-
      day, edited by Robert B. Downs and Ralph E. McCoy.   Chicago:
      American Library Association, 1984.   pp. 265-270.
         Bagdikian reviews the implications of the U.S. Supreme
      Court decision in the "Pentagon Papers" case.   Despite this
      victory, the press must remain constantly vigilant in the fight
      to protect its First Amendment rights.

295. "'The Pentagon Papers' Case," The New York Times.   (July
      1, 1971) Reprinted in: The First Freedom Today, edited by
      Robert B. Downs and Ralph E. McCoy.   Chicago: American
      Library Association, 1984.   pp. 264-265.
         The article states that the Supreme Court decision to lift
      the restraining order that had prevented newspapers from pub-
      lishing the hitherto secret "Pentagon Papers" reaffirmed the
      guarantee of the people's right to know.

296. Witcover, Jules, et al.   "The First Amendment on Trial," Colum-
      bia Journalism Review.   10:3 (September/October 1971) 7-50.
         A collection of articles concerned with the publication of
      the "Pentagon Papers."

LIBRARIANSHIP

A. THE ADVOCATION OF CENSORSHIP IN LIBRARIES

297. Cowley, Malcolm. "Dirty Books," Virginia Librarian. 14 (Winter 1967) 8-17 Reprinted in: The First Freedom Today, edited by Robert B. Downs and Ralph E. McCoy. Chicago: American Library Association, 1984. pp. 248-255.
    Cowley, in a speech before the Virginia Library Association, advocates the discriminating use of censorship by librarians to fight obscenity.

298. Molz, Kathleen. "The Public Custody of the High Pornography," Library Journal. 92:17 (October 1, 1967) 3373-3376.
    Molz notes that it may seem unfortunate that librarians have traditionally placed a greater reliance in these matters on the literature of jurisprudence than on the literature of criticism, for pornography is essentially an aesthetic, not judicial, problem. In conclusion, she voices the hope that the public library will resist the banalities of a literature squalid in style, poor in effect.

B. LIBRARIANS AS CENSORS

299. Bailey, Bill. "The Literature of Conservatism," Collection Building. 7:1 (Spring 1984) 11-13.
    Bailey analyzes the accusation of Cal Thomas, vice president of the Moral Majority, that librarians have turned a cold shoulder to books by conservatives. He concludes that, most likely, Thomas is correct in his complaints; an unfortunate situation because libraries should provide materials and information presenting all points of view on current and historical issues.

300. Boisse, Joseph A., et al. "Intellectual Freedom in Wisconsin," Wisconsin Library Bulletin. 67 (July/August 1971) 241-253.
    A collection of articles focusing on censorship within a library context. Topics include the selection process as censorship, the film medium, and conditions in the Wisconsin scene.

301. Bostwick, Arthur E. "The Librarian as a Censor," Library
      Journal. 33 (1908) 257-264.
          The text of Bostwick's 1908 presidential address to the
      American Library Association reflects the exclusionist stance
      still holding sway within large segments of the profession at
      that time. His speech reveals a shift from the earlier elitist
      pronouncements of genteel America, which had dominated li-
      brarianship in the nineteenth century, to the more "scientific"
      rhetoric typifying the Progressive era.

302. Daily, Jay E. "Afterwords: Censorship and Management After
      Mid-1973," Journal of Library Administration. 4:1 (Spring
      1983) 7-11.
          Daily surveys censorship in the library field since the land-
      mark Miller vs. California cases. He attempts to heighten the
      sensitivity of library managers to the issues involved and
      recommends ways of dealing with censorship in a professional
      manner.

303. Garrison, Dee. Apostles of Culture: The Public Librarian and
      American Society, 1876-1920. New York: Free Press, 1979.
          Garrison notes the varied strategems employed by public
      librarians to protect their clientele from objectionable books.

304. Hagist, Barbara. "Resistance and Reluctance in Record Selec-
      tion," Library Journal. 93:3 (February 1, 1968) 518-520.
          Hagist notes that if book collections had been developed
      with the principles of selection used by today's record librarians,
      libraries would contain only incunabula and classic literature.
      A survey sent out to all public libraries serving cities of over
      100,000 population (130), indicated that libraries were not
      keeping abreast of public tastes or technological advance-
      ments in the selection of newer media.

305. Peck, A. L. "What May a Librarian Do...," Library Journal.
      22 (1897) 77-90.
          The inclination of librarians in that period to support con-
      temporary community standards and acquiesce to societal pres-
      sures is reflected in the author's advocacy of controlling con-
      troversial titles.

306. Sayers, Frances C. "If the Trumpet Be Not Sounded," Wilson
      Library Bulletin. 39 (1965) 659-662.
          The author charts a wavering line regarding the role of
      librarians in fighting censorship since the late nineteenth cen-
      tury. Sayers speaks from personal experience; she and a
      friend lost their jobs at the New York Public Library during
      World War II as a result of the paranoid pressures of the Home
      Front with its liberty cabbage and Creal Committee.

307. Serebnick, Judith. "Self-Censorship by Librarians: An Analysis

of Checklist-Based Research," Drexel Library Quarterly. 18:1
(Winter 1982) 35-56.

Serebnick delineates checklist-based research designed to
determine whether particular books, periodicals, and films
deemed controversial by the investigators are in the collections
of certain types of libraries. The article includes a discussion of self-censorship and relevant references.

308. Stielow, Frederick J. "Censorship in the Early Professionaliza-
tion of American Libraries, 1876 to 1929," The Journal of Library History. 18:1 (Winter 1983) 37-54. Reprinted in: Library Lit. 14--The Best of 1983, edited by Bill Katz. Metuchen,
N.J.: Scarecrow, 1984. pp. 326-341.

Stielow surveys the gradual evolution of the attitudes of
of librarians toward censorship. He concludes that "by 1925,
censorship policies, while not totally dismissed, had been
altered from an accepted standard into an issue to be attached
or at least challenged in public--a substantial development in
the history of librarianship."

309. Thomas, Cal, and Nat Hentoff. "Are Librarians Fair? Preselection Censorship in a Time of Resurgent Conservatism," Newsletter on Intellectual Freedom. 31:5 (September 1982) 151,
181-188. Reprinted in: The First Freedom Today, edited by
Robert B. Downs and Ralph E. McCoy. Chicago: American
Library Association, 1984. pp. 117-123.

Thomas, Vice-president of the Moral Majority, and columnist
Hentoff provide divergent points of view with respect to a
preselection censorship by librarians. Excerpts from a program
presented at the 1982 ALA annual conference.

310. Watson, Jerry. "Self-Censorship: the Proof is in the Selection," Newsletter on Intellectual Freedom. 30:2 (March 1981)
35, 53-54.

A study, employing a sample of undergraduate and graduate
students taking children's literature classes at the University
of Iowa and Michigan State University (most of whom were Education and Library Science majors), found that book selectors
avoid selecting children's books containing objectionable content
as identified by someone else. Watson concludes that education
in the areas of book selection, book evaluation, and book protection in censorship cases needs immediate practical and
thorough attention.

311. Williams, Patrick, and J. T. Pearce. "Common Sense and Censorship: A Call For Revision," Library Journal. 98:15 (September 1, 1973) 2399-2400.

The authors posit that the current theoretical position of
the library profession on censorship is a disaster. The values
of freedom of expression and inquiry are not unlimited but
rather are relative to the rights of others, to time, place,

circumstances, and any other factor which can legitimately be
introduced.

C. CENSORSHIP BY TYPE OF LIBRARY

Academic Libraries

312. Ashley, Edwin M. "Sensing Censoring," Community & Junior
      College Libraries. 2:1 (Fall 1983) 75-76.
          Ashley notes the vulnerability of U.S. community colleges
      to threats of censorship in that many students are minors.
      He provides recommendations as to how to overcome this vul-
      nerability; e.g., the drafting of a selection policy incorporat-
      ing the American Library Association's Library Bill of Rights
      and supported by the school board.

313. Gore, Daniel. "A Skirmish with the Censors," ALA Bulletin.
      63 (February 1969) 193-203.
          The article conveys the message that anyone working in a
      private, religiously-supported college should expect to find a
      compromised view of the principle of free inquiry. Herein lies
      the distinction between a publicly-supported library, with a
      mandate to uphold first Amendment rights, and a private li-
      brary.

Public Libraries

314. Allain, Alex P. "Public Library Governing Bodies and Intel-
      lectual Freedom," Library Trends. 19:1 (July 1970) 47-63.
          Allain, an attorney and public library trustee, outlines an
      enlightened path for the governing bodies of libraries in deal-
      ing with civil rights issues. He concludes that "it is not
      pornography ... which causes emotional imbalance which impels
      a child or an adult to seek pornography."

315. Allain, Alex P., and Ervin J. Gaines. "Trustees and Censor-
      ship," In: Library Trustee: A Practical Guidebook, edited
      by Virginia G. Young. New York: Bowker, 1969. pp. 149-
      154.
          The authors outline the role of the trustee with respect to
      censorship.

316. Becker, Loftus E. "The First Amendment and Public Libraries,"
      Newsletter on Intellectual Freedom. 27:4 (July 1978) 83-84,
      105-107.
          The text of a speech presented by Becker at a program on
      intellectual freedom sponsored by the Metro Washington Council

of Governments' Library Council, the Maryland Library Association, and the Virginia Library Association. He concludes that
librarians have thought more than any other profession about
the reasons why broad and open access to information is important; if they cannot mobilize support for that proposition in
their communities, then lawyers and judges can't be expected
to assist to any great extent.

317.   "A Dime-Store Paul Revere; A New Trustee Plunges a Thriving
        Young Library on Long Island Into Chaos," Library Journal.
        92:17 (October 1, 1967) 3380-3384.
            Case study in which a John Birch Society member is elected
        to the board of the Farmingdale Public Library and proceeds
        to harrass its staff on a variety of fronts, including the con-
        fiscation of a journal title and a petition to seek direct access
        to library records "at all hours of the day."

318.   Galvin, Hoyt R.   "Freedom of Access, Partially Achieved,"
        Library Trends.   19:1 (July 1970) 89-95.
            Galvin posits that "Freedom of access, in itself, is not the
        only responsibility of librarianship. Until the service is actu-
        ally rendered, and the informational, inspirational, and educa-
        tional needs of the entire community are met, the job is not
        done." He compares the public library to a retail establishment;
        if individuals are not adequately served, their use of--and
        loyalty to--a particular institution will inevitably be curtailed.

319.   Geller, Evelyn.   Forbidden Books in American Public Libraries,
        1876-1939.   Westport, Conn.: Greenwood, 1984.
            Geller depicts the evolution of the library profession's stance
        from the position of guardians of access to all information.

320.   Ladof, Nina Sydney.   "Intellectual Freedom," ALA Bulletin.
        63 (July/August 1969) 903.
            Coverage of the attempt by the VFW, the American Legion,
        the Lion's Club, and a local church to force the St. Charles
        County Library System to label "subversive" and "un-American"
        materials.

321.   Roberts, Don.   Report on Past and Present Censorship of Non-
        Book Median in Public Libraries. Washington, D.C.: Council
        on Library Resources, Inc., 1976. ERIC report, ED 194 096.
            In this 37-page monograph, Roberts analyzes selected cen-
        sorship cases and examines libraries' attitudes and policies
        toward nonprint materials. He concludes that a "primacy of
        print" attitude represents a de facto form of censorship, and
        recommends seven correctional courses of action.

322.   Robinson, Charles W.   "From the Administrator's Desk," Top
        of the News.   31 (April 1975) 313-316.
            Robinson recommends strategies which might facilitate a

greater understanding on issues of intellectual freedom between
public library administrators and the parents of the children
they serve.

School Libraries

323. Bartlett, Larry. "The Iowa Model Policy and Rules for Selec-
      tion of Instructional Materials," In: Dealing With Censorship,
      edited by James E. Davis. Urbana, Ill.: National Council of
      Teachers of English, 1979. pp. 202-214.
          Bartlett outlines the essentials of a model school board
      policy regarding the selection of instructional materials. He
      sees a policy as being a vital source of direction for school
      boards, and ultimately a means of fighting off attempts at cen-
      sorship.

324. Bradley, Julia Turnquist. "Censoring the School Library:
      Do Students Have the Right to Read?" Connecticut Law Re-
      view. 10 (Spring 1978) 747-774.
          A study of school censorship cases. Distinguishing between
      the book selection process and censorship, Bradley focuses on
      a constitutional formula by which the First Amendment rights
      to read may be ensured without damaging school boards' in-
      terests in the selection of instructional materials.

325. Bryson, Joseph E., and Elizabeth W. Detty. The Legal Aspects
      of Censorship of Public School Library and Instructional Ma-
      terials. Charlottesville, Virginia: Michie Company, 1982.
          The overall aim of the work is to provide appropriate in-
      formation to assist educational decision makers in matters con-
      cerning legal aspects of censorship. The information is also
      intended to provide guidance in the selection of appropriate
      educational materials and preparation of policies and procedures,
      thereby minimizing the litigation and adverse public relations
      associated with censoring situations.

326. Censorship, Libraries and the Law, compiled and with an intro-
      duction by Haig Bosmajian. Foreword by Nat Hentoff. New
      York: Neal-Schuman, 1983.
          A compilation of landmark court cases concerned with book
      censorship in school libraries; its aim is to make librarians
      more confident of their ability to deal with any future assaults
      on their freedom to read as well as to discourage self censor-
      ship. The work is divided into two parts: (1) School Library
      Censorship Cases, and (2) United States Supreme Court Deci-
      sions Relied On by the Lower Courts in Library Censorship
      Cases.

327. Censorship Litigation and the Schools. Chicago: American
      Library Association, Office of Intellectual Freedom, 1983.

The work is comprised of papers presented at the Colloquium
on School and School Library Book Censorship Litigation, Janu-
ary 1981. Contents: "Current Social and Political Trends and
Their Implications for Future Litigation," by Robert O'Neil;
"The State as Editor or Censor: Book Selection and the Public
Schools," by Mark G. Yadov; "Schoolbook Censorship Litiga-
tion: a Litigator's Overview," by Floyd Abrams; "A First
Amendment Perspective," by Floyd Abrams.

328.   Clark, Elyse. "A Slow, Subtle Exercise in Censorship," School
Library Journal. 32:7 (March 1986) 93-96.
         Clark, a Middle School Librarian for the Hanover (Pa.)
Public School District, recounts the successful efforts of the
Hanover Board of Education and school administrators to re-
move six books from library shelves. She concludes by saying,
"The repression of knowledge sets a dangerous precedent. In
the words of Edmund Burke, 'All that is needed for the triumph
of evil is that good men do nothing.' "

329.   Lawhorne, Clifton O. "Library Censorship and the Law,"
Arkansas Libraries. 38:2 (June 1981) 8-13.
         The author discusses the decisions in various court cases
involving censorship of library materials. The article possesses
a predominantly school library orientation.

Minarcini v. Strongsville City School District

330.   Koletsky, Joy. "Limit of School Board's Discretion in Curriculum Choice--the Public School Library as a Marketplace of
Ideas," Case Western Law Review. 27 (1977) 1034-1055.
         A study of Minarcini v. Strongsville City School District,
in which the U.S. Court of appeals for the Sixth Circuit held
that the removal of certain library books represented an abridge-
ment of the First Amendment rights of students.

331.   Seitz, William John. "Removal of Books From School Libraries
Violates Students' First Amendment Rights," University of Cincinnati Law Review. 45 (1976) 701-709.
         Seitz analyzes cases concerned with the censorship of school
library materials, with a particular emphasis upon Minarcini v.
Strongsville School District.

332.   Simpson, William Kennedy. "Constitutional Aspects of Removing Books from School Libraries," Kentucky Law Journal. 66
(1978) 127-149.
         Simpson analyzes the conflicting decisions reached in Presi-
dent's Council District 25 v. Community School Board No. 25
and Minarcini v. Strongsville City School District.

333.   "The Strongsville Decision," School Library Journal. 23:3
(November 1976) 23-28.

The article covers the U.S. District Court's decision which
required the Strongsville (Ohio) board of education to replace
the books it had ordered removed from the library at an earlier
date.

D. ADVOCATION OF A STANCE OPPOSED TO CENSORSHIP

334. Asheim, Lester. "Not Censorship but Selection," Wilson Library Bulletin. (September 1953)
      Asheim focuses upon the distinction between censorship and
selection. He concludes that "selection is democratic while censorship is authoritarian, and in our democracy we have tradi-
tionally tended to put our trust in the selector rather than in
the censor." The article remains as relevant today as in the
day it was written.

335. Berninghausen, David K. "Intellectual Freedom in Librarianship: Advances and Retreats," In: Advances in Librarianship, edited by Michael H. Harris. Volume 9. Seminar Press,
1979. pp. 1-29.
      Berninghausen's essay focuses on two major areas: (1) the
philosophical stance of the profession with respect to intellectual
freedom, and (2) the application of that concept in practice.
He asserts that the future is doubtful; the question of whether
free inquiry for library users will survive depends upon the
the vigor and effectiveness of those who defend it when it is
challenged.

336. Berninghausen, David K. "The Librarian's Commitment to the
Library Bill of Rights," Library Trends. 19:1 (July 1970)
19-38.
      A historical survey of the librarian's role in the support of
intellectual freedom, beginning with the institution of the Library's Bill of Rights in 1939. Berninghausen also provides
a philosophical framework for this stance on the part of the
profession.

337. Busha, Charles. An Intellectual Freedom Primer. Littleton,
Colo." Libraries Unlimited, 1977.
      The book is comprised of essays covering some of the most
significant aspects of censorship and intellectual freedom in
the present day. Contents include: Busha's summary of the
state of intellectual freedom in the U.S. in the twentieth century; Stephen Harter's "Privacy and Security in Automated
Personal Data Systems," which notes the potential dangers of
centralized national data centers; Yvonne Linnert Morse's "Freedom of the Visual Arts," which documents the widespread
governmental censorship of pictures, photos, and sculpture at

the local level; Rebecca Dixon's "Bibliographical Control of
Erotica," which calls for the selection, acquisition, and organization of erotica so as to make it more readily available to scholars
and other interested parties.

338. Castagna, Edwin. "Censorship, Intellectual Freedom, and Libraries," In: Advances in Librarianship. Volume 2. Seminar
Press, 1971. pp. 215-251.
  Castagna surveys the historical background and issues with
respect to librarianship and intellectual freedom.

339. De Grazia, Edward. "Sex and the Stuffy Librarian," Library
Journal. 90 (June 1, 1965) 2183-2485.
  De Grazia challenges librarians to resist the impulse to self-
censorship.

340. Donelson, Ken. "Censorship Today and Probably Tomorrow,"
Canadian Library Journal. 40:2 (April 1983) 83-89.
  The article examines preconceptions on censorship, citing
problems posed to librarians and teachers. Donelson covers
censored books, individual censors (e.g., the Gablers), organized groups (e.g., Save Our Schools, Phyllis Schlafly's Eagle
Forum, the Moral Majority), teachers and librarians as censors,
and others who aid and abet censors.

341. Ficociello, T. "Censorship, Book Selection, and the Marketplace of Ideas," Top of the News. 41:1 (Fall 1984) 33-38.
  Ficociello addresses issues raised in Carol Hole's article,
"Who Me, Censor?" (See item number 345) with respect to
library collection development and censorship.

342. Gaines, Ervin J. "The Crucial Error in Censorship," Library
Journal. 92:17 (October 1, 1967) 3377-3379.
  Gaines notes that censorship is, a priori, undemocratic because it runs counter to the fundamental assumption that all
men have a right to be heard and that, in the marketplace of
ideas, all thoughts are permissible. In his opinion, the free
flow of ideas is a librarian's most cherished ideal, the very
heart and soul of his/her professional activity.

343. Gaines, Ervin J. "Libraries and the Climate of Opinion," Library Trends. 19:1 (July 1970) 39-46.
  Gaines provides a brief survey of censorship in the Western
world, with a primary emphasis on the United States. He discusses the implications of these developments to libraries.
While the climate seems to have improved significantly in the
sixties, particular areas of concern remain within the profession. Public and school libraries are in the most exposed position of all because (1) they are most accessible to democratic
control, and (2) children constitute a substantial portion of
their target audience.

344. Ginger, Ann Fagen, and Celeste MacLeod. "The Rights of the
     People and the Role of Librarians," Library Trends. 19:1
     (July 1970) 96-105.
        The authors feel that librarians can perform a vital service
     for both their patrons and the democracy of our country by
     recognizing the importance of the people's need to know their
     rights, and by providing them with the necessary materials
     and information. The following suggestions are provided as a
     means of accomplishing this goal: (1) collect the laws; (2)
     collect secondary materials, particularly those which relate to
     the needs of your library's clientele; (3) keep a list of agency
     referrals and help patrons use them; (4) publicize the collec-
     tion.

345. Hole, Carol. "Who Me, Censor?" Top of the News. 40:2
     (Winter 1984) 147-153.
        Hole asserts that librarians must not select materials on the
     basis of applying a professional code of ethics or an institutional
     selection policy; rather, the mandate for creating a balanced
     collection necessitates the selection of sexist and racist books.
     The ultimate guideline for librarians should be personal moral
     judgment.

346. McCoy, Ralph E. "Social Responsibility vs. the Library Bill
     of Rights," In: The First Freedom Today, edited by Robert
     B. Downs and Ralph E. McCoy. Chicago: American Library
     Association, 1984. pp. 114-116.
        McCoy examines the interrelationship of social responsibility
     and intellectual freedom concepts.

347. Merritt, LeRoy C. "Book Selection and Intellectual Freedom,"
     In: Book Selection and Intellectual Freedom, New York: Wilson,
     1970. Reprinted in: The First Freedom Today, edited by Robert
     B. Downs and Ralph E. McCoy. Chicago: American Library As-
     sociation, 1984, pp. 103-109.
        An examination of the problems of book selection with re-
     spect to intellectual freedom.

348. Oboler, Eli M. Defending Intellectual Freedom; The Library
     and the Censor. Westport, Conn.: Greenwood Press, 1980.
     (Contributions in Librarianship and Information Science, Number
     32)
        A collection of previously published articles, editorials, let-
     ters, and reviews, as well as new material, developed around
     the theme "that man is by nature free in mind as well as body,
     and that librarians, of all mankind, are (or should be) the
     leaders in explanation, defense, promotion, and practice of in-
     tellectual freedom." Noteworthy chapters include: "The Free
     Mind: Intellectual Freedom's Perils and Prospects"; "The
     Politics of Censorship"; "The Fear of Science: Back of 'The
     Speaker' Controversy"; "The Etiology of Censorship"; "Public
     Relations and Fighting Censorship"; "The Censorship Battle in

a Conservative State." Excellent bibliographic survey--con-
sisting of a book review section and two separate booklists--
of the censorship literature published between 1959-1979.

349. O'Neil, Robert M. "Libraries, Librarians, and First Amendment Freedoms," In: The First Freedom Today, edited by
Robert B. Downs and Ralph E. McCoy. Chicago: American
Library Association, 1984. pp. 124-133.
O'Neil states that constitutional safeguards comparable to
those defining the free expression of professors, teachers,
reporters, theatrical performere, authors, and others cannot
be found in the library world. He feels that there exist per-
suasive, if untested, legal bases for a new and badly needed
First Amendment freedom.

350. Swan, John C. "Untruth or Consequences," Library Journal.
111:12 (July 1986) 44-52.
An impassioned plea for librarians to uphold the true spirit
of intellectual freedom. According to Swan, "We are caught in
a dilemma that we have generally failed to appreciate. We are
committed both to the search for the truth and to the freedom
of expression of untruth."

E. PREPARATIONS FOR DEALING WITH THE CENSOR

351. American Library Association. Office for Intellectual Freedom.
Intellectual Freedom Manual. Chicago: American Library Association, 1974.
The work has been designed to answer the many practical
questions that confront librarians in applying the principles of
intellectual freedom to library service. The contents include:
ALA and Intellectual Freedom: A Historical Overview: Library
Bill of Rights; Freedom to Read; Intellectual Freedom; Before
the Censor Comes: Essential Preparations; Intellectual Freedom
and the Law; Assistance from ALA.

352. American Library Association. Office for Intellectual Freedom.
"What to Do Before the Censor Comes--And After," Newsletter
on Intellectual Freedom. 21 (March 1972) 49-56.
The article includes the following headings: How Libraries
Can Resist Censorship; Library Bill of Rights; School Library
Bill of Rights; Statement on Labeling; Resolution on Challenged
Material; What the American Library Association Can Do For
You to Help Combat Censorship. This material forms an in-
tegral part of the Intellectual Freedom Manual.

353. Asher, Thomas R. "A Lawyer Looks at Libraries and Censorship," Library Journal. 95 (October 1, 1970) 3247-3249.

152910

An American Civil Liberties Union official provides a blue-
print for dealing with threats to intellectual freedom.

354. Bazzell, Charles. "Libraries and Theatre Owners Have Something in Common: The Threat of Censorship," LLA Bulletin.
36 (Spring 1974) 6-10.
Bazzell recommends cooperative efforts between librarians
and movie house proprietors in order to achieve legislation
protecting the First Amendment rights of the public.

355. Dempsey, David. "Teaching Librarians to Fight Back," Saturday Review. 48 (February 27, 1965) 20-21ff.
Dempsey discusses how the recent censorship decisions by
the Supreme Court have impacted upon librarians. In his words,
"The Court has, in effect, asked the librarian to be a liber-
tarian as well. What was once proscribed is now legal, and
the burden of choice has been shifted from the law to the
school, the library, and the bookseller. By the same token,
the frustrations of the censor have been deflected from the
Court (impeach Earl Warren) to the house of books (fire Blanche
Collins)." Dempsey touches on strategies which librarians can
employ in order to survive these new pressures.

356. Hough, Maxine L. "Censorship: Where Will You Be When It
Hits the Fan," Michigan Librarian. 39:2 (Summer 1973) 5-7.
Hough provides recommendations to librarians on what to do
before the censor arrives.

357. Jones, Frances M. Defusing Censorship: The Librarian's
Guide to Handling Censorship Conflicts. Phoenix: Oryx, 1983.
The work emphasizes the importance of meeting censoring
actions with knowledgeable planning rather than unprepared,
defensive reaction. Step-by-step guidelines are given for
handling conflict in school and public libraries.

358. Stavely, Keith, and Lani Gerson. "We Didn't Wait for the Censor," Library Journal. (September 1, 1983) 1654-1658.
The authors provide constructive steps for responding to
censoring attempts.

359. Moon, Eric, ed. Book Selection and Censorship in the Sixties.
New York: Bowker, 1969.
An anthology of 55 articles published in Library Journal
during the sixties. Part I deals with book selection; Part II
is concerned with book censorship.

360. Robotham, John, and Gerald Shields. Freedom of Access to
Library Materials. New York: Neal-Schuman, 1982.
The stated purpose of the work is to move librarians and
others "to think about issues and philosophies relating to freedom of access to the graphic records stored in libraries." The

table of contents includes: What is Freedom?; Freedom and the
Type of Library; At What Age Freedom?; Freedom Denied;
Racism, Sexism and Other "Isms"; Freedom in the Media; Con-
trolling the Complainant; Freedom Attacked: A Case Study;
Freedom Defended; Freedom and the Library--and Information--
Professional; Selected Bibliography; Appendix (Forms: Book
Selection Inquiry; Book Selection Inquiry [For Book Not in
Library]; Request for Review of Material; Citizen's Request
for Reconsideration of a Book; Patron Comment on Library Ma-
terials; Citizen's Request Form for Re-Evaluation of Learning
Resource Center Materials).

361. Berninghausen, David K. The Flight from Reason; Essays on
Intellectual Freedom in the Academy, the Press, and the Library. Chicago: American Library Association, 1975.
      A collection of essays focusing upon the need for intellectual
freedom to increase an individual's objective understanding of
the world at large. Contents include: (1) Educating Librarians
for Intellectual Freedom; (2) Intellectual Freedom and the Communication Process; (3) The Threat to Liberal Values in the
Communications Institutions; (4) Problem Cases of Library Censorship; (5) The Flight from Reason; (6) Theories of the Press
as Bases for Intellectual Freedom; (7) The Social Responsibility
Concept of Librarianship Versus the Library Bill of Rights
Concept; (8) ALA's Program for Defenders of Intellectual Freedom.

362. Berninghausen, David K. "Teaching a Commitment to Intellectual Freedom," Library Journal. 92 (October 15, 1967)
3601-3605.
      The author notes that library education in America has
long been based upon an assumption that students who have
been awarded a Bachelor's degree have acquired the appropri-
ate prerequisite for entrance into an M.L.S. program. Unfortunately, undergraduate programs have not always succeeded
in providing their students with the liberal education necessary
to appreciate the importance of intellectual freedom. Accordingly, library schools must emphasize the fighting of censorship
in their course offerings.

363. Kister, Kenneth F. "Educating Librarians in Intellectual Freedom," Library Trends. 19:1 (July 1970) 159-168.
      Kister discusses trends within library schools which relate
to intellectual freedom principles and censorship problems.

364. Merritt, LeRoy C. "Informing the Profession About Intellectual
Freedom," Library Trends. 19:1 (July 1970) 158-168.
      Merritt surveys the most effective ways of providing infor-
mation and assistance to librarians with respect to intellectual
freedom issues; e.g., access to relevant publications, conferences, the services of professional association, legal and financial support groups (e.g. Freedom to Read Foundation).

F. RESEARCH AND CENSORSHIP IN LIBRARIES

365. Busha, Charles H. Freedom versus Suppression and Censor-
      ship. Littleton, Colo.: Libraries Unlimited, 1972.
          An expansion of Busha's doctoral dissertation. Chapters
      1-5 survey the historical background and literature of intel-
      lectual freedom. Chapters 6-8 focus upon the results of his
      study of midwestern librarians in which he established that
      they profess a more liberal attitude regarding intellectual free-
      dom than they apparently practice. The work also includes an
      exhaustive bibliography, the letters and survey instrument
      sent to participants in the study, and the intellectual freedom
      statements adopted by ALA.

366. "Censorship in the South," Newsletter on Intellectual Freedom.
      35:2 (March 1985) 29, 56.
          According to an American Civil Liberties Union survey of
      1,127 librarians in Alabama, Georgia, Louisiana, and Tennessee,
      44.9 percent of public libraries and 30.9 percent of public
      school libraries have been targets of attempts to censor books,
      magazines, or films since 1980. The study did not find a clear
      relationship between the adoption of written policies to handle
      challenges and the retention of challenged materials. A wealth
      of anecdotes on isolated cases of censorship are included.

367. Chepesiuk, Ron. "On Assignment," Wilson Library Bulletin.
      61:1 (September 1986) 49-50.
          Chepesiuk summarizes the American Civil Liberties Union
      study, Censorship in the South: A Report of Four States,
      1980-1985. ACLU officials are quoted as carrying out the sur-
      vey of school and public libraries in order to bring attention
      to the censorship problem which exists not only in the South
      but on a national scale. Recommendations as to how to combat
      censorship are also excerpted from the report.

368. Serebnick, Judith. "A Review of Research Related to Censor-
      ship in Libraries," Library Research. (Summer 1975) 95-118.
          Serebnick notes that most studies are concerned with the
      opinions and practices of librarians rather than with the
      American public as a whole.

369. White, Howard D. "Library Censorship and the Permissive
      Minority," Library Quarterly. (April 1981) 192-207.
          White's study finds that the majority of Americans are op-
      posed to the library distribution of pornography.

370. White, Howard D. "Majorities for Censorship," Library Journal.
      111:12 (July 1986) 31-38.
          Utilizing data drawn from several General Social Surveys
      conducted between 1972-1983 by the National Opinion Research

Center in Chicago under the sponsorship of the National Science
Foundation, White finds that the American people as a whole
do support censorship of library books. He provides a variety
of statistical chart breakdowns covering types of controversial
authors people would remove from public libraries, opinions on
the availability of sexual information, attitudes toward the distribution of pornography, etc.; these topics are cross-tabled
by demographic characteristics such as sex, geographic locale,
age, amount of education, race, and religious denomination.

371.   Woods, L. B.   A Decade of Censorship in America; The Threat
       to Classrooms and Libraries, 1966-1975.   Metuchen, N.J.:
       Scarecrow, 1979.
          This study, originally a Ph.D. thesis, sought to gather
       quantitative data regarding censorship which might provide
       answers to the following questions: (1) When did the censor-
       ship attempts occur?; (2) Where did the censorship attempts
       occur?; (3) How many items were censored?; (4) What formats
       of materials were censored?; (5) What types of educational in-
       stitutions were affected by the censorship attempts?; (6) What
       were the titles of the censored materials?; (7) What were the
       sources of the censorship attempts?; (8) What were the reasons
       for the censorship attempts?; (9) What was the final disposition
       of the censorship attempts?   The study was motivated by (1)
       the limited empirical knowledge available about censorship, (2)
       the chaos resulting out of a shift in the First Amendment inter-
       pretation of obscenity regulations, and (3) Woods' conviction
       that censorship is far more prevalent than many librarians and
       educators believe.   In short, Woods' goal is to provide the in-
       formation needed to aid those confronted with the specter of
       censorship.

372.   Woods, L. B.   "For SEX: See Librarian," Library Journal.
       103:15 (September 1, 1978) 1561-1566.
          The article interprets the findings of a survey of censor-
       ing activities in U.S. libraries and educational institutions
       sponsored by the American Library Association's Office of In-
       tellectual Freedom.   The study reveals that censorship is on
       the rise and its proponents are employing improved planning
       techniques in pursuing their aims.

373.   Woods, L. B.   "Patterns in the Censorship of Children's Ma-
       terials," Newsletter on Intellectual Freedom.   28:2 (March 1979)
       25-26, 40-41.
          The study--expanded later into a Ph.D. thesis--examines
       censorship attempts directed toward children's collections in
       public libraries and elementary schools.   Woods notes the rea-
       sons for censorship efforts as well as the results of these at-
       tempts; he concludes that censorship is on the rise.   Two
       tables--"Titles of Children's Materials Censored in Public Li-
       braries and Elementary Schools 1966-75" and "Types of Materials

Censored in Elementary Schools in the U.S., 1966-75"--have been included.

374. Woods, L. B., and Cynthia Robinson. "Censorship: Changing Reality," Paper presented at the annual Convention of the American Library Association, Philadelphia, July 13, 1982. Avaliable from ERIC, ED 226 740.

   Based on data compiled from issues of the American Library Association's Newsletter on Intellectual Freedom, the report analyzes over 500 censorship cases occurring in U.S. educational institutions and public libraries from 1976 through 1980, and compares them with a previous study of U.S. censorship covering 1966 to 1976. Information is presented on censorship attempts by year and level of educational institution affected; number of items covered by year; formats of censored material; sources of censorship attempts; reasons for censorship attempts; and titles of censored books, dictionaries, and films. The authors have also included eight tables and a censorship index by state and geographical region.

POLITICS AND GOVERNMENT SERVICE

A. GOVERNMENTAL CONTROL OF AMERICAN SOCIETY

375. Adamo, S. J. "Let Freedom Zing," America. 127 (October 28, 1972) 346-347.
    Adamo criticizes the concerted efforts of the Nixon Administration to suppress freedom of the press.

376. Aronson, James. Packaging the News: A Critical Survey of Press, Radio, TV. New York: International, 1971.
    Aronson chronicles the concerted attacks by the Nixon Administration on the freedom of the press. He argues that the mass media must actively resist such challenges in order to retain its constitutional prerogatives.

377. Aronson, James. The Press and the Cold War. Indianapolis: Bobbs-Merrill, 1970.
    Aronson contends that the newspaper industry has compromised its responsibility as a purveyor of information to the public by becoming a willing pawn of governmental policy makers, particularly during times of crisis.

378. Arthur, William B. "Freedom of the Press and the Phenomenon Called Agnewism," Quill. 59 (June 1971) 22-27.
    Arthur notes that some consider the Nixon Administration's treatment of press freedom as "the bitterest attack in history." He considers the ultimate danger to be to the freedom of society as a whole.

379. Ashmore, Harry S., ed. The William O. Douglas Inquiry into the State of Individual Freedom. Center for the Study of Democratic Institutions/Westview Press, 1979.
    The collection of essays focuses on four headings within the general rubric of political and human rights: (1) aspects of human behavior immune from governmental regulation: (2) individual freedom and restraint on law enforcement; (2) freedom and governmental expenditures promoting the public welfare; (4) freedom and governmental control over private power.

380. Bagdikian, Ben H. "Governmental Suppression of the Media," University of Miami Law Review, 29 (Spring 1975) 447-455.

Bagdikian argues that the firm commitment to a voluntary
press council--on the part of both the public and journalists
alike--is essential in combating governmental assaults on First
Amendment rights of the media.

381. Bagdikian, Ben H.   "Don't Let Them Scare You," Quill.   60:8
(August 1972) 12-15.
Bagdikian states that the press has been neutralized by
government intimidation.   As a result, the citizenry is being
denied access to the information needed to facilitate enlightened
decision making.

382. Belknap, Michal R.   Cold War Political Justice: the Smith Act,
The Communist Party, and American Civil Liberties.   Westport,
Conn.:   Greenwood Press, 1977.
A scholarly study of the legal suppression of the Communist
Party through the application of the Smith Act, a law enacted
prior to World War II which made it a crime to advocate violent
overthrow of the government, to organize a group to do so, or
to become a member of such a group knowing of its purpose.

383. Blackstock, Nelson.   COINTELPRO: The FBI's Secret War on
Political Freedom.   New York: Vintage, 1976.
Blackstone contends that the FBI has abused its responsibility to protect U.S. citizens from "certain subversive political
groups that would jeopardize our freedom."   He provides docu-
mentation that the agency conducted covert and illegal investigations of individuals such as Martin Luther King, Jr. and
groups such as the Socialist Workers Party.

384. "Do Loose Lips Sink Ships?"   New Republic.   193:21 (November
18, 1985) 7-8.
The editorial notes that the Reagan Administration efforts
to plug all leaks believed to be a threat to U.S. national security go against the letter of the law, even apart from First
Amendment considerations.

385. Oboler, Eli M.   "Congress as Censor," Library Trends.   19:1
(July 1970) 64-73.
The article provides a historical survey of the role of Congress as a censoring force.   Oboler concludes that "the threat
of censorship from Congress is perennial, and seemingly will
continue to be so.   Though laws are not actually always passed,
at the very least sensational hearings are held which get national publicity, and are often reflected in state and local laws
and more rigid administration of laws already on the books."

386. Porter, William E.   Assault on the Media: The Nixon Years.
Ann Arbor: University of Michigan Press, 1976.
Porter surveys attempts on the part of the Nixon Adminis-
tration to control and intimidate the mass media.

387. Sarnoff, Robert W. "The Threat to Freedom of Information,"
      Vital Speeches. 39 (July 1, 1973) 551-554.
         RCA chairman Sarnoff accuses the federal government--most
      notably through the Office of Telecommunication in the White
      House--of attacking the news media with the aim of damaging
      its credibility.

                   B. U.S. COMMISSION ON OBSCENITY AND
                       PORNOGRAPHY (1970)

388. Blount, Winton M. "Case Against the Commission on Obscenity
      and Pornography," Congressional Record. 116 (October 14,
      1970) 36943-36945.
         The Postmaster General argues that pornography can only
      be legalized through the legislative process.

389. Kauffmann, Stanley. "On Obscenity," In: The First Freedom
      Today, edited by Robert B. Downs and Ralph E. McCoy. Chi-
      cago: American Library Association, 1984.
         Kauffmann assesses the impact of the Report of the U.S.
      Commission on Obscenity and Pornography. He notes that "we
      have here the astonishing phenomenon of a commission appointed
      by a President of the United States voting twelve to five for
      a report whose gist, as little as ten years ago, could have
      been read only in the most liberal journals."

390. Krug, Judith F. "Statement of the American Library Associa-
      tion," Newsletter on Intellectual Freedom. 19:4 (July 1970)
      59-62. Reprinted in: The First Freedom Today, edited by
      Robert B. Downs and Ralph E. McCoy. Chicago: American
      Library Association, 1984.
         A commentary prepared for the U.S. Commission on Obscenity
      and Pornography while it was in session reflects the point of
      view of the American Library Association. In essence, Krug
      urges the Commission not to recommend any further controls
      on the public's access to information.

391. Packer, Herbert L. "The Pornography Caper," Commentary.
      (February 1971). Reprinted in: The First Freedom Today,
      edited by Robert B. Downs and Ralph E. McCoy. Chicago:
      American Library Association, 1984.
         Packer assesses the impact of the Report of the U.S. Com-
      mission on Obscenity and Pornography. He identifies his bias
      to be "that of a lawyer who believes pornography to be a
      nuisance rather than a menace. Effective legal controls for
      this nuisance I consider to be a worse nuisance than what
      they attempt to suppress, which a democratic, open society
      can ill afford."

392. U.S. Commission on Obscenity and Pornography. "Report,"
      In: The First Freedom Today, edited by Robert B. Downs and
      Ralph McCoy. Chicago: American Library Association, 1984.
      pp. 201-214.
         The article reproduces the Preface, the nonlegislative recom-
      mendations, and legislative recommendations of the Commission's
      1970 report.

393. U.S. Commission on Obscenity and Pornography. The Report
      of The Commission on Obscenity and Pornography, September
      1970. Washington, D.C.: U.S. Government Printing Office,
      1970.
         Because Congress found the traffic in obscenity and pornog-
      raphy to be "a matter of national concern," it established an
      advisory commission whose purpose was, "after a thorough
      study which shall include a study of the causal relationship of
      such materials to antisocial behavior, to recommend advisable,
      appropriate, effective, and constitutional means to deal effec-
      tively with such traffic in obscenity and pornography."
         The Commission's Report consists of a Preface; an overview
      of the findings of the Commission; a set of nonlegislative and
      legislative recommendations; the full reports of the four work-
      ing panels--legal, traffic and distribution, effects, and posi-
      tive approaches; separate statements of the Commission mem-
      bers; and pertinent appendices--(A) Public Law 90-100 (Oc-
      tober 3, 1967), which provided the impetus for the study, (B)
      Biographies of Commission Members, (C) Contractors, and (D)
      Hearings and Witnesses.

394. U.S. Commission on Obscenity and Pornography. Technical
      Report of The Commission on Obscenity and Pornography:
      Volume I; Preliminary Studies. Washington, D.C.: U.S.
      Government Printing Office, 1970.
         Table of Contents: (I) Literature Reviews--"Psychological
      Assumptions in Sex Censorship: An Evaluative Review of Re-
      cent Research (1961-1968)," by Robert B. Cairns, J.C.N. Paul,
      and J. Wishner; "Experimental Induction of Human Sexual
      Arousal," by Jay Mann; "Physiological Measures of Sexual
      Arousal in the Human," by Marvin Zuckerman; "The Role of
      Pornography in the Etiology of Juvenile Delinquency: A Re-
      view of the Research Literature," by Lenore Kupperstein; (II)
      Theoretical analyses--"Pornography and Mechanisms of Defense,"
      by Norman N. Holland; "Erotic Materials: A Commodity Theory
      Analysis of Availability and Desirability," by Timothy C. Brock;
      (III) Preliminary Empirical Observations--"Moral Reasoning
      About Sexual Dilemmas: The Development of an Interview and
      Scoring System," by Carol Gilligan et al.; "Exposure to Porno-
      graphy and Juvenile Delinquency: The Relationship as Indi-
      cated by Juvenile Court Records," by Terrence P. Thornberry
      and Robert A. Silverman; "College Students' Attitudes on
      Pornography: A Pilot Study," by David Manning White and

Lewis D. Barnett; "Westchester College Students' Views on Pornography," by William J. Roach and Louise Kreisberg; "Effects of Mass Media on the Sexual Behavior of Adolescent Females," by Patricia Schiller.

395.   U.S. Commission on Obscenity and Pornography. Technical Report of The Commission on Obscenity and Pornography: Volume II; Legal Analysis. Washington, D.C.:   U.S. Government Printing Office, 1970.
    Table of Contents: (I) Obscenity Law in the United States-- "Definition of 'Obscene' Under Existing Law," by Paul Bender; "Implications of Stanley v. Georgia," by Paul Bender; "State Obscenity Statutes: Description and Analysis," by Jane E. Friedman; (II) Historical and Philosophical Perspective--"Origins of the Law of Obscenity," by Martha Alschuler; "Theoretical Approach to 'Morals' Legislation," by Martha Alschuler; (III) Comparative Perspectives--"Argentina," by Helen Silving; "Australia," by Bryan Bromberger; "Denmark, Sweden, and Norway," by Knud Wasben; "France," by Mirjan Damaska; "Hungary and the Soviet Union," by Mirjan Damaska; "Israel," by Dr. Ernest Livneh; "Italy," by Mirjan Damaska; "Japan," by Peter Hocker; "Mexico," by Helen Silving; "United Kingdom," by Bryan Bromberger; "West Germany," by Mirjan Damaska; "Yugoslavia," by Mirjan Damaska.

396.   U.S. Commission of Obscenity and Pornography. Technical Report of The Commission on Obscenity and Pornography: Volume III; The Marketplace: The Industry. Washington, D.C.: U.S. Government Printing Office, 1970.
    Table of Contents: "Commercial Traffic in Sexually Oriented Materials in the United States (1969-1970)," by John J. Sampson. Includes the following headings: Motion Pictures; Books and Magazines; Mail Order; "Under-the-Counter" or "Hard-Core" Pornography; Conclusions.

397.   U.S. Commission on Obscenity and Pornography. Technical Report of The Commission on Obscenity and Pornography: Volume IV; The Marketplace: Empirical Studies. Washington, D.C.: U.S. Government Printing Office, 1970.
    Table of Contents: "A Matching Analysis of Sex-Oriented Materials in Denver, August 1969: A Pilot Study," by Morris E. Massey; "The Traffic in Sex-Oriented Materials in Boston," by M. Marvin Finkelstein; "The San Francisco Erotic Marketplace," by Harold Nawy; "Some Observations on Characteristics of Patrons of Adult Theaters and Bookstores," by Charles Winick; "A Study of Consumers of Explicitly Sexual Materials: Some Functions Served by Adult Movies," by Charles Winick; "Pornography in Denmark: Pieces of a Jigsaw Puzzle Collected Around New York 1970," by Berl Kutschinsky.

398.   U.S. Commission on Obscenity and Pornography. Technical

Report of The Commission on Obscenity and Pornography: Volume V; Societal Control Mechanisms.   Washington, D.C.:   U.S. Government Printing Office, 1970.

   Table of Contents: (I) Law Enforcement--"Gravity of the Pornography Situation and Problems of Control: A Survey of Prosecuting Attorneys," by W. Cody Wilson, Jane Friedman, and Bernard Horowitz; "Regulation of Obscenity by Federal Agencies," by Jane Friedman; "Problems in Arrest and Prosecutions for Obscenity and Pornography: Response of Police and Prosecutors," by Alexander B. Smith and Bernard Locke; "Traffic in Sex-Oriented Materials and Criminality and Organized Crime: The Relationship," by M. Marvin Finkelstein; (II) Citizen Action Groups--"Collective Dynamics of Ad Hoc Antipornography Organiziations," by Louis A. Zurcher and R. George Kirkpatrick; "Participants in Ad Hoc Antipornography Organizations: Some Individual Characteristics," by Louis A. Zurcher and Robert G. Cushing; (III) Industry Self-Regulation--"Classification by the Motion Picture Industry," by Richard S. Randall; (IV) Sex Education--"Sex Education Programs in the Public Schools of the United States," by Quality Educational Development, Inc.; "The Positive and Constructive Approach to Pornography: In General Sex Education, in the Home, and in Sexological Counseling," by John Money; "Effects of Erotic Stimuli Used in National Sex Forum Training Courses in Human Sexuality," by the Glide Foundation; "Pornography and Youth: A Survey of Sex Educators and Counselors," by W. Cody Wilson and Sylvia Jacobs.

399.   U.S. Commission on Obscenity and Pornography. Technical Report of The Commission on Obscenity and Pornography: Volume VI; National Survey of Public Attitudes Toward and Experience With Erotic Materials. Washington, D.C.:   U.S. Government Printing Office, 1970.

   Table of Contents: "Findings," by H. Abelson et al.; "Methodological Report," by L. LoSciuto et al.

400.   U.S. Commission on Obscenity and Pornography. Technical Report of The Commission on Obscenity and Pornography: Volume VII; Erotics and Antisocial Behavior. Washington, D.C.:   U.S. Government Printing Office, 1970.

   Table of Contents: "Exposure to Pornography and Sexual Behavior in Deviant and Normal Groups," by Michael J. Goldstein et al.; "Erotic Stimuli and the Aggressive Sexual Offender," by C. Eugene Walker; "Pornography and the Sex Offender: Patterns of Exposure and Immediate Arousal Effects of Pornographic Stimuli," by Robert F. Cook and Robert H. Fosen; "Sex Offenders' Experience With Erotica," by Waldon T. Johnson, Lenore R. Rupperstein, and Joseph J. Peters; "Exposure to Pornography, Character, and Sexual Deviance: A Retrospective Survey," by Keith E. Davis and George N. Braucht; "Pornography and Sex Crime: The Danish Experience," by

Richard Ben-Veniste; "Towards an Explanation of the Decrease
in Registered Sex Crimes in Copenhagen," by Berl Kutschinsky;
"Erotica and Antisocial Behavior: An Analysis of Selected So-
cial Indicator Statistics," by Lenore R. Kupperstein and W.
Cody Wilson; "A Pilot Comparison of Two Research Instruments
Measuring Exposure to Pornography," by Harold S. Kant,
Michael J. Goldstein, and Derek J. Lepper.

401.   U.S. Commission on Obscenity and Pornography, Technical Report of The Commission on Obscenity and Pornography: Volume
VIII; Erotica and Social Behavior.   Washington, D.C.:   U.S.
Government Printing Office, 1970.
       Table of Contents: "An Investigation of Behavioral, Psycho-
logical, and Physiological Reactions to Pornographic Stimuli,"
by Donald M. Amoroso et al.; "The Effect of Erotic Stimuli on
Sex Arousal, Evaluative Responses, and Subsequent Behavior,"
by Donn Byrne and John Lamberth; "Reactions to Viewing Films
of Erotically Realistic Heterosexual Behavior," by Keith E.
Davis and George N. Braucht; "Effects of Exposure to Porno-
graphy," by James L. Howard, Clifford B. Reifler, and Myron
B. Liptzin; "The Effect of Pornography: A Pilot Experiment
on Perception, Behavior, and Attitudes," by Berl Kutchinsky;
"Effects of Erotic Films and the Sexual Behavior of Married
Couples," by Jay Mann, Jack Sidman, and Sheldon Starr;
"Psychological Reactions to Pornographic Films," by Donald L.
Mosher; "Sex Callousness Toward Woman," by Donald L. Mo-
sher; "Emotional Arousal as a Mediator of Erotic Communication
Effects," by Percy H. Tannenbaum; "Pornographic Films, Male
Verbal Aggression Against Women, and Guilt," by Donald L.
Mosher and Harvey Katz.

402.   U.S. Commission on Obscenity and Pornography.   Technical Re-
port of The Commission on Obscenity and Pornography: Volume
IX; The Consumer and the Community.   Washington, D.C.:
U.S. Government Printing Office, 1970.
       Table of Contents: "Relationship of Socioeconomic Back-
ground to Judgments of Sexual Stimulation: Correlation With
Judgments of Obscenity," by Marshall Katzman; "Photograph
Characteristics Influencing the Judgment of Obscenity," by
Marshall Katzman; "Contemporary Community Standards of Visual
Erotica," by Douglas Wallace, Gerald Wehmer, and Edward Po-
dany; "Sex-Related Themes in the Underground Press: A Con-
tent Analysis," by Jack Levin; "A Study of Mass Media Erotica:
The Romance or Confession Magazine," by David Sonenschein
et al.; "Pornography: High School and College Years," by Alan
S. Berger, John H. Gagnon, and William Simon; "Urban Working-
Class Adolescents and Sexually Explicit Media," by Alan S.
Berger, John H. Gagnon, and William Simon; "Exposure to
Adolescents to Erotic Materials," by James Elias; "Exposure to
Sexually Oriented Materials Among Young Male Prisoners," by
Martin H. Propper; "A Cross-Cultural Study of Modesty and

Obscenity," by William N. Stephens; "The Consumers of Pornography Where it is Easily Available: the Swedish Experience,"
by Hans L. Zetterberg.

C. THE MEESE COMMISSION (1986)

403. "AAP Testimony to Meese Commission," Newsletter on Intellectual
Freedom. 35:2 (March 1986) 34-35, 64-66.
       The article reproduces the complete texts of the statements
by Heather Grant Florence, a vice president of Bantam Books,
and J. D. Landis, author of The Sisters Impossible, before
the Meese Commission. Both commentaries make an impassioned--
and rational--plea for support of our nation's heritage of free
speech.

404. "ACLU Report Condemns Work of Meese Commission," Newsletter
on Intellectual Freedom. 35:3 (May 1986) 73, 100-106.
       The article focuses on the contents of a 30-page report
prepared by American Civil Liberties Union legislative counsel
Barry W. Lynn (and issued on February 23, 1986). The report charges that the procedures used by the Meese Commission
have been "so intellectually indefensible that they taint the integrity and credibility of any final recommendations."

405. Baker, John F. "The Meese Commission--And After," Publishers
Weekly. 230:2 (July 11, 1986) 30-31.
       The editorial assesses the work of the Meese Commission.
The verdict is a mixed one--e.g., Baker supports the effort
to control child pornography but questions the use of pressure
tactics, harassment and intimidation with respect to materials
not found to be legally obscene.

406. "The Commission Speaks: Some Key Excerpts From the Meese
Report," Publishers Weekly. 230:2 (July 11, 1986) 32-35.
       An encapsulated overview of the Meese Report--its method-
ology, its philosophical stance, and some key recommendations.

407. Fields, Howard. "'A More Difficult Climate': First Reactions
From Publishers and the ACLU View the Report With Alarm,"
Publishers Weekly. 230:2 (July 11, 1986) 36-37.
       Spokesmen for the Association of American Publishers (Bruce
Rich, Nicholas Veliotes, and Ervin A. Glikes) and the American
Civil Liberties Union (Barry Lynn) react to various portions
of the Meese Report.

408. Green, Michelle, et al. "The Shame of America," People. (June
30, 1986) 28-33.
       A report on the controversy surrounding the institution of

the Meese Commission. Two subfeatures are appended to the
article: "Does Porn Panel Nix Pix? Hollywood Sees Big Chill";
A Preacher's Scattershot 'Porn' Charges Lead to Lawsuits and
Allegations of Government Intimidation."

409. Hefner, Christie. "The Meese Commission: Sex, Violence,
      and Censorship," The Humanist. 47:1 (January/February
      1987) 25-29, 46.
          Hefner, president of Playboy Enterprises, Inc., attacks the
      aims and methods of the Commission. She considers the ulti-
      mate public policy danger and tragedy of the Meese report to
      be that "it misdirects sincere people's attention away from
      thinking about the real causes of violence and abuse."

410. Hertzberg, Hendrik. "Big Boobs; Ed Meese and His Porno-
      graphy Commission," The New Republic. (July 14/21, 1986)
      21-24.
          An assessment of the probable impact of the Meese Commis-
      sion's report. Hertzberg concludes that "despite its many as-
      sertions to the contrary, the Meese commission has simply failed
      to demonstrate that pornography constitutes a meaningful threat
      to the public interest. At a minimum, the commission is guilty
      of what Levine and Becker, in their dissent, call 'unacceptable
      efforts' to 'tease the current data into proof of a causal link.'
      But even if some such showing could be made, it would not
      follow that freedom of speech and of the press ought therefore
      to be abridged."

411. Lillienstein, Maxwell J. "Meese Commission Vigilantes; They
      Preach What They Practice," Publishers Weekly. 203:2 (July
      11, 1986) 43-44.
          Lillienstein, a counsel to the American Booksellers Associa-
      tion, concludes that the Meese Commission, by its conduct and
      by its report, has revealed little regard for the First Amend-
      ment. He adds that misfeasance, like pornography, is hard
      to define, but you know it when you see it, and you don't
      have to be a fan of pornography to be a foe of this kind of
      officially inspired vigilantism.

412. Marshner, Connaught. "Inside Look at Pornography and the
      Commission," Conservative Digest. (August 1986) 27-36.
          Marshner provides a sympathetic analysis of the Meese Com-
      mission's role in attacking the pornography industry.

413. The Meese Commission Exposed, Proceedings of a National
      Coalition Against Censorship Public Information Briefing on the
      Attorney General's Commission on Pornography, January 16,
      1986. New York: National Coalition Against Censorship, 1986.
          A compendium of the statements made by well-known writers,
      feminists, actors, psychiatrists, lawyers, and psychologists--
      including Kurt Vonnegut, Betty Friedan, and Colleen Dewhurst--

opposed to the Meese Commission's findings and the growing
wave of attacks on sexually related expression.

414. "Meese Moves Against Porn," Newsletter on Intellectual Freedom.
      36:1 (January 1987) 3-4.
          The article focuses on the seven-point plan, "designed to
      curb the growth of child pornography and obscenity," an-
      nounced by Attorney General Meese at an October 22, 1986,
      press conference in response to increasing fire by antiporno-
      graphy activists seeking implementation of the Attorney General's
      Commission on Pornography.

415. Stengel, Richard, et al. "Sex Busters," Time. (July 21,
      1986) 12-22.
          The article notes that the Meese Commission report and a
      series of restrictive Supreme Court decisions (e.g., allowing
      states to outlaw homosexual sodomy) seem emblematic of a new
      moral militancy evident in communities around the country and
      of a willingness of government officials to help enforce tradi-
      tional values. However, the authors warn that "Political and
      social leaders who carry their moral zeal too far are in danger
      of being left stranded when the pendulum swings the other
      way. And it always does." The following subfeatures have
      been appended to the article: "Reagan's Moral Point Man";
      "Pornography: The Feminist Dilemma"; "Pornography: A Poll."

416. "Storm Continues Around Porn Commission," Newsletter on In-
      tellectual Freedom. 35:4 (July 1986) 111-112, 137-138.
          The article notes that as draft reports and working papers
      have become available, critics (e.g., the American Civil Liber-
      ties Union, the American Booksellers Association, the Council
      for Periodical Distributors Associations, and at least two mem-
      bers of the Commission itself) of the Meese Commission have
      stepped up attacks on the validity of the latter's methodology
      and conclusions.

417. United States Department of Justice. Attorney General's Com-
      mission on Pornography. Final Report, July 1986. 2 Volumes.
      Washington, D.C.: U.S. Government Printing Office, 1986.
          Table of Contents: Part One--Commissioner Biographies;
      Acknowledgments and Notes; Individual Commissioner State-
      ments; Part Two--Introduction; The History of Pornography;
      The Constraints of the First Amendment; The Market and the
      Industry; The Question of Harm; Laws and Their Enforcement;
      Child Pornography; The Role of Private Action; Part Three--
      Introduction; Law Enforcement Agencies and the Justice Depart-
      ment; Child Pornography; Victimization; Civil Rights; Nuisance
      Laws; Anti-Display Laws; Part Four--Victimization; Performers;
      Social and Behavioral Science Research Analysis; Organized
      Crime; The History of the Regulation of Pornography; First
      Amendment Considerations; Citizen and Community Action and

Corporate Responsibility; Production and Distribution of Sex-
ually Explicit Materials; The Imagery Found Among Magazines,
Books and Films, in "Adults Only" Pornographic Outlets; Sam-
ple Forms; Witnesses Testifying Before the Commission; Wit-
nesses Invited But Unable to Appear Before the Commission;
Persons Submitting Written Statements; Part Five--Bibliography,
Additional Suggested Reading Materials; Staff Listing; Part
Six--Photographs; Appendix A--Commission Charter.

418.   United States Department of Justice. Attorney General's Com-
       mission on Pornography. Final Report of the Attorney General's
       Commission on Pornography. Nashville, Tenn.: Rutledge Hill
       Press, 1986.
           A reprint of the Final Report; certain deletions or conden-
       sations--designated in the text by a "scissors" symbol--have
       been made. The Introduction, written by Michael J. McManus,
       is a summary, analysis, and commentary on the substance of
       the Final Report as well as a story of some of the drama of
       the Commission and the aftermath of the initial publication of
       the work. The work is 571 pages in length.

419.   Yen, Marianne. "Two Members Reveal Porn Commission's Ap-
       proach," Publishers Weekly. 230:2 (July 11, 1986) 18.
           Two members of the Meese Commission--Dr. Judith Becker
       and Ellen Levine--explain why they agreed to participate,
       criticize its methods of fact-finding, and defend its work in
       the area of child pornography at a luncheon hosted by the Na-
       tional Coalition against Censorship.

                       D. U.S. POST OFFICE

420.   Fowler, Dorothy G. Unmailable: Congress and the Post Of-
       fice. Athens: University of Georgia Press, 1977.
           A survey of the U.S. Post Office's role as a censor through-
       out U.S. history. Fowler notes that the responsibility for
       deciding what materials are sent via the mail has gradually
       shifted from the government to private citizens.

421.   Paul, James C. N., and Murray L. Schwartz. Federal Censor-
       ship: Obscenity in the Mail. New York: Free Press of Glen-
       coe, 1971.
           The book surveys the role of the U.S. Post Office in sup-
       pressing access to information and materials.

422.   Robertus, Patricia E. Postal Control of Obscene Literature
       1942-1957. Seattle: University of Washington, 1974. Ph.D.
       dissertation, available from University Microfilms, no. 75-28,
       433.

The research focuses on three major forms of control: non-mailable orders, limitations on second-class mailing privileges, and mail blocks.

E. THE SUPREME COURT

423. Alfange, Dean, Jr. The Role of the Supreme Court in the Protection of Freedom of Expression in the United States. Ithaca, N.Y.: Cornell University, 1967. Ph.D. dissertation, available from University Microfilms, no. 67-8751.
      Alfange analyzes the respective merits of the doctrine of constitutional absolutism versus the doctrine of self-restraint in relation to First Amendment rights. He concludes that a compromise doctrine, the "balancing of interest," holds the greatest potential for ensuring an enlightened interpretation of the First Amendment by the Court.

424. Navasky, Victor. "Ronald Reagan and the Supremes," Esquire. 107:4 (April 1987) 77-84.
      Navasky notes that as the sun sets on the Reagan era, the impact of his Supreme Court appointments on our civil rights is only beginning to be felt.

June 21, 1973, Supreme Court Obscenity Decisions

425. Berger, Gertrude. "Hester Prynne and Linda Lovelace, Pure or Prurient," In: Dealing With Censorship, edited by James E. Davis. Urbana, Ill.: National Council of Teachers of English, 1979. pp. 125-130.
      Berger discusses the implications of the June 21, 1973, Supreme Court decisions on obscenity which yield jurisdiction in such matters to communities. She concludes that "communities will now have to make decisions on questions of morality in sexual behavior, standards of what is art and what is pornography, and judgments about the relationship of books and films to behavior.
      "There are clear indications throughout the country that an assault on intellectual freedom will accompany the search for the obscene."

426. Blake, Richard A. "Will Fig Leaves Blossom Again?" America. 129 (August 18, 1973) 82-84.
      Blake cites two major concerns arising out of the 1973 Supreme Court obscenity decisions: (1) the future development of "community standards," and (2) how to apply the "serious merit" test.

427.   Oboler, Eli M.   "Paternalistic Morality and Censorship," Li-
       brary Journal.   98:15 (September 1, 1973) 2395-2398.
          In light of the 1973 Supreme Court decisions on obscenity--
       particularly the localization of contemporary standards and the
       denial of the significance of social importance--librarians are
       in real danger of becoming criminal if they are found guilty of
       distributing what some court defines as obscene and/or porno-
       graphic reading and viewing materials.   Oboler's rather ambigu-
       ous answer to this dilemma is to have each librarian live by
       both public morality (as conveyed in laws and attitudes) and
       private morality (i.e., one's respective morality as a profes-
       sional).

PART IV:

PRO-CENSORSHIP/ANTI-CENSORSHIP: REPRESENTATIVE INDIVIDUALS AND GROUPS

The struggle between proponents and opponents of intellectual freedom is not only an ongoing process, but reaches into virtually every segment of American society. The issues most likely to elicit controversy--politics, social values and traditions, sexuality, and religion--have stimulated the rise of individuals and groups espousing a diversified array of interpretations with respect to the role First Amendment rights should play in contemporary life.

Generally speaking, the actions and ideas identified with these individuals and groups can be classified as either infringing upon or upholding the unqualified guarantees of the First Amendment. While few Americans would outwardly admit to being opposed to the U.S. Constitution--or, more specifically, the First Amendment--many contradict such protestations by means of the activities in which they are engaged. Any attempts at ascertaining the motivations of those in opposition to a clash of values, cynicism, or opportunism--are inevitably doomed to failure; to endeavor to force the issue would, in fact, run contrary to the Bill of Rights.

The term "censor" evokes a picture of irrational, belligerent behavior. But such a picture can be misleading. It could be argued that most censors are concerned citizens who are sincerely interested in the future well-being of their respective communities. [1] However, one characteristic of censors and would-be censors is harder to defend.

> Regardless of specific motives, all would-be censors share one belief--that they can recognize "evil" and that other people must be protected from it. Censors do not necessarily believe their own morals should be protected, but they do feel compelled to save their fellows. [2]

Those opposed to censorship, likewise, may be motivated by any number of a diverse set of factors, including personal values, professional commitments, a political agenda, business interests, etc.

These motivations may produce an inherent clash within a given individual or group. For example, liberals are not necessarily above
resorting to censoring activities; on the other hand, conservatives
may be opposed to the majority of infringements upon First Amendment rights. The dilemma faced by feminists with respect to pornography illustrates the complexity of the censorship phenomenon.
While those within the movement are unanimous in their assessment
of pornography as degrading in its treatment of women as sex ob-
jects, groups such as the Feminists Anti-Censorship Task Force consider any attempts at undercutting the First Amendment to represent
an even greater evil. Other organizations--e.g., Feminists Against
Pornography--are willing to risk categorically compromising intellectual freedom in order to enhance the likelihood of realizing the
movement's aims. Such a nod in favor of expediency would appear
to typify the modus operandi of most individuals and groups practicing some form of censorship.

    The sources included in this chapter will assist in identifying
notable censors and intellectual freedom advocates as well as delineating their respective outlooks, goals, and programs. The individuals
and groups included within the bibliography represent a list that is
far from complete.

    In addition to those groups cited in the bibliography, the fol-
lowing organizations also advocate censorship in one form or another:
Action for Children's Television; the American-Arab Anti-Discrimina-
tion Committee; the American Baptist Home Mission Society; the American Coalition for Traditional Values; the American Legion; the American Renewal Foundation; Back in Control (Orange County, California);
the Board for Brotherhood Concerns; the Boy Scouts of America; the
Brethren in Christ Church; Citizens for Excellence in Education;
Daughters of the American Revolution; Feminists Against Pornography;
Florida Coalition for Clean Cable; Illinois Baptist State Association;
John Birch Society; NAB Code Review Board; the National Association
of Christian Educators; the National Legal Foundation; the National
Woman's Christian Temperance Union; New York-Connecticut Americans
for Morality; New York State Pro-Family Coalition; Parents Watching
the Schools; Save Our Schools; and Texans for America.

    The following groups--not listed in the bibliography--are dedi-
cated to fighting censorship: the AAUP Commission on Academic
Freedom and Pre-College Education; the American Association of
School Administrators; the American Federation of Teachers; The
American Library Association; the American National News Service;
American Newspaper Publishers Association; Americans for Constitu-
tional Freedom; the Association for Education in Journalism and Mass
Communication; the Association of American Publishers; the Council
for Periodical Distributors Associations; the Feminists Anti-Censorship
Task Force; the Freedom of Expression Foundation; Freedom to Read
Committee; the International Reading Association; the Magazine Pub-
lishers Association; the Media Coalition; the National Cable Television

Association; the National Coalition Against Censorship; the National Council of Teachers of English; the National Council of the Social Studies; the National Education Association; and the Speech Communication Association.

Those individuals notable for either practicing censorship or supporting intellectual freedom are far too numerous to list here. Numerous examples can be found by reading the reports and commentaries concerned with the respective censorship cases.

NOTES

1. Intellectual Freedom Manual, compiled by the Office for Intellectual Freedom of the American Library Association. 2d ed. Chicago: American Library Association, 1983. p. 173.

2. Ibid.

A. VIEWPOINTS: PRO-CENSORSHIP

428. Anchell, Melvin. "Pornography Anyone?" Social Justice. 66
      (October 1973) 194-198.
         Anchell argues that pornography does indeed harm indi-
      viduals, regardless of their demographic characteristics.

429. Armstrong, O. K. "The Problems of Pornography," American
      Legion Magazine. 87 (August 1969) 22-25ff.
         An indictment of protective court decisions which, according
      to Armstrong, have resulted in a society overrun with obscenity.

430. Berns, Walter. The First Amendment and the Future of Ameri-
      can Democracy. New York: Basic Books, 1976.
         Berns argues that the Supreme Court, in the name of civil
      liberty, is compromising the nation's moral fiber, thereby un-
      dermining the democratic way of life which the Constitution
      was supposed to defend.

431. Berns, Walter. Freedom, Virtue and the First Amendment.
      Westport, Conn.: Greenwood, 1969.
         Berns asserts that "the complete absence of all forms of
      censorship ... is theoretically untenable and practically inde-
      fensible. Civil society is impossible if every man retains an
      absolute freedom of opinion." He views law as the means of
      promoting virtue. This edition is a reprint of the 1957 edition.

432. Berns, Walter. "Pornography and Democracy: The Case for
      Censorship," Public Interest. (Winter 1971)
         Berns asserts that there is a "necessity for the law to
      make a modest effort to promote good character."

433. Bickel, Alexander M. "Pornography, Censorship and Common
      Sense," Reader's Digest. 104:2 (February 1974) 115-118.
         The interview format is employed. Bickel defends Supreme
      Court efforts to suppress hard-core pornography. He appears
      to view the relevant constitutional issues from the standpoint
      of a moralist who has been backed into a corner.

434. Blount, Winton M. "Let's Put the Smut Merchants Out of Busi-
      ness," Nation's Business. 59 (September 1971) 34-36, 39. Re-
      printed in: Marriage and Family Living. (February 1972)

Blount condemns the pornography industry. He advocates
the utilization of various defenses so as to undercut its influence; e.g., the postal obscenity statute, legislation enabling
citizens to prosecute anyone mailing unsolicited obscene materials.

435. Clor, Harry M. Obscenity and Public Morality: Censorship
in a Liberal Society. Chicago: University of Chicago Press,
1969. Reprinted in 1985.
Clor establishes a threefold purpose for this study: (1) to
analyze and evaluate the argument, evidence, and assumptions
employed in the controversy over obscenity; (2) to explore the
difficulties encountered by the law when it seeks to define
public morality in a constitutional democracy and in a society
characterized by pluralism and rapid change; (3) to contribute
to the development of a philosophy of censorship and a test of
obscenity which will do justice to the public interests in morality,
in free expression, and in literature. His argument for legal
control of obscenity--while systematic and devoid of blatantly
non-rational considerations--reveals a narrow-mindedness and
puritanical bias absent from truly objective research on the
subject.

436. Comstock, Anthony. Traps for the Young. Cambridge: Belknap Press/Harvard University, 1967. Reprint of the 1883
edition.
Comstock is commonly viewed as the quintessential censor.
His ideas have fallen into disrepute due to his heavy-handed
moralizing, as evidenced in the following statement: "I un-
hesitatingly declare, there is at present no more active agent
employed by Satan in civilized communities to ruin the human
family and subject the nations to himself than EVIL READING."

437. Coyne, John R., Jr. "The Pornographic Convention," Library
Journal. 91:11 (June 1, 1966) 2768-2773.
Coyne accuses ALA of helping to destroy standards which
once prevented pornography from gaining any great literary
acceptance. His advice for libraries: to analyze and speak
out rather than merely ban books.

438. Elliot, George P. Conversions. New York: Dutton, 1971.
Elliott considers pornography to represent an attack on
"society as such" because it subverts the institution of the
family. He views "erotic nihilists" such as Henry Miller as a
particular threat in that their work possesses "literary value
... enough to redeem its pornography but not enough to make
one ignore its destructive intent."

439. Gardiner, Harold C., S. J. Catholic Viewpoint on Censorship.
Garden City, N.Y.: Doubleday/Image Paperbacks, 1961.
The work is essentially an apology for limited censorship

on moral grounds. Nevertheless, it represents an objective and thought-provoking study.

440. Hausknecht, Murray, and others. "The Problem of Pornography: A discussion," Dissent. (Spring 1978) 193-208. Reprinted in: Library Lit. 9--The Best of 1978, edited by Bill Katz. Metuchen, N.J.: Scarecrow, 1979. pp. 373-397.

Hausknecht proposes zoning as a means of controlling pornography. He states, "The proposal assumes that once the X-rated movie and the material that normally appears in 'adult bookshops' are limited to a few sections of the city there will be fewer complaints about pornography and significantly less demand for complete censorship. Zoning would still leave us with the 'moral ugliness' of pornography, but in an imperfect world that is preferable to the certainties imposed on us by a Robespierre."

Reactions to his essay are provided by Lionel Abel, George P. Elliott, Cynthia Fuchs Epstein, Irving Howe, and David Spitz--along with a final rejoinder by Hausknecht.

441. Holbrook, David, ed. The Case Against Pornography. La-Salle, Ill.: Open Court, 1973.

The work's premise could be summarized as follows: "I am ... prepared to accept that obscenity is sometimes necessary within the whole content of a serious work of art. Only I believe those works which really need obscenity are few and far between."

442. Kirk, Jerry. The Mind Polluters. Nashville, TN: Thomas Nelson, 1985.

The first five chapters delineate the seriousness of the pornography issue, followed by five chapters outlining specific things people can do--individually and in groups--to rid their communities of pornography. Essentially, a story of Kirk's career as a porn fighter in Cincinnati where he has served two decades as senior pastor of a Presbyterian church.

443. Kilpatrick, James J. The Smut Peddlers. Westport, Conn.: Greenwood Press, 1973. Reprint of the 1960 edition.

Kilpatrick's prime message is that "a free society should find nothing inconsistent with its freedom in seeking to keep from its reservoirs the merchants of filth." "The Case for Censorship" represents the pivotal chapter in the book; herein Kilpatrick elucidates the principal contentions of the proponents of obscenity statutes: (1) Of course laws punishing obscenity are constitutional; it is absurd to contend they are not constitutional. (2) The term "obscenity" is no more vague or elusive than many another concept of law; objections on this score are captious. (3) A causal relationship between obscene materials and antisocial behavior may not be susceptible to statistical proof--by its very nature, the relationship is unprovable--but the common sense of mankind, supported by the opinions of experts, holds strongly that such a relationship exists. (4) It is no more futile to combat obscenity than it is to combat other social evils that may gain allure from the fact of their suppression.

444. Kuh, Richard H. Foolish Figleaves? Pornography Figleaves? Pornography In and Out of Court. New York: Macmillan, 1967.
    The book represents an indictment of the liberal trend characterizing court cases at that time. Kuh sets forth an ominous warning in the following statement: "When the law provides no adequate redress the citizenry may not always be rational in its resort to self-help."

445. Kuh, Richard H. "Obscenity, Censorship, and the Nondoctrin-aire Liberal," Wilson Library Bulletin. (May 1968). Reprinted in: The First Freedom Today, edited by Robert B. Downs and Ralph E. McCoy. Chicago: American Library Association, 1984. pp. 238-244.
    Kuh, an advocate of legislation to protect the moral fiber of society without threatening intellectual freedom, posits the need for a "thinking man's censorship."

446. Penetar, Michael P. "Pornography and Censorship," Social Justice Review. 60 (March 1968) 412-413.
    Penetar argues that pornography has contributed to rising delinquency, drug addiction, divorce, etc. He calls for pro-tection of the home from inroads by pornography.

447. Rushdvony, Rousas J. The Politics of Pornography. New Rochelle, New York: Arlington House, 1974.
    Rushdvony places himself firmly in the moralist camp as evidenced by the following observation: "The new pornography ... is ... a crusade for a new freedom and an all-out war against God and His law."

448. Schechner, Richard. "Pornography and the New Expression," Atlantic. 219:1 (January 1967) 74-78.
    Schechner states that an atavistic, cohesive, and participa-tory "revolution of the flesh" is the new expression; the revolu-tion threatens to radically transform virtually all forms of cul-tural expression. His conclusion--i.e., no one knows what to do about it--acknowledges the possible desirability of regulat-ing sexuality and artistic expression. Freedom, in his words, is merely "an agreement on what to suppress."

449. Sunderland, Land V. Obscenity: the Court, the Congress and the President's Commission. Washington, D.C.: American Enterprise Institute, 1975.
    The author argues that the "resolution of obscenity cases will still depend, finally, on the subtle quality of judicial judg-ment."

B. STUDIES OF THE CENSORING MIND

450. Haney, Robert W. Comstockery in America: Patterns of Censorship and Control. New York: Da Capo Press, 1974. Reprint of the 1960 edition.

The work is designed to introduce the reader to censorship and restraints--public and private--placed on the mass media, as they have existed throughout history, thereby encouraging deeper thought about social norms, the meaning of art in all its forms, and the place of the questioning mind in human society. In Anthony Comstock, the former crusader against "devil-traps" in literature, Haney finds an apt model for his exploration of the censoring mentality. The bibliography exhaustively documents notable articles from the late 1940s and 1950s dealing with censorship.

451. Nelson, Jack. "Censors and Their Tactics," Library Journal. 88 (December 15, 1963) 4809-4812ff.

Nelson delineates the mind of the censor. He stresses the importance of maximum public exposure through the cooperation of teachers, librarians, and the press as a means of combating censorship.

452. Poppel, Norman, and Edwin M. Ashley. "Toward an Understanding of the Censor," Library Journal. 111:12 (July 1986) 39-43.

The authors delineate the nature of the censoring mind as well as the strategies to be employed by libraries in dealing with the phenomenon.

453. White, Howard D. "Are Americans Censorship-Minded?" Publishers Weekly. 203:2 (July 11, 1986) 40-41.

White analyzes data drawn from recent General Social Surveys conducted by the national Opinion Research Center at the University of Chicago. He discerns a clear picture of intolerance, measured by willingness to censor, showing up strongly only in certain groups, and these generally not those that, taken nationally, would be considered the most advantaged.

C. PRO-CENSORSHIP: GROUPS

General

454. Benedict, John. "Pornography, a Political Weapon," American Mercury. 90 (February 1960) 3-21.

Benedict decries the growing permissiveness of American society. He cites those groups actually fighting pornography as well as providing guidelines for grassroots protest activities.

455. Boyer, Paul S. Purity in Print; The Vice-Society Movement
      and Book Censorship in America. New York: Scribner, 1968.
          The work spans the post-Civil War period which witnessed
      the founding of the vice societies--largely a response to deep-
      seated fears about the drift of urban life--up to their decline
      in the thirties. Boyer provides a scholarly, but engaging,
      narrative of the progression toward a more liberal view of the
      literary realm on the part of American society. His biblio-
      graphy is exhaustive in its documentation of this seventy-odd-
      year period.

456. Nelson, Jack, and Gene Roberts, Jr. The Censors and the
      Schools. Boston: Little, Brown, 1963.
          The authors examine the methods of pressure groups in at-
      tempting to influence the outcome of textbook selection.

457. People for the American Way. "Mind Control in the Schools:
      The Censorship Battle," In: The First Freedom Today, edited
      by Robert B. Downs and Ralph E. McCoy. Chicago: American
      Library Association, 1984. pp. 54-57
          An indictment of the attempts of the radical religious right
      to impress their view of the world on all Americans.

458. Park, J. Charles. "Clouds on the Right: A Review of Pend-
      ing Pressures Against Education," In: Dealing With Censor-
      ship, edited by James E. Davis. Urbana, Ill.: National Coun-
      cil of Teachers of English, 1979. pp. 96-107.
          Park warns that the climate exists for a resurgence of po-
      litical ultra conservatism. He profiles the chief components
      of this emerging right-wing coalition. Park states that "whether
      we like it or not, American education can never be entirely
      removed from the political process."

459. Wingfield, William. "California's New Vigilantes," The Progres-
      sive. 32:2 (February 1968) 30-33.
          Wingfield surveys the various right-wing pressure groups
      in Southern California involved in attacking school textbooks,
      college newspapers, and radio talk shows. These attacks seem
      to be on the upsurge.

460. Zurcher, Louis A., Jr., and R. George Kirkpatrick. Citizens
      for Decency: Antipornography Crusades as Status Defense.
      Austin: University of Texas Press, 1976.
          The work examines two antipornography crusades, one in
      the Midwest and the other in the Southwest. Particular atten-
      tion is paid to the evolution and impact of such crusades, the
      satisfaction derived from participating, and the relevant charac-
      teristics of the participants and their opponents. Intended
      for students in the social sciences, particularly for courses in
      collective behavior, social movements, social change, social
      problems, political sociology, deviant behavior, and social con-
      trol.

Accuracy in Academia

461. Ashworth, Kenneth H. "McCarthyism in the Classroom; Anti-
      Intellectualism at Its Worst," Change. 17:6 (November/Decem-
      ber 1985) 10.
          The article delineates the role of the newly formed Accuracy
      in Academia--an offshoot of Accuracy in Media--in monitoring
      classroom activities in American colleges and universities. He
      compares the group's agenda to the McCarthy witch hunts of
      the early fifties.

462. Lawrence, Malcolm. "Accuracy in Academia: Is it a Threat
      to Academic Freedom?" Vital Speeches of the Day. 52 (Novem-
      ber 1, 1985) 44-49.
          The article is comprised of the text of Lawrence's September
      25, 1985, address delivered at Iowa State University. Law-
      rence, the president of Accuracy in Academia, provides back-
      ground information about the organization's genesis and mission.

463. Ledbetter, James. "Campus Double Agent: I Was A Spy for
      Accuracy in Academia," New Republic. 193:27 (December 30,
      1985) 14-16.
          A somewhat jaundiced expose of the group's methods and
      intent.

464. Marshall, E. "New Group Targets Political Bias on Campus,"
      Science. 229 (August 30, 1985) 841-842.
          Marshall profiles Accuracy in Academia and discusses its
      platform.

465. Verkuil, Paul R. "Monitoring Academic Activity of Professors:
      Is There A Necessity?" Vital Speeches of the Day. 52 (Janu-
      ary 1, 1986) 174-177.
          The text of President Verkuil's inaugural address at William
      and Mary College, delivered on October 20, 1985. He argues
      that an organization like Accuracy in Academia could, if suc-
      cessful, undermine academic freedom.

Accuracy in Media

466. "AIM Claims PBS Has Double Standard," Broadcasting. (Janu-
      ary 27, 1986) 72-74.
          The organization alleges that public television's liberal bias
      precludes a fair hearing for conservative viewpoints.

467. AIM Report. Washington, D.C.: Accuracy in Media, Inc.,
      1972-. Monthly.
          The vehicle by which AIM cites cases of bias, misinforma-
      tion, omissions, etc., revealing a strong liberal bent in the
      newspaper and electronic press.

468. D'Souza, Dinesh. "Eye on the Press: Accuracy in Media,"
      National Review. 36 (November 2, 1984) 36-37.
          The article analyzes the organization's role in advocating
      the representation of conservative ideas within the media.

469. Epstein, Daniel. The Anatomy of AIM. Columbia: Freedom
      of Information Center, School of Journalism, University of Mis-
      souri, 1973. Report no. 313.
          A six-page profile of the pressure group. Epstein con-
      siders charges of AIM's critics that the organization has a
      strong right-wing bias of its own.

470. Massing, Michael. "Who's Afraid of Reed Irvine? The Rise
      and Decline of Accuracy in Media," Nation. (September 13,
      1986) 200ff.
          An in-depth portrait of the organization, emphasizing its
      aims and modus operandi.

471. Morris, Roger. "Taking AIM at Jack Anderson," Columbia
      Journalism Review. 14:1 (May/June 1975) 19-23.
          Morris recounts AIM's attacks on Jack Anderson in the form
      of complaints before the National News Council.

Action for Children's Television

472. Engelhardt, Tom. "Saturday Morning Fever: The Hard Sell
      Takeover of Kids TV," Mother Jones. (September 1986) 38ff.
          Englehardt surveys the rise of programming which exists
      primarily to promote toys and related products. He delineates
      the role of Action for Children's Television in fighting this
      trend.

American Library Association

473. Kister, Ken, and Sanford Berman. "Right Here in River City:
      A.L.A., Censorship, and Alternatives," CALL (Current Aware-
      ness--Library Literature). (January/February 1978) 3-5. Re-
      printed in: Library Lit. 9--The Best of 1978, edited by Bill
      Katz. Metuchen, N.J.: Scarecrow, 1979. pp. 398-405.
          Kister and Berman provide an expose on the censorious
      activities of the Reference & Subscription Books Review Com-
      mittee of the American Library Association, a pattern of be-
      havior which mocks the organization's lofty preachments on
      intellectual freedom.

474. Young, Arthur P. "World War I, ALA, and Censorship,"
      Newsletter on Intellectual Freedom. 26:4 (July 1977) 95-97,
      123.
          Young surveys ALA's role as a censor of the library materi-
      als provided to U.S. soldiers during World War I.

California League Enlisting Action Now

475. Wingfield, William. "California's Dirty Book Caper: The Po-
      litics of Smut," Nation. 202 (April 18, 1966) 456-459.
          A profile of California League Enlisting Action Now (CLEAN),
      with a particular emphasis on its anti-pornography program.

Christian Voice

476. Guth, James L. "The New Christian Right," In: The New
      Christian Right; Mobilization and Legitimation, edited by Robert
      C. Liebman and Robert Wuthnow. New York: Aldine, 1983.
      pp. 31-45.
          A profile of the three major Christian Right Organizations--
      Christian Voice, the Moral Majority, and the Religious Round-
      table. Following concise historical surveys of each group, the
      following topics are covered: (1) Lobbying: Issues and
      Strategies; (2) Electoral Strategies; (3) Potential and Limita-
      tions.

Citizens' Committee for Better Juvenile Literature of Chicago
(See: Censorship Cases--Comic Books, Comic Strips, etc.)

Citizens for Decent Literature (Cincinnati)

477. Armstrong, O. D. "Landmark Decision in the War on Porno-
      graphy," Reader's Digest. 91 (September 1967) 93-97.
          Ample space is given to covering the role of CDL in the
      successful prosecution of newsstand pornography in Cincinnati
      via the Polly King case.

478. Gaines, Ervin, J. "CDL on the Local Scene," ALA Bulletin.
      59 (January 1965) 17-18.
          Gaines surveys the negative impact of the Citizens for De-
      cent Literature. He states that the organization "seems to
      have established a kind of canned doctrine for use in local
      brouhahas over 'dirty books.' "

Citizens for Decency Through Law
(Formerly: Citizens for Decent Literature)

479. Citizens for Decency Through Law. How to Start an Anti-
      Pornography Drive in Your Community. Cleveland: Citizens
      for Decency Through Law, 1975? Available from Citizens for
      Decency Through Law, 11000 North Scottsdale Road, Suite
      210, Scottsdale, AZ. 85254, (602) 483-8787.
          The twelve-page pamphlet is a primer for instituting a

subsidiary of CDL in one's community. It includes guidelines
for fighting pornography. An update of Procedures Handbook
for Establishing a Citizens for Decent Literature Group in Your
Town (Cincinnati: Citizens for Decent Literature, n.d.).

480. Gordon, Maryl. "The Dirty Little War at the Newsstand,"
Savvy. (November 1986) 38-43.
Gordon surveys the efforts of the CDL and other pressure
groups to orchestrate a crackdown on porn retailers.

481. Yen, Marianne, compiler. "A Morality Who's Who; The People
and Policies of Citizen Groups Currently in Pursuit of Pornography," Publishers Weekly. 203:2 (July 11, 1986) 42.
A thumbnail sketch of the group, its aims and activities.

Concerned Women for America

482. Miller, Holly G. "Concerned Women for America: Soft Voices
With Clout," Saturday Evening Post. 257 (October 1985) 70-
71ff.
Laudatory profile of the group. Its agenda for fighting the
rampant permissiveness in American society is discussed at
length.

483. Yen, Marianne, compiler. "A Morality Who's Who; The People
and Policies of Citizen Groups Currently in Pursuit of Pornography," Publishers Weekly. 203:2 (July 11, 1986) 42.
A concise portrait of the group, its goals and activities.

The Eagle Forum

484. Wall, J. M. "A New Right Tool Distorts Regulations," Christian
Century. 102 (April 24, 1985) 403.
Wall delineates the methods employed by the Eagle Forum in
protesting public school curricula.

485. Yen, Marianne, compiler. "A Morality Who's Who; The People
and Policies of Citizen Groups Currently in Pursuit of Pornography," Publishers Weekly. 203:2 (July 11, 1986) 42.
A thumbnail sketch of the organization, its objectives and
modus operandi.

Educational Research Analysts

486. Jenkinson, Edward B. "How the Mel Gablers Have Put Textbooks on Trial," In: Dealing With Censorship, edited by
James E. Davis. Urbana, Ill.: National Council of Teachers
of English, 1979. pp. 108-116.

Jenkinson delineates the history and agenda of Norma and
Mel Gabler's Educational Research Analysts, "the nation's
largest textbook review clearing house."

487. Jenkinson, Edward B. "How to Condemn a Book Without Reading It," Newsletter on Intellectual Freedom. 27:3 (May 1978)
49, 69-72.
Jenkinson describes the methods by which Norma and Mel
Gabler of Educational Research Analysts foster textbook censorship.

488. People for the American Way. "The Texas Connection: Counter-
ing the Textbook Censorship Crusade," In: The First Freedom
Today, edited by Robert B. Downs and Ralph E. McCoy. Chicago: American Library Association, 1984. pp. 94-96.
The article is, in essence, a profile of the censoring platform set forth by Mel and Norma Gabler. P.A.W. announces
the launching of the Texas Textbook Project, which is dedicated
to protecting students' access to information and ideas in the
public schools.

Freedom Council (See: Pat Robertson)

Greater Cincinnati Committee on Evaluation of Comic Books
(See: Censorship Cases--Comic Books, Comic Strips, etc.)

The Legion of Decency

489. Corliss, Richard. "The Legion of Decency," Film Comment.
4:4 (Summer 1968) 24-61.
Corliss surveys the history and policies of the organization.

490. Facey, Paul W. The Legion of Decency: A Sociological Analysis of the Emergence and Development of a Social Pressure
Group. New York: Arno/New York Times, 1974. Reprint of
Ph.D. dissertation, Fordham University, 1945.
A sympathetic portrayal of the organization. Facey concludes his study by stating that "the system of directive control through the community seems a distinct improvement over
direct control through the state." The Table of Contents includes: Introduction (The Social Problem of the Motion Picture) Previous Attempts at Control; Relevant Sociological Concepts); The Structure of the Legion of Decency; The Ends of
the Legion of Decency; Means Used By the Legion of Decency;
The Legion of Decency in Relation to Other Groups in Society.

491. Little, Thomas F. "Why Film Control?" Journal of Screen
Producers Guild. (Spring 1961) 15-16.

The executive secretary of the organization discusses its
system of film classification. He recommends that the industry
adopt a self-imposed rating system.

492. National Legion of Decency. Motion Pictures Classified. New
      York: National Legion of Decency, 1951.
      A compilation of Catholic moral classifications of films re-
      leased between 1936-1950.

493. Walsh, M. "Right Conscience About Films," America. 110
      (May 9/16, 1964) 657-658ff.
      Walsh defends the organization's film-rating policy.

The Liberty Federation (Lynchburg, Virginia)

494 Yen, Marianne, compiler. "A Morality Who's Who; The People
     and Policies of Citizen Groups Currently in Pursuit of Porno-
     graphy," Publishers Weekly. 203:12 (July 11, 1986) 42.
     A concise portrait of the group, its aims and activities.

The Moral Majority

495. Beis, Richard H. "The Moral Majority: Misguided Effort,"
      The Humanist. 41:5 (September/October 1981) 44, 58.
      Beis posits that the Moral Majority mistakenly considers
      moral change to be synonymous with moral breakdown. He
      concludes that the Moral Majority's energies would be far bet-
      ter spent if the organization were to grapple with the moral
      problems of the present.

496. Klein, J. "Moral Majority's Man in New York," New York. 14
      (May 18, 1981) 26-30.
      A profile of the Reverend D.C. Fore.

497. Lamont, Corliss. "Answering the Moral Majority," The Human-
      ist. 41:4 (July/August 1981) 19.
      Lamont argues for the need to mount a concerted counter-
      attack against the false doctrines and malicious propaganda of
      the Moral Majority.

498. Liebman, Robert C. "Mobilizing the Moral Majority," In: The
      New Christian Right; Mobilization and Legitimation, edited by
      Robert C. Liebman and Robert Wuthnow. New York: Aldine,
      1983. pp. 49-73.
      A historical survey of the first major effort to build a na-
      tional movement of conservative evangelicals. Liebman's ex-
      amination of the group includes the following topics: Mobilizing
      the Moral Majority; The Determinants of Success; The Majority's
      National Network; The Fundamentalist Connection.

499.   Negri, Maxine. "The Moral Majority vs. Humanism," The
       Humanist. 41:2 (March/April 1981) 4-7.
           Negri notes the threat which the Moral Majority and the
       New Right represents with respect to the rights of humanists.
       Appended to the article are examples of recent attacks on hu-
       manism appearing in newspapers and magazines: "Falwell
       'Gospel Hour' In Jeopardy;" "Enforcing God's Law in the Vot-
       ing Booth," by Jerry Falwell; "Humanist View Is Challenged,"
       by Phyllis Schlafly; "The New State Religion," by Jeff Calkine;
       "Moral Majority: Voting the 'Godly' Way," by Fred Olson;
       "Baptist Calls Humanism One of World's Most Dangerous Reli-
       gions," by David Becker; "Humanists' Fears Rising As Funda-
       mentalists Attack," by Steve Haner.

500.   "North Carolina Moral Majority Listing 'Harmful' School Books,"
       Newsletter on Intellectual Freedom. 30:2 (March 1981) 29, 32.
           A report on the statewide campaign being conducted by the
       North Carolina chapter of the Moral Majority to remove text-
       books and library books it deems unfit from North Carolina
       public schools.

501.   Radl, Shirley Rogers. The Invisible Woman: Target of the
       Religious New Right. New York: Delacorte, 1983.
           Radl analyzes the war being waged by right-wing religious
       sects to undermine the freedom of women and to redefine the
       family in authoritarian nineteenth-century terms.

502.   Shupe, Anson, and William Stacey. Born Again Politics and
       The Moral Majority: What Social Surveys Really Show. New
       York: Edwin Mellen Press, 1982.
           An expanded analysis of the findings included as a chapter
       in Liebman and Wuthnow's The New Christian Right (see Items
       498, 503/4).

503.   Shupe, Anson, and William Stacey. "The Moral Majority Con-
       stituency," In: The New Christian Right; Mobilization and
       Legitimation, edited by Robert C. Liebman and Robert Wuthnow.
       New York: Aldine, 1983. pp. 103-116.
           An analysis of Moral Majority support in a Bible Belt metro-
       politan area, Dallas-Fort Worth, offers the following conclusions:
       (1) there is no evidence of a sizable constituency in support
       of religious involvement in politics; (2) Falwell and other
       leaders of the New Christian Right seriously overestimate the
       amount of agreement among sympathizers on the issues they
       hold dear; (3) while Falwell claims that the Moral Majority is
       a political, not a religious, movement, the analysis of its grass-
       roots support indicates otherwise.

504.   Simpson, John H. "Moral Issues and Status Politics," In: The
       New Christian Right; Mobilization and Legitimation, edited by
       Robert C. Liebman and Robert Wuthnow. New York: Aldine,
       1983. pp. 187-205.

Simpson addresses the following questions about the Moral
Majority: (1) How should support for the sociomoral platform
of the organization be measured and, given a measurement
method, what proportion of the American population is positively oriented toward the platform? (2) How is support for
the platform distributed in terms of the social characteristics
of the population and what is the meaning of the pattern of
relationships? (3) What stimulated some Fundamentalist Christians to take advantage of a public mood that is supportive of
their sociomoral platform and enter the American political arena
in the late 1970s via an organization such as the Moral Majority?

505. Thomas, Cal. Book Burning. Good News, 1983.
Thomas, vice president of the Moral Majority, accuses the
liberal establishment--well represented among the nation's
publishing houses, literary critics, bookstones, and libraries--
of censoring the writings of conservatives.

Morality in Media (New York City)

506. Yen, Marianne, compiler. "A Morality Who's Who; The People
and Politics of Citizen Groups Currently in Pursuit of Pornography," Publishers Weekly. 203:2 (July 11, 1986) 42.
A thumbnail sketch of the organization, its goals and activities.

National Board of Review of Motion Pictures

507. Ramsaye, Terry. "Forty Years of the National Board," Films
in Review. 1 (February 1950) 23-24.
An examination of the forces which led to the formation of
the group.

508. "Your Town and the Movies," Films in Review. 2 (April 1951)
1-5.
The organization advocates the establishment of more motion
picture councils; the activities and benefits of these councils
are outlined.

National Catholic Office for Motion Pictures

509. Corliss, R. "Still Legion, Still Decent?" Commonweal. 90
(May 23, 1969) 288-293.
Corliss critiques the past judgments of the organization.

510. Phelan, John. The National Catholic Office for Motion Pictures:
An Investigation of the Policy and Practice of Film Classification.

New York: New York University, 1968. Ph.D. dissertation, available from University Microfilms.
  Phelan surveys the historical background and practices of the organization.

National Citizens Committee for Broadcasting

511. **Access**. Washington, D.C.: National Citizens Committee for Broadcasting, 1975-. Biweekly.
  The vehicle of a watchdog organization representing individuals and groups who feel their views have been under-represented in the mass media.

National Coalition Against Pornography (Cincinnati)

512. Koenig, Richard. "Success of Crusade to Rid City of Smut Has Made Cincinnati a Model for Anti-Pornography Forces," Wall Street Journal. (December 1, 1986) 38, 44.
  The article focuses on the role played by the National Coalition Against Pornography in this clean-up campaign.

513. Minnery, T. "Antipornography Conference Signals Growing Commitment to Combat Obscenity," Christianity Today. 29 (October 18, 1985) 37ff.
  Minnery outlines the agenda of the NCAP in its fight to suppress obscenity.

514. Yen, Marianne, compiler. "A Morality Who's Who; The People and Policies of Citizen Groups Currently in Pursuit of Pornography," Publishers Weekly, 203:2 (July 11, 1986) 42-43.
  A concise portrait of the group, its aims and activities.

National Federation for Decency (Tupelo, Miss.)

515. Conley, Heather. "Protests Lead to Removal of Pornographic Magazine From More Than 5,000 Stores," Christianity Today. (February 1, 1985) 50.
  The article includes coverage of the NFD's contribution to the campaign against convenience stores which sell porn titles.

516. Davis, Rod. "Disciples of Decency: They Say They're Not Censors. They Just Want to Control What You Read, Buy, See, and Do," Houston City Magazine. (November 1986) 42-45, 98.
  A profile of the Houston Federation for Decency, a chapter of the National Federation for Decency. David notes that "if the federation is right, the pendulum in Houston has swung so far into debauchery that only a massive and systematic effort

encompassing picket lines, prosecutors, and long-suffering
citizenry can push it back."

517. Rabey, Steve. "Christian Leaders Take Steps To Combat the
      Porn Epidemic," Christianity Today. (October 19, 1984) 47-
      48.
          Rabey notes the role of the group in the boycott of 7-
      Eleven stores.

518. Yen, Marianne, compiler. "A Morality Who's Who; The People
      and Policies of Citizen Groups Currently in Pursuit of Porno-
      graphy," Publishers Weekly. 203:2 (July 11, 1986) 43.
          A thumbnail sketch of the group, its goals and activities.

National Organization for Decent Literature

519. American Civil Liberties Union. "Statement on Censorship Ac-
      tivity by Private Organizations and the National Organization
      for Decent Literature," In: The First Freedom, edited by
      Robert B. Downs. Chicago: American Library Association,
      1960. pp. 134-138.
          An examination of the NODL--its character and mode of
      operation. The article includes an appendix listing books
      banned by the NODL and literary prize-winning authors who
      have been blacklisted by that organization.

Parent Teacher Association (See: Parents Music Resource Center)

Parents Music Resource Center

520. Goodman, Fred. "Parents, RIAA In Lyrics Accord," Billboard.
      97:45 (November 9, 1985) 1, 87.
          An agreement was reached on November 1, 1985, between
      twenty RIAA-member companies, the PMRC, and the PTA re-
      garding the identification of recordings with lyrics dealing with
      sex, violence, or drugs and alcohol. The companies will either
      apply the inscription "Explicit Lyrics--Parental Advisory" or
      display a printed lyric sheet under the LP shrinkwrap when
      deemed appropriate.

521. Harrington, Richard. "The Capitol Hill Rock War; Emotions
      Run High as Musicians Confront Parents' Group at Hearing,"
      Washington Post. (September 20, 1985) B1, B6.
          Concise play-by-play coverage of the September 19, 1985,
      Senate Commerce Committee hearing on "porn rock."

522. Hentoff, Nat. "The Disc Washers," The Progressive. 49:11
      (November 1983) 29-31.

Hentoff criticizes the aims and methods of the PMRC. He discusses the broader implications of the group's work: "If a rating code comes to pass ... what will become of future songs in the (political) mode of 'Born in the U.S.A.,' 'What's Going On?,' 'Street Fighting Man,' 'Authority Song,' and 'Beat It.' Each of these describes or discusses instances of great violance. At best, under the new regime of rating, their audience would be restricted."

523. Holland, Bill. "PMRC Calls For Uniform Labeling; Cites Good Faith of Record Companies," Billboard. 98:50 (December 20, 1986) 3, 67.
Press statements issued by the PMRC and the national PTA have accused some of the twenty-two record companies previously submitting to the labeling of records with explicit lyrics of "blatantly ignoring, sidestepping, or mocking" the November 1985 agreement. However, the overall tone at a November 10 press conference was conciliatory, expressing faith in the record industry's capacity to act responsibility in living up to the letter of its commitment.

524. Hoyt, Mary Finch. "How Parents Can Stop Obscene Rock Songs," Good Housekeeping. 201 (November 1985) 120ff.
A sympathetic portrayal of the PMRC's policies to protect youth from exposure to obscene rock song lyrics.

525. Isler, Scott. "Parent Terror; Insidious Rock Lyrics: The Inquisition Begins," Musician. n86 (December 1985) 50-62.
Isler provides in-depth coverage of porn rock hearing before the Senate Committee on Commerce, Science and Transportation. The article includes the subfeature, "The Artists Speak: We're Not Gonna Take It ... Never Did and Never Will," in which noteworthy artists reflect on the specter of censorship.

526. Morthland, John. "Rock 'n' Roll Feels the Fire," High Fidelity. 35 (December 1985) 74-75ff.
Morthland discusses PMRC efforts to effect a change from the permissiveness of today's rock lyrics to a more responsible industry-wide stance.

527. "PMRC Still Active," Newsletter on Intellectual Freedom. 35:4 (July 1986) 116.
An update on PMRC activities since reaching an agreement in November 1985 with the RIAA on voluntary labeling. Earlier articles on the NIF are cited (July 1985, p. 138; September 1985, p. 183; November 1985, p. 189; January 1986, p. 3).

528. "'Settlement' Reached in Rock Lyric Dispute," Newsletter on Intellectual Freedom. 35:1 (January 1986) 3-4, 23-25.
The PMRC and its allies scored a victory with the RIAA's

announcement that many American record companies would begin
including warnings on albums containing potentially offensive
lyrics. Events leading up to the announcement as well as
reactions to it on the part of industry spokesmen are noted.
The article includes a special section containing the full text
of rock star Frank Zappa's September 19, 1985, statements
before the Senate Commerce Committee defending the First
Amendment rights of recording artists.

Religious Alliance Against Pornography

529. "Clerics Say President Vows a Major Drive to Curb Smut,"
The New York Times. (November 15, 1986) 9L.
    Spokesmen for the organization cite Reagan's verbal promise
to help in the nationwide crusade being waged against pornography. Covers the implications of the administration's long-
range commitment to the cause.

530. Marshner, Connaught. "Religious Alliance Against Pornography
Represents Millions," Conservative Digest. 13:2 (February
1987) 71, 80.
    An interview with Dr. Jerry Kirk, chairman of the Religious
Alliance Against Pornography, which focuses on his role in
organizing the leaders of all the religious denominations in
America to fight porn.

The Religious Roundtable
(See Also: Christian Voice)

531. Clymer, Adam. "Religious Oriented Right-Wing Group Plans
Driver," The New York Times. (April 12, 1981) 13.
    A report on founder Ed McAteer's efforts to extend his
work by organizing local units of the organization.

Women Against Pornography

532. Yen, Marianne, compiler. "A Morality Who's Who: The People
and Policies of Citizen Groups Currently in Pursuit of Pornography," Publishers Weekly. 203:2 (July 11, 1986) 43.
    A concise portrait of the group, its goals and modus operandi.

D. PRO-CENSORSHIP: INDIVIDUALS

Patrick Buchanan

533. Judis, John B. "Whate House Vigilante: Pat Buchanan Takes

Matters Into His Own Hands," New Republic. 196:4 (January 26, 1987) 17-22.
   Judis surveys Buchanan's life and career. Despite his left-of-center bias, Judis succeeds in capturing the essence of Buchanan's character.

Anthony Comstock

534. Andrist, Ralph K. "Paladin of Purity," American Heritage. 24:6 (October 1973) 4-7, 84-89.
   An engaging account of Comstock's lifelong crusade to fight obscenity.

535. Brown, Heywood, and Margaret Leech. Anthony Comstock: Roundsman of the Lord. New York: Literary Guild of America, 1927.
   The book remains the definitive character study of Comstock.

Jerry Falwell
(See Also: Moral Majority; Pat Robertson)

536. Conway, Flo, and Jim Siegelman. "The Prince of the Power of the Air," In: Holy Terror. Garden City, N.Y.: Doubleday, 1982. pp. 66-80.
   The authors survey Falwell's rise to prominence, focusing on the reasons for his success.

537. "Jerry Falwell," In: Current Biography Yearbook, 1981. New York: H. W. Wilson, 1981. pp. 139-143.
   The career profile focuses on Falwell's role as founder and spokesman for the Moral Majority. A list of biographical references have been included for further study.

538. Solod, Lisa. "The Nutshell Interview: Jerry Falwell," Nutshell. (1981/82) 34-41.
   Falwell reflects on his role as a leader of the New Right.

539. Strober, Gerald, and Ruth Tomczak. Jerry Falwell: Aflame for God. Nashville: Thomas Nelson, 1979.
   The biography provides ample insights into Falwell's vision as a leader of the New Right.

Timothy LaHaye

540. Conway, Flo, and Jim Siegelman. "The World's Greatest Evil," In: Holy Terror. Garden City, N.Y.: Doubleday, 1982. pp. 128-135.
   A profile of LaHaye, termed "the foremost purveyor of fundamentalist hysteria over secular humanism."

James Robison (See: Pat Robertson)

Pat Robertson

541.   Aufderheide, Pat.   "The Next Voice You Hear," The Progres-
       sive.   49:9 (September 1985) 34-37.
           A career profile of the evangelical leader.   The article
       cites First Amendment abuses by the Robertson empire, includ-
       ing CBN programming and his grass-roots pressure group, the
       Freedom Council.

542.   Jenkins, John W.   "Toward the Anti-Humanist New Christian
       Nation," The Humanist.   41:4 (July/August 1981) 20-23, 52.
           Jenkins notes that cable TV and satellite transmission
       threaten a massive evangelical transformation of society, with
       implications transcending politics.   He focuses on the words
       and deeds of three TV preachers--Pat Robertson, James Robi-
       son, and Jerry Falwell--as a means of illustrating how the ar-
       chitects of the New Christian Nation are working.

Jimmy Swaggart

543.   Conway, Flo, and Jim Siegelman.   "The Old-Timers: Jimmy
       Swaggart," In: Holy Terror.   Garden City, N.Y.:   Double-
       day, 1982.   pp. 48-49.
           A concise depiction of the methods employed by Swaggart;
       his old-time ministry is contrasted with the newcomers work-
       ing in the area known as the "electronic church."

Richard A. Viguerie

544.   Conway, Flo, and Jim Siegelman.   "The Gang of Three: Viguere--
       Mail Chauvinist," In: Holy Terror.   Garden City, N.Y.:
       Doubleday, 1982.   pp. 83-90.
           The authors state that Viguerie may be the most important
       individual in the fundamentalist right network.   The role played
       by Viguerie--as fund raiser, manager of a vast information
       clearing house, and publicist--is outlined at length.

545.   "Richard A(rt) Viguerie," In: Current Biography Yearbook,
       1983.   New York: H. W. Wilson, 1983.   pp. 427-430.
           A career profile of the "Godfather of the New Right."   The
       article documents Viguerie's influence via direct-mail advertis-
       ing, political fund raising, and publishing.   A list of biographi-
       cal references have been included for further study.

546.   Viguerie, Richard A.   The New Right: We're Ready to Lead.
       Falls Church, Va.:   The Viguerie Company, 1980.

Viguerie delineates the socio-political agenda of the New Right.

Paul Weyrich

547. Conway, Flo, and Jim Siegelman.   "The Gang of Three: Wey-
rich--'Mr. Big,'" In: Holy Terror. Garden City, N.Y.:
Doubleday, 1982. pp. 90-95.
A profile of Weyrich, termed "the architect of the preachers-
into-politics movement."

548. Edwards, Lee. "Paul Weyrich: Conscience of the New Right,"
Conservative Digest. 7:7 (1981) 2-8.
A career portrait of Weyrich, focusing on his role as strate-
gist and coordinator of activities within the New Right.

E.   VIEWPOINTS: ANTI-CENSORSHIP

549. Ackerman, Margaret B. "Arguments Against Censorship: Milton and Mill," Arizona English Bulletin. 11 (February 1969)
23-27.
A comparative analysis of two seminal works concerned with
intellectual freedom--Milton's Areopagitica and Mill's Of the
Liberty of Thought and Discussion.

550. Bender, Paul. "The Obscenity Muddle: A Guide to the Supreme Court's Latest Sexual Crisis," Harper's. 246 (February
1973) 46, 50-52.
Bender recommends that the Supreme Court "broaden the
permissible meaning of 'obscene,' while narrowing the permissible situations where that categorization is legally relevant."
He notes that this would inhibit the sexual exploitation of
children while allowing adults to purchase sexual materials.

551. Burstyn, Varda, editor. Women Against Censorship. Van-
couver: Douglas & McIntyre, 1985.
The collection of essays in this book attempt to convey the
conflict within the women's movement over explicit sexual material. Topics include: Censorship and Law Reform: Will
Changing the Laws Mean a Change for the Better?; Women and
Images: Toward a Feminist Analysis of Censorship; Retrench-
ment versus Transformation: The Politics of the Antipornography Movement; False Promises: Feminist Antipornography
Legislation in the U.S.

552. Darling, Richard L. "Censorship--An Old Story," Elementary
English. 51 (May 1974) 691-696. Reprinted in The First

Freedom Today, edited by Robert B. Downs and Ralph E.
McCoy. Chicago: American Library Association, 1984. pp.
109-114.

Darling argues that censorship will not solve the real problems of society. He notes that "when librarians, or teachers,
begin to censor books because those books reflect the social
climate and conscience of the era in which they were produced,
it sounds ominously as though they adopted the philosophy of
1984."

553. Gaines, Ervin J. "The New Censorship--Social Responsibility
and Moral Righteousness," Minnesota English Journal. 12:1
(Winter 1976) 3-8.

Gaines contends that censorship on the grounds of obscenity
is under control; political censorship now poses the greatest
threat to freedom of expression. He states that any suppression of ideas is undesirable; liberal intellectuals are often as
guilty as the ultra-conservative element in allowing the ends
to justify the means.

554. Kaminer, Wendy. "A Woman's Guide to Pornography and the
Law," The Nation. (June 21, 1980) Reprinted in: The First
Freedom Today, edited by Robert B. Downs and Ralph E.
McCoy. Chicago: American Library Association, 1984. pp.
244-247.

Kaminer argues against legislative or judicial suppression
of pornography because it is "simply not possible without
breaking down the legal principles and procedures that are essential to our own right to speak and, ultimately, our freedom
to control our own lives."

555. Kendall, Roy. "Rogue Valley Humanists Fight Back," The
Humanist. 41:2 (March/April 1981) 8-9, 60.

The article is comprised of two letters written by a member
of the American Humanist Association Watchdog Committee on
Fairness in Religious Broadcasting: the first was sent August
28, 1980, to a local (Ashland, Oregon) Christian radio station
that had been making derogatory statements about humanists;
and the second, dated September 10, 1980, confirms the offend-
ing pastor's offer of air time for a rebuttal. Kendall feels that
these two letters exemplify just what can be done to combat
public attacks by fundamentalists which violate FCC guidelines
(e.g. Fairness doctrine, personal attack rule).

556. Levin, Harry. "The Unbanning of the Books," Atlantic. 217:2
(February 1966) 77-81.

Levin assesses the current trend in our society--and, more
specifically, our courts--toward increased permissiveness regarding previously banned materials. He states that if we
abandon censorship, we depend all the more imperatively upon
criticism. He concludes that one of the wholesome results of our

hard-won candor may be to drive the pornographers out of
business.

557.   Michalsky, Walt.   "The Masquerade of Fundamentalism," The
Humanist.   41:4 (July/August 1981) 15-18, 52.
       Michalsky offers the following assessment of the upsurge
of fundamentalism as a political force: "The separation of
church and state seems to be melting into a pot out of which
rises the fumes of an in-name-only secular state that reflects
the revealed truths of fundamentalist religion.   The political
issues become religio-political issues.
       "For many silent observers, this is a frightening situation
that signals the possible return of a Puritan-type philosophy.
The message: It's time to run the sinners out; Sinner defined
as someone with whom the militant Christians don't agree."
He concludes that media messiahs and classroom evangelists
must be confronted in order to avoid repeating history's mistakes.

558.   Pilpel, Harriet F.   "Obscenity and the Constitution," In: The
First Freedom Today, edited by Robert B. Downs and Ralph
E. McCoy.   Chicago: American Library Association, 1984.
pp. 228-237.
       Pilpel surveys the legal treatment of obscenity in the courts
since the mid-nineteenth century.   She provides recommendations as to how to fight censorship both on the legislative and
court fronts.

559.   "A Plague of Censors," The Progressive.   (July 1986) 9-10.
       The editorial asserts that the newly revived crusade against
"pornography" is of a piece with the Reagan Administration's
crusade against the disclosure of "secrets" in that "both assume that the state should have the last word on what citizens
may or may not read, see, hear, or--ultimately--think."

560.   "Writers Speak Out," Newsletter on Intellectual Freedom.   35:3
(May 1986) 75-77, 99-100.
       The article consists of lengthy statements from four noted
contemporary authors--John Irving, Susan Isaacs, William Kennedy, and John Updike--in support of intellectual freedom.   All
contributors agree that the current climate of censorship
threatens creativity as well as the individual's pursuit of enlightenment and happiness.

                F.   ANTI-CENSORSHIP: GROUPS

General

561.   Shugert, Diane P.   "A Body of Well-Instructed Men and Women:

Organizations Active for Intellectual Freedom," In: Dealing
With Censorship, edited by James E. Davis. Urbana, Ill.:
National Council of Teachers of English, 1979. pp. 215-221.
   Shugert delineates the people and organizations dedicated
to fighting censorship.

American Booksellers Association

562.   Baker, John F.   "On the Front Line in the Censorship Struggle;
       Booksellers Offer Advice, Share Experiences and Urge Mutual
       Support Systems," Publishers Weekly.   203:2 (July 11, 1986)
       45-46.
          Highlights of a panel session at the 1986 annual convention
       of the American Booksellers Association which addressed the
       problems of book retailers with censorship, local vigilante ac-
       tivity and the religious right.

563.   Noyes, Richard P.   "The ABA's Involvement in the Long Strug-
       gle Against Censorship," Publishers Weekly.   207:20 (May 19,
       1975) 129-130.
          Noyes surveys the role played by the ABA in fighting cen-
       sorship since the Ulysses case in the thirties.

American Civil Liberties Union

564.   Mayer, Milton.   The Trouble With the ACLU," The Progressive.
       44 (February 1980) 48-50.
          The text of Mayer's October 1979 speech to the Monterey,
       California chapter of the ACLU, which presented him with its
       Ralph Atkinson Civil Liberties Award for 1979.   He states that
       "Civil liberties do not civilize a society; the Bill of Rights was
       amended into the Constitution and it can be amended out.
       What civilizes society is the determination above all else to be
       civilized."

People for the American Way
(See Also: Norman Lear)

565.   Marty, Martin E.   "A Profile of Norman Lear; Another Pilgrim's
       Progress," The Christian Century.   104:2 (January 21, 1987)
       55-58.
          In light of negative portraits provided by leaders of the
       religious New Right, Marty attempts to provide a more objective
       view of Lear and his crusade for intellectual freedom via People
       for the American Way.   The author proposes that Lear's most
       important contribution may be to assist his most public enemies
       in becoming more empathetic and open as they make their own
       way.

566.   "People for the American Way Offers Help in Legal Fights Over
       School Books," Phi Delta Kappan. (May 1986) 686.
          The article reports on the organization's role in fighting
       school censorship.

The Reporters Committee for Freedom of the Press

567.   Witcover, Jules. "A Reporters' Committee That Works," Colum-
       bia Journalism Review. 12:1 (May/June 1973) 26-30, 43.
          Witcover profiles the activities of The Reporters Committee
       for Freedom of the Press in support of the press' First Amend-
       ment rights.

G.   ANTI-CENSORSHIP: INDIVIDUALS

Alan Dershowitz

568.   "Alan M(orton) Dershowitz," In: Current Biography Yearbook,
       1986. New York: H. W. Wilson, 1986. pp. 108-112.
          Career profile focuses on his litigation of antiwar and free
       speech causes. It is noted that "Dershowitz finds that most
       agents of the American justice system--judges, prosecutors,
       and defense attorneys alike--are distinctly apathetic in their
       pursuit of truth and justice and in their respect for the Con-
       stitution." Includes a list of biographical references for fur-
       ther study.

Hugh Hefner

569.   Leerheen, Charles, et al. "Aging Playboy," Newsweek. (Au-
       gust 4, 1986) 50-56.
          A profile of Hefner's life and career. Despite recent set-
       backs (e.g., the Dorothy Stratten scandal, a stroke in 1985,
       attacks by the Meese Commission), he faces current challenges
       with a renewed sense of purpose. The article includes the
       subfeature, "The Bunnymaster and His Mistresses."

Norman Lear
(See Also: People for the American Way)

570.   Stein, Ben. "Norman Lear vs. the Moral Majority: The War
       to Clean Up TV," Saturday Review. 8:2 (February 1981) 22-
       27.
          The author outlines Lear's concern about the burgeoning
       power of the combined new Christian right and the new political

right. Lear's role in making TV a more intelligent medium is
also noted.

571. "Norman (Milton) Lear," In: Current Biography Yearbook,
      1974. New York: H. W. Wilson, 1974. pp. 229-232.
         The career profile focuses on his accomplishments in the
      entertainment business. While the essay was published prior
      to his founding of People for the American Way, his role as
      president of the American Civil Liberties Union Foundation is
      noted. A list of biographical references has been included for
      further study.

PART V:

CASES OF CENSORSHIP IN THE MASS MEDIA

The intent of this chapter is to provide documented instances in which the censorship--or attempted censorship--of materials, programs, presentations, etc., has occurred. The bibliographic listing is selective by a number of criteria, including location of occurrence (the United States), date of occurrence (the twentieth century, with preference given to the post-World War II period), and quality and comprehensiveness of the article, book, etc., covering the incident. It should also be noted that at least two additional factors have limited those instances included in the bibliography: (1) the failure of many cases to receive adequate coverage in the mass media--some are reported only on a local basis, and others not at all--and (2) the fact that many incidents are never outwardly diagnosed as censorship (e.g., self-censorship, the use of implied threats by the censor to achieve the desired effect).

A considerable number of studies have documented the categories in which censorship has taken place in contemporary American history (as well as the motivations behind these attempts to suppress various materials, ideas, etc.). L. B. Woods, in his work, A Decade of Censorship, has done a particularly admirable job of codifying both the stimuli for censorship in addition to the subjects and formats victimized by the phenomenon.

> The topics or subjects of materials under censorship attack are varied, but can be categorized. Reasons cited for censorship have included drugs, governmental or administrative criticism, language, morals, politics, racism, religion, sex, and war. The materials involved have been described as being biased, communistic, controversial, filthy, immoral, inaccurate, lascivious, lewd, obscene, poorly written, pornographic, pro-Chicano or pro-Negro, questionable, racy, radical, risque, sacrilegious, "smut," un-American, and violent, and may deal with topics such as abortion, alcoholism, divorce, early marriage, homosexuality, nudity, the police, pregnancy, prostitution, racial unrest, religion, school dropouts, sex, suicide, or the Vietnam War. The protection

of children is one of the most common concerns expressed,
yet the problem is compounded because today's youth are
increasingly seeking materials that reflect the world as it
is. Children's literature increasingly deals with such issues
as cruelty, drug abuse, race relations, and social problems.
And young adults, confronting a world that is different
from the world of their parents, want literature relevant to
their lives in contemporary society.

Woods determined that the formats subjected to censorship attacks vary extensively, from the written word to films, people, the
fine arts, music, dramatic works, symbols, subjects, groups, exhibits, places and things. More specifically, he has cited the following categories as victims of censorship: administrators, art works,
booklets, books, bulletins (handbills, leaflets, pamphlets, etc.),
card catalogs, choral grounds, library circulation records, citizens,
college bands, comics, the confederate flag, courses, dance groups,
displays, editors of school publications, essays, films, filmstrips,
gay student organizations, government documents, graffiti, handouts,
laboratories, lectures, librarians, libraries, library meeting rooms,
magazines, materials selection policies, mime troupes, the Nazi Party/
National Socialists White Peoples Party, newspapers, nude models,
organizations, panels, peace symbols, photographs, picketers, plays,
poems, posters/pictures, radio stations, recordings, religious observ-
ances, rock operas/musicals, sex surveys, slide shows, songs,
speakers, speeches, students, teachers, television stations, textbooks, trustees, video tapes and yearbooks.

For those who find the entries to be too limited for their liking,
the additional titles in Table 4 have been provided as a starting point
for further research. In addition, sources such as Banned Books,
Banned Films, and the Newsletter on Intellectual Freedom, which have
provided concise references to either current or retrospective cases
of censorship, are highly recommended to the reader.

TABLE 4:   Mass Media Titles Which Have Been Censored in the U.S.

BOOKS [1]

The Abortion: An Historical Romance; About David; The Accommoda-
tion: The Politics of Race in an American City; Across 110th; Across
the River and In to the Trees; Adolescents Today (Scott Foresman,
1982); The Adventures of Sherlock Holmes; Albert Herbert Hawkins;
Albert Herbert Hawkins and the Space Rocket; Alice in Wonderland;
All About Eggs; An American Tragedy; Ancient Evenings; Anderson-
ville; Ann Vickers; Antic Hay; Are You There God, It's Me Margaret;
As I Lay Dying; Autumn Street; Be Ready with Bells and Drums (A

TABLE 4 (cont.)

Patch of Blue); Beastly Boys and Ghostly Girls; Beat the Turtle
Drum; Beggar Man, Thief; Biology (Holt, Rinehart and Winston,
1975); Black Boy; The Black Stallion; Black Like Me; Blackbriar;
Blood Brothers; Blueschild Baby; Breaking the Sex Role Barrier;
The Burros of Mavrick Gulch; The Call of the Wild; Came a Spider;
The Case for India; Catch-22; Changes; Changing Bodies, Changing
Lives; Chocolate to Morphine; Christine; Cinderella; Citizen Tom Paine;
Claudia, Where are You?; The Color Purple; Concepts in Biology
(Brown, 1979); Confessions of an Only Child; Contemporary Living
(Goodheart, 1981); Crossings; Cujo; Dark Laughter; Daybreak; The
Death Penalty (Putnam, 1978); Delta Star; The Devil's Own Dear
Son; Diary of a Frantic Kid Sister; Dinky Hocker Shoots Smack; The
Divorce Express (Delacorte, 1982); Don't Tell Me Your Name; The
Doors of Perception; Dreamland Lake; Elmer Gantry; The Encyclo-
pedia of Psychoactive Drugs; End as a Man; Endless Enemies; Esther
Waters; The Eternal Anti-Semite; Exploring Science (Laidlaw Brothers,
1975); Eyeless in Gaza; Facts About Sex for Today's Youth (Ed-U
Press, 1981); The Facts of Love, Living, Loving and Growing Up
(Crown, 1979); Family Matters (Pergamon, 1983); The Fate of the
Earth; Father Christmas; The Fixer; A Fleet in Being; Flowers for
Algernon; The Fog Comes in on Little Pig's Feet; Forever Amber;
From Here to Eternity; The Future of Motherhood; The Games of
Wizards; The Genius; Girls Are Equal, Too; The Glitter Dome; The
God Makers; The Godfather; Goodbye Jeanette; The Great Religions
by Which Men Live (Fawcett, 1977); A Green Desire; The Green
Pastures; Grendel; Gun Control; The Hamlet, Hanging Out With Cici;
Happiness in Marriage; Haunting of America; Health (Prentice-Hall,
1976); Health, a Way of Life (Scott Foresman, 1978); The Hobbit;
Horses and Men; Howl; The Humanities; Cultural Roots and Continui-
ties; Humorous Poetry for Children; I Am the Cheese; Ice and Fire;
Illustrated Encyclopedia of Family Health; Image of the Beast; In a
Dark, Dark Room; In the Night Kitchen; In the Spirit of Crazy
Horse; Inner City Mother Goose; Inside Mom; It Can't Happen Here;
Jelly Belly; A Journey to the Arctic; The Joy of Sex; Jude the Ob-
scure; The Jungle; Jurgen; A Kid's First Book About Sex; Kings-
blood Royal; Last Exit to Brooklyn; The Last Mission; Lesbian Nuns:
Breaking Silence; Let's Talk About Health; A Light in the Attic; Lis-
ten to the Silence; Literature of the Supernatural; Little Big Man;
Longarm in Virginia City (Jove, 1984); Love Among the Haystacks;
The Love Machine; Macbeth; Man and Superman; Man, Myth and
Magic; Many Marriages; Married and Single Life (Bennett, 1984);
Married Love; Masculinity and Femininity (Houghton Mifflin, 1971);
The Me Nobody Knows--Children's Voices From the Ghetto; Meet
the Vampire; Memoirs of Hecate County; The Merchant of Venice;
Metrication, American Style; The Miller's Tale; Mistral's Daughter;
Modern Human Sexuality (Houghton Mifflin, 1976); A Modern Lover;
Modern Sex Education (Holt, Rinehart and Winston, 1972); Mom, the
Wolfman, and Me; Monsters; Mosquitoes; Mrs. Warren's Profession;
My Fights for Birth Control; My Life and Work, by Henry Ford; My

TABLE 4 (cont.)

Sweet Audrine; The Naked and the Dead; The Naked Ape Naomi in
the Middle; Native Son; The New Centurions; The New Our Bodies,
Ourselves; Nicodemus and the Houn' Dog; Nigger; Nightwork; Notes
of Two Trips with the Channel Squadron; Nuclear War, What's in it
for You?; Nutshell Library; Occult America; Oil; The Old Man and
the Sea; On the Road; One Sad Day; Our Land, Our Time; Out of
the Cauldron; The Outsiders; Parenting and Children (McGraw,
1980); Person to Person (Bennett, 1981); The Philanderers; The Pig-
man; The Pill vs. the Springhill Mine Disaster; Point Counter Point;
The Popular History of Witchcraft; Portnoy's Complaint; Possible Im-
possibilities (Houghton Mifflin, 1977); The Price of Power; The Prize;
Pylon; The Quartzsite Trip; Rabbit Is Rich; Rabbit Run; The Rain-
bow; The Revolt of Mother; Revolution for the Hell of It; The Rights
of Gay People; Rommel Drives on Deep into Egypt; Salem's Lot; Salome;
Sanctuary; The Satanist; Secrets of the Shopping Mall; The Seduction of Peter S.; See How They Grow; The Sensuous Woman; Seven
Arrows; Sexual Behavior in the Human Female; The Shining; The
Shoemaker; Shoplifting (Lodestar Books, 1980); Shuttlecock; Single
and Pregnant (Beacon, 1970); Sister Carrie; The Sisters Impossible;
Slugs; Soldier's Pay; Songs and Stories of the Netsilik Eskimos;
Sons and Lovers; Spoon River Anthology; Star Witness; The Story
of Passover for Children; Strange Fruit; Strange Interlude; Studies
in the Psychology of Sex; Studs Lonigan; The Stupids Die; The
Stupids Step Out; Summer of '42; The Sun Also Rises; Superfudge;
The Tall Man From Boston; Tell Me That You Love Me, Junie Moon;
Tess of the D'Urbervilles; That Was Then, This Is Now; Three Poor
Tailors; Three Weeks; Timberlaine; To Have and Have Not; Tobacco
Road; Today's Teen; Tom Sawyer; Topics for the Restless; Towards
an East European Marxism; Trig; Tropic of Capricorn; Trout Fishing
in America; The Truth in Crisis; Understanding Psychology (Random
House, 1983); Undress the City; Unicorns in the Rain; User's Guide
to Computer Crime; Valley of the Dolls; Valley of the Horses; War
on Villa Street; The Wayward Bus; Webster's Ninth Collegiate Dic-
tionary; The Well of Loneliness; Where do Babies Come From; Where
the Sidewalk Ends; Where the Wild Things Are; Why Are We in Viet-
nam?; Wide is the Gate; Wifey; The Wild Palms; Winning; Wise Parenthood; Witches (Harper and Row, 1975); The Wizard of Oz; Women in
Love; A World I Never Made; A Wrinkle in Time; Your Health and
Your Future (Laidlaw Brothers, 1976); Zodiac and Swastika.

FILMS [2]

1908-1919

Birth Control; The Brand; The Easiest Way; Fit to Win; the Hand
That Rocks the Cradle; The James Boys in Missouri; Night Riders;
The Ordeal; The Sex Lure; The Spirit of '76; The Spy; Willard-
Johnson Boxing Match.

TABLE 4 (cont.)

1920-1939

Alibi; The Birth of a Baby; Ecstasy; The Naked Truth; Professor
Hamlock; Remous; The Road to Ruin; Spain in Flames; Tomorrow's
Children; The Youth of Maxim.

1940-1959

Amok; The Anatomy of a Murder; Curley; Desire Under the Elms;
Don Juan; The Game of Love; The Garden of Eden; La Ronde; Latuko;
The Lovers; M; The Man with the Golden Arm; Miss Julie; Mom and
Dad; The Moon Is Blue; Naked Amazon; Native Son; The Outlaw;
Pinky; Victory in the West; Wild Weed.

1960-1969

Alimony Lovers; Angelique in Black Leather; Bachelor Tom Peeping;
The Bedford Incident; Blue Movie; Body of a Female; Bunny Lake Is
Missing; Carmen, Baby; The Connection; The Dirty Girls; The Fe-
male; 491; The Fox; Have Figure Will Travel; I, a Woman; Lorna;
Mondo Freudo; Never on Sunday; Odd Triangle; Pattern of Evil;
Rent-a-Girl; Revenge at Daybreak; A Stranger Knocks; Therese
and Isabelle; This Picture Is Censored; The Twilight Girls; Un Chant
d'Amour; The Unsatisfied; The Virgin Spring; Viva Maria; The
Wicked Die Slow; A Woman's Urge; Women of the World; Yellow Bird.

1970-1981

The Art of Marriage; Bad News Bears; Behind the Green Door;
Caligula; Carnal Knowledge; Cindy and Donna; Class of '74; A Clockwork Orange; The Collection; Computer Game; Cry Uncle; The Devil
in Miss Jones; Emmanuelle; Grease; Gun Runners; I Am Sandra; It
All Comes Out in the End; The Killing of Sister George; The Last
Picture Show; The Libertine; Lysistrata; Magic Mirror; Naked Comes
the Stranger; The Newcomers; Pink Flamingo; Pornography in Den-
mark; Rocky Horror Picture Show; School Girl; The Secret Sex Lives
of Romeo and Juliet; Sexual Sinderella; Starlet, Stewardesses; The
Vixen; Where Eagles Dare; Without a Stitch; Woodstock.

1982-present

About Last Night (Sexual Perversity in Chicago); Acid From Heaven;
Acid Rain; Requiem or Recovery; All American Girls; Born American;
The Breakfast Club; California Valley Girl; A Christmas Story; Cobra;
Debbie Does Dallas; Dracula Blows His Cool; Ecocide: A Strategy of

TABLE 4 (cont.)

War; Faces of Death; Faces of War; From the Ashes ... Nicaragua
Today; Hail Mary; The Headless Cupid; Hearts and Minds; If You
Love This Planet; In Our Own Backyards; Mishima; Monsters and
Other Science Mysteries; Mystery of Astrology; Mystery of ESP;
Mystery of Witchcraft; Never Cry Wolf; Occupied Palestine; A Pas-
sage to India; Peace; A Conscious Choice; Pink Floyd--The Wall;
Rambo; Rajiv's India; Return to Oz; Romeo and Juliet; Salo--The
120 Days of Sodom; Save the Planet; The Silent Scream; Soldier
Girls; Splash; The Story of O; The Sword and the Sorcerer; Taboo;
Taboo II; Testament; Victor, Victoria; Whatever Happened to Child-
hood?

MAGAZINES/NEWSPAPERS [3]

The Advocate; Among Friends; Anal Leather; Battle of the Stars,
Round Two; Berkeley Barb; Chic; Circus; Common Lives/Lesbian
Lives; Creem; Criterion (Mesa College); Cue (Harvard University);
Daily Nebraskan; Eidos; Fetish Fantasies; A Few Good Men; Forum;
Gallery; Genesis; Harbor Hawk (Harbor College); Harper's; Hit
Parader; Holiday; The Humanist; Hustler; Illini Chronicle (University
of Illinois); International Life; Issues and Answers; Lumberjack (Hum-
boldt State University); Mademoiselle; Ms.; National Geographic; Na-
tional Vanguard; New Voice (Hofstra University); Newlook; News-
week; Not for Profit; Our Own; Our Paper; Pace Press (Pace Uni-
versity); Penthouse; Philadelphia Bulletin; Philadelphia Inquirer;
Playboy; Playgirl; Providence Journal; Redbook; The Religious Herald;
Rolling Stone; Scholastic Scope; South End; South Shore Record;
Spice (Temple University); Sports Illustrated; Super Teen; Swank;
Tampa Tribune; Texas Review; Tiger Beat; Time; Washington Journal
of Sex and Politics; The Washington Post; The Weekly News; Weekly
Reader; Young Miss.

SONGS/SOUND RECORDINGS [4]

"Am I Black Enough For You"--Billy Paul [lyrics]; "Animal (F**k
Beast)"--W.A.S.P. [lyrics]; Below the Belt--Boxer [cover]; Blind
Faith--Blind Faith [cover]; Country Life--Roxy Music [cover]; "Darl-
ing Nikki"--Prince [lyrics]; "Dixie" [lyrics]; "Eight Miles High"--
Byrds [lyrics]; Electric Ladyland--Jimi Hendrix Experience [cover];
"The Fish Cheer & I-Feel-Like-I'm-Fixin'-to-Die Rag"--Country Joe
and the Fish [lyrics]; "Heroin"--Velvet Underground [lyrics]; "Honey
Love"--Drifters [lyrics]; "Kick Out the Jams"--MC5 [lyrics]; "Louie
Louie"--Kingsmen [lyrics]; Moby Grape--Moby Grape [poster insert];
"Rhapsody in the Rain"--Lou Christie [lyrics]; "Short People"--Randy
Newman [lyrics]; "Sink the Pink"--AC/DC [lyrics]; "Sixty Minute
Man"--Dominoes [lyrics]; Slippery When Wet--Bon Jovi [cover];
"Stairway to Heaven"--Led Zeppelin [backmasking]; "Sugar Walls"--
Sheena Easton [lyrics]; Two Virgins--John Lennon & Yoko Ono [cover];

TABLE 4 (cont.)

"Volunteers"--Jefferson Airplane [lyrics]; "Woman Love"--Gene Vincent [vocal delivery]; You Axed For It!--Mentors [lyrics].

TELEVISION [5]

Acts of Violence (HBO documentary); American Bandstand; Badge of
the Assassin (CBS docudrama); Charlie's Angels; Dallas; The Dating
Game; Death of a Princess; Dukes of Hazzard; Flashpoint; It's a
Living; Ladies' Man; Mary Hartman, Mary Hartman; The Newlywed
Game; Playboy Channel; Playing for Time; Saturday Night Live; Soap;
Taxi; Three's Company; Vegas; WKRP in Cincinnati.

THEATRICAL PRESENTATIONS [6]

Animal Farm; Butterflies are Free; The Children's Hour; A Chorus
Line; Coser y Cantar; The Curse of the Starving Class; Equus; The
Good Doctor; Grease; Hair; Jesus Christ, Superstar; Judevine; Ly--
sistrada; Merry Wives of Windsor; Oh Calcutta!; One Flew Over the
Cuckoo's Nest; The Persecution and Assassination of Jean-Paul Marat
as Performed by the Inmates of the Asylum of Charenton Under the
Direction of the Marquis de Sade; Sister Mary Ignatius Explains It
All for You; Sorcerer and Friends; Working.

VIDEO CLIPS/FEATURES [7]

"Girls on Film"--Duran Duran; "Sex (I'm a ...)"--Berlin; Sun City--
Various Artists; "Too Much Blood"--Rolling Stones.

It should be noted that the chapter is concerned only with the
mass media titles censored in schools, libraries, retail outlets, and
other public places.   The vast panorama of censorship restraints--
e.g., post office seizure and blockage, customs confiscation, civil
injunction, police and citizen group blacklist--involving a focus upon
issues other than the treatment of particular mass media materials
and presentations are covered in the other sections of the work.

NOTES

1.   The listing is largely based upon the Newsletter on Intellectual
     Freedom ("Targets of the Censor--Books"); Freedom and Culture,
     compiled by Eleanor Widmer ("Censored Books"); A Decade of
     Censorship in America, by L. B. Woods ("List of Most Censored
     Items in Educational Institutions in the U.S. and Their Reviews,

1966-75"; and "Children's Materials Censored in Educational Institutions, 1966-75").

2. The listing is largely based upon the Newsletter on Intellectual Freedom ("Targets of the Censor--Films"); Banned Films, by De Grazia and Newman ("Appendix F"); and A Decade of Censorship in America, by L. B. Woods ("List of Most Censored Items in Educational Institutions in the U.S. and Their Reviews, 1966-75").

3. The listing is largely based upon the Newsletter on Intellectual Freedom ("Targets of the Censor--Periodicals") and A Decade of Censorship in America, by L. B. Woods ("List of Most Censored Items in Educations in the U.S. and Their Reviews, 1966-75"). Many instances involving high school papers were left out of this compilation.

4. The listing is based upon news briefs and features culled from a variety of entertainment trade magazines and music fanzines.

5. The listing is based upon the Newsletter on Intellectual Freedom ("Targets of the Censor--Broadcasting").

6. The listing is largely based upon the Newsletter on Intellectual Freedom ("Targets of the Censor--Theatre").

7. The listing is based upon news briefs culled from a variety of entertainment trade journals.

A. THE MASS MEDIA: GENERAL

572. Cirino, Robert. Don't Blame the People: How the News Media Use Bias, Distortion and Censorship to Manipulate Public Opinion. Los Angeles; Diversity, 1971; New York: Random House, 1972.

Based upon his analysis of the news coverage by The New York Times, the Los Angeles Times, the three major TV networks, four radio networks, and Reader's Digest, Cirino argues that the media establishment "has prevented real public participation by not allowing all ideas to compete fairly for public acceptance."

573. Hohenberg, John. Free Press/Free People; the Best Cause. New York: Columbia University Press, 1971.

Hohenberg surveys the development of the concept of a free press, beginning with communications in pre-print days.

574a. McCoy, Ralph E. Freedom of the Press: An Annotated Bibliography. With a Foreword by Robert B. Downs. Carbondale: Southern Illinois University Press, 1968.

According to McCoy's preface, the work represents "an annotated bibliography of some 8,000 books, pamphlets, journal articles, films, and other material relating to freedom of the press in English-speaking countries, from the beginning of printing to the present. 'Press' is used generally to include all media of mass communications: books, pamphlets, periodicals, newspapers, motion pictures, photograph records, radio, television, and, to a limited extent, stage plays. Subjects include heresy, sedition, blasphemy, obscenity, personal libel, and both positive and negative expressions on freedom of the press."

574b. McCoy, Ralph E. Freedom of the Press: A Bibliocyclopedia. Ten-Year Supplement (1967-77). Foreword by Robert B. Downs. Carbondale: Southern Illinois University Press, 1979.

The work updates McCoy's Freedom of the Press: An Annotated Bibliography (1968). The compilation includes over 6,500 items--print and nonprint--dealing with censorship and intellectual freedom that were published between 1967-1977. The arrangement is alphabetical; exhaustive index is thirty-nine pages in length.

575. Mosco, Vincent. Broadcasting in the United States. Norwood,
     N.J.: Ablex, 1979.
        Mosco argues that radio and television franchise owners
     have induced the FCC to act conservatively with respect to
     FM radio, UHF TV, cable TV, and subscription TV. He feels
     this has led to the concentration of political and economic power
     in the hands of the broadcasting industry, thereby restricting
     the audiences' choice of programs. Proposals to change the
     regulatory structure are examined.

576. Stuart, Reginald. "F.C.C. Acts to Restrict Indecent Program-
     ming," The New York Times. 47:112 (April 17, 1987) A1,
     C30.
        The FCC, responding to public complaints, unanimously
     adopted measures on April 17, 1987, which are intended to
     sharply restrict explicit language about sex and bodily func-
     tions on radio, television, and telephone services. The agency,
     in determining whether enforcement steps should be taken
     against a license holder, will apply the definition of indecent
     language set forth in a 1976 FCC order (and upheld in 1978 by
     the Supreme Court) in place of a narrower "seven dirty words"
     yardstick that was part of the 1976 order. The definition is
     as follows: " ... language or material that depicts or describes,
     in terms patently offensive as measured by contemporary com-
     munity standards for the broadcast medium, sexual or excretory
     activities or organs." Letters of warning are to be sent to
     three radio stations alleged to have made indecent broadcasts:
     KPFN-FM, Los Angeles, KCSB-FM, Santa Barbara, and WYSP-
     FM, Philadelphia.

Fairness Doctrine

577. Barron, Jerome A. "Access to the Press: A New First Amend-
     ment Right," Harvard Law Review. (June 1967) Reprinted
     in The First Freedom Today, edited by Robert B. Downs and
     Ralph E. McCoy. Chicago: American Library Association,
     1984. pp. 321-324.
        Barron argues that the First Amendment gives constitutional
     protection not to the "press" but to "freedom of the press,"
     and that this protection encompasses the right of the people
     to have access to the newspaper press as they now have to
     the electronic press under the "fairness doctrine."

578. Daniel, Clifton. "Rights of Access and Reply," In: The First
     Freedom Today, edited by Robert B. Downs and Ralph E. McCoy.
     Chicago: American Library Association, 1984. pp. 325-328.
        Daniel argues that mandating the right of access and right
     of reply to the press would prove to be unworkable. He sets
     forth other alternatives for achieving fairness; e.g., appoint
     a full-time ombudsman on the paper/station to track down

complaints, organize a local press council of community repre-
sentatives.

579. Daniels, Bruce E. "Fairness Doctrine--Public Access Vs. First
Amendment," Newsletter on Intellectual Freedom. 34:3 (May
1985) 68-69.
    Daniels traces the historical development of the Fairness
Doctrine of the Communications Act of 1934 through various
FCC rulings, legislative amendments, and judicial interpretations. He posits that factors such as improved technology,
the need to justify performance to the federal government, and
the present imperative for vigorous debate of controversial new
ideas necessitate the elimination of the Fairness Doctrine.

580. Daniels, Bruce E., compiler. "Fairness Doctrine--Public Access Vs. First Amendment: An Annotated Bibliography," Newsletter on Intellectual Freedom. 34:3 (May 1985) 70-71.
    The highly selective listing includes books and articles pub-
lished between 1964-1984 which touch upon some aspect of the
Fairness Doctrine.

581. Friendly, Fred W. The Good Guys, the Bad Guys and the First
Amendment: Free Speech vs. Fairness in Broadcasting. New
York: Random House, 1975; New York: Vintage, 1978.
    Friendly's analysis of the issues surrounding the Fairness
Doctrine is enhanced by those insights gained from his former
tenure as director of CBS News. He reveals how government
regulations concerned with fairness in broadcasting influence
the right to free speech; noting the mixed reviews received
by the Fairness Doctrine, he recommends that television take
control of its own destiny by means of a voluntary long-term
commitment to presenting differing viewpoints on a given issue.

582. Jencks, Richard, and Robert Lewis Shayon. "Does the Fairness Doctrine Violate the First Amendment?" Public Telecom-
munications Review. (December 1974) 46-58.
    Jencks and Shayon provide opposing viewpoints regarding
the constitutionality of the Fairness Doctrine in a National Association of Educational Broadcasters debate.

583. Johnson, Nicholas. "Defending the Fairness Doctrine," Review
of General Semantics. 32:4 (December 1975) 397-399.
    Johnson, an ex-member of the FCC, supports the need for
the Fairness Doctrine or some comparable legislation so as to
safeguard the public's right to be exposed to diversified outlooks via the mass media.

584. Kaufman, Irving. "Reassessing the Fairness Doctrine: Should
the First Amendment Apply Equally to the Print and Broadcast
Media?" New York Times Magazine. 132 (June 19, 1983) 16-
18.

Kaufmann dispassionately lays out the arguments favored by both proponents and critics of the Fairness Doctrine.

585. Rowan, Carl T. Broadcast Fairness: Doctrine, Practice, Prospects. Longman, 1984.
A thorough analysis of the arguments and issues surrounding the Fairness Doctrine controversy. While Rowan favors its continued existence, he feels that the application of federal policy in recent Fairness Doctrine cases has been inconsistent.

586. Sommons, Steven J. The Fairness Doctrine and the Media. Berkeley: University of California Press, 1978.
The author surveys the development of the Fairness Doctrine as well as the problems arising out of its implementation.

Self Censorship Within the Mass Media

587. "'Most Censored' Stories of 1985," Newsletter on Intellectual Freedom. 35:4 (July 1986) 109, 139.
Project Censored, a national media research project in its tenth year, identifies and elaborates on the most under-reported stories of the past year. The top ten "censored" stories are as follows: (1) fierce serial war in El Salvador, (2) military wastes, (3) ten years of genocide in East Timor, (4) the Reagan Revolution: Liberty under siege, (5) media merger mania threatens information flow, (6) terata: the birth defect epidemic, (7) phony "Stars Wars" test result, (8) nuclear decapitation study, (9) federal government rips off the homeless, and (10) high-tech health hazards. According to its originator, Dr. Carl Jensen, the project has functioned as a "distant early warning system for society's problems."

588. "'Most Censored' News Stories of 1984 Named," Newsletter on Intellectual Freedom. 34:4 (July 1985) 103-104.
According to Project Censored, the ten most under-reported stories of 1984 were: (1) the well-publicized Soviet military buildup was a lie, (2) Reagan's attacks on civil liberties, (3) Nicaragua's fair elections, (4) CIA and the death squads, (5) worst radiation spill in North America, (6) the red-herring of "left-wing" terrorism, (7) death of a nation: the tragedy of Transkei, (8) NSDD-84: Reagan's Orwellian censorship law, (9) potentially explosive political stories about Paul Laxalt, Edwin Meese, and Charles Wick that might have changed the course of the 1984 election, (10) the myth of the peaceful atom: U.S. & U.K. break nuclear treaty. Fifteen additional stories victimized by governmental disinformation, the questionable priorities of the press, etc., are also noted.

B. THE MASS MEDIA: INDIVIDUAL CENSORSHIP CASES

Books

a. General Background

589.   Blumenthal, Walter H.   "American Book Burnings," American
       Book Collector.   6:10 (Summer 1956) 13-19.
           Blumenthal chronicles book burnings in America from the
       Colonial period through the Eisenhower Administration.

590.   Bogart, Max.   A Study of Certain Legally Banned Novels in
       the United States, 1900-1950.   New York: New York Univer-
       sity, 1956.   Ph.D. dissertation, available from University
       Microfilms, no. 57-1356.
           Bogart limits his study to novels noteworthy for their social
       and/or aesthetic impact in the first half of the twentieth cen-
       tury.   He parlays these examples into an analysis of the trends
       in literary censorship.

591.   Daniels, Walter M.   The Censorship of Books.   New York:
       H. W. Wilson, 1954.
           While dated, the anthology remains a useful resource, pro-
       viding a diverse array of viewpoints on the topic.   Articles
       are organized under the following headings: The Nature of
       the Problem; Moral Censorship; Political Censorship; United
       States Libraries Abroad; Textbooks; The Censors and the Li-
       brarian.

592.   Downs, Robert B., editor.   The First Freedom; Liberty and
       Justice in the World of Books and Reading.   Chicago: Ameri-
       can Library Association, 1960.
           The work delineates major aspects of intellectual freedom
       with the practical aim of providing ammunition for use by li-
       brarians, publishers, bookdealers, authors, and other members
       of the book world who may come under fire from the censor.
       The essays--contributed by such luminaries as William O. Doug-
       las, Havelock Ellis, D. H. Lawrence, Aldous Huxley, Harry
       Steele Commager, George Bernard Shaw, and John Steinbeck--
       have been organized under the following headings: (1) We
       have been here before: a historical retrospective; (2) The is-
       sues at stake; (3) The courts look at books; (4) Giving others
       the courage of our convictions: pressure groups; (5) Who or
       what is obscene?; (6) Political subversion and censorship; (7)
       The writers fight back; (8) The librarians take a stand; (9)
       The schools under attack; (10) Censorship in Ireland; (11)
       Books under dictators red and black; (12) The broad views
       past, present, future.   Downs has provided introductions to
       each chapter and each selection.

593. Eshelman, William R.   "The Behemoths and the Book Publishers,"
      Library Trends. 19:1 (July 1970) 106-114.
          Eshelman contends that the steady increase in the number
      of publishing houses being swallowed up by conglomerate
      owners may well undermine freedom of expression in our so-
      ciety. He also notes some trends which could counteract such
      a restriction to freedom to publish; e.g., increased publishing
      by the university presses, the establishment of new publishing
      houses.

594. Haight, Anne Lyon. Banned Books, 387 B.C. to 1978 A.D.
      Updated and enlarged by Chandler B. Grannis. New York:
      Bowker, 1978.
          The intent of the work is to document censorship's past
      triumphs and defeats as a means of helping to prevent a future
      wave of book supression. The core of the text is comprised
      of an annotated listing--in rough chronological order--of not-
      able print titles which have been censored. The list includes
      titles which have been censored. The list includes The Odyssey,
      Aristophanes' plays, The Bible and other scriptural works,
      Dante's The Divine Comedy, Shakespeare's King Lear, Twain's
      The Adventures of Huckleberry Finn, Disney's comic strip ver-
      sion of Mickey Mouse, Thomas' Down These Mean Streets; and
      the American Heritage Dictionary. Banned Books also includes
      an essay by Charles Rembar, "Censorship in America: The
      Legal Picture," and the following appendices: (1) Trends in
      Censorship, (2) Statements on Freedom of the Press, (3) Ex-
      cerpts from Important Court Decisions, (4) Commission on Ob-
      scenity and Pornography (excerpts), and (5) Selected U.S.
      Laws and Regulations.

595. Lewis, Felice Flanery. Literature, Obscenity, & Law. Car-
      bondale: Southern Illinois University Press, 1976.
          The book offers the reader a broad retrospective view of
      literature's involvement in the obscenity question by present-
      ing a systematic, comparative investigation of (1) Works of
      imaginative literature that are known to have been the subject
      of obscenity litigation in the United States; (2) trends in
      sexual content, explicit language, and moral values that are
      reflected in that fiction; and (3) judicial opinions concerning
      that fiction, and the literary implications of the opinions.

                    b. Rating Systems for Books

596. Bogutz, Allan D. "Protection of the Adults' Rights to Porno-
      graphy," Arizona Law Review. 11 (Winter 1969) 792-806.
          Bogutz advocates a self-imposed rating system for print
      materials which draws from the established model within the
      film industry.

597. Hentoff, Nat. "Any Writer Who Follows Anyone Else's Guide-

lines Ought To Be In Advertising," School Library Journal.
24:3 (November 1977) 27-29.

Hentoff criticizes the Council on Interracial Books for Children's 1976 volume, Human (and Anti-Human) Values in Children's Books: A Content Rating Instrument for Educators and
Concerned Parents See Item 598. He notes that all censorship
is the same; it suppresses free speech and inhibits creative
imagination. He concludes, "What it comes down to is that
the Council on Interracial Books for Children not only distrusts
individualism ('should be discouraged as a highly negative
force'), but it also greatly distrusts children."

598. Human (and Anti-Human) Values in Children's Books: A Con-
      tent Rating Instrument for Educators and Concerned Parents.
      Council for Interracial Books for Children, 1976.

Arguing that books for children generally transmit the values
of their creators, the Council sets forth an "instrument" presenting a report card-like checklist of criteria for evaluating
the content of selected titles which educators and parents are
urged to examine for evidences of racism, elitism, materialism,
conformity, escapism, ageism, and negative images of females
and minorities. The reviews of 235 books published for children and young adults during 1975 accompany the checklist;
thirty-nine percent of these titles were rated low for being
racist, ageist, sexist, etc. The ultimate question posed by the
work is whether it proposes censorship or selectivity of children's books.

c. Dictionaries

599. Jenkinson, Edward B. "'Across-the-board' and 'Bed' are Dirty
      Words?" Newsletter on Intellectual Freedom. 28:4 (July 1979)
      71-72, 92-93.

Jenkinson reports on recent efforts to censor dictionaries
and textbooks in public schools. He discusses the tactics employed by groups such as Educational Research Analysts in
Longview, Texas. He offers six steps to prevent the removal
of these materials from the schools.

d. Individual Titles

--The Adventures of Huckleberry Finn, by Mark Twain

600. Cloonan, Michele V. "The Censorship of The Adventures of
      Huckleberry Finn: An Investigation," Top of the News. 40:2
      (Winter 1984) 189-196.

Part 1 of a two-part article examining the reasons the book
has been continuously censored since its publication.

601. "Huck and Jim Still Making Waves," EPIEgram Materials. 13
      (April/May/June 1985) 1-2.

A report on recent attempts at suppressing the work. The
focus is upon public schools.

602. Kean, John M. A Rationale for Teaching Huckleberry Finn,"
In: Celebrating Censored Books, edited by Nicholas J. Karolides and Lee Burress. Racine, Wisc.: Wisconsin Council of
Teachers of English, 1985. pp. 6-9.
     Kean cites--and elaborates on--the following reasons for in-
cluding the novel within the humanities and social sciences
curricula: (1) Twain is one of America's greatest authors;
(2) The novel is believed by many to have truly started an
American literature tradition; (3) It is a fictionalized historical
description of the antebellum South with a particular emphasis
on class and race; (4) It presents a classic portrayal of a
youth's "rites of passage"; (5) It is an exciting adventure
story; (6) It provides a means to study literary elements used
by the novel writer.

603. Lynn, Kenneth S. Huckleberry Finn: Text, Sources, and
Criticism. New York: Harcourt, Brace and World, 1961.
     Lynn cites the controversial nature of his subject matter;
However, these considerations are secondary to his thorough
analysis of the aesthetic and socio-cultural features of the
work.

604. Mitchell, Arlene Harris. "Historical Perspective of the Huck
Finn Challenge," In: Celebrating Censored Books, edited by
Nicholas J. Karolides and Lee Burress. Racine, Wisc.: Wisconsin Council of Teachers of English, 1985. pp. 10-11.
     A concise survey of attacks and censoring actions against
the work during the hundred years since its publication.
Mitchell notes that the precipitating factor in censorship challenges of the eighties--the portrayal of Jim--has largely been
the result of the rising economical, political, educational and
social status of blacks. She cites authoritative sources which
oppose such efforts at suppression: "Michael Hearn (The Nation, 1982) claims that 'no work of American literature exposes
the corruption of the peculiar institution more eloquently than
does Mark Train's novel' ... David Bradley, author of the
Chaneysville Incident, says that he rereads Huckleberry Finn
every year and 'I don't see how anybody can read the book and
find it racist.' Bradley is black."

605. Stanek, Lou Willett. "Huck Finn: 100 Years of Durn Fool
Problems," School Library Journal. 31:6 (February 1985) 19-
22.
     Stanek surveys the novel's history of censorship since it
was first published in 1885. She notes that "although a conservative estimate says Huck Finn has sold 20 million copies in
100 editions in 30 languages, for the last century someone has
always managed to find something wrong with Huck's character.

He has been banned from more libraries and schools than any
other book in history. Nat Hentoff has even written a young
adult novel about his problems, called The Day They Came to
Arrest the Book (Delacorte, 1982). Either Huck represents
something the world does not want to know or there have been
many cooperative censors in the schools and libraries who find
it easier to go along or who have not read the story and therefore cannot defend it. It was Twain himself who, perhaps
prophetically, said a classic is something everybody wants to
have read and nobody wants to read."

606. Stavely, Keith, and Lani Gerson. "We Didn't Wait for the Cen-
      sor: Intellectual Freedom at the Watertown Public Library,"
      Library Journal. 103:15 (September 1983) 1654-1658.
         An account of censorship of the novel. The authors express
      concern over the changing face of censorship; i.e., from ex-
      plicit suppression of heterodox points of view to vehement
      moral censure of them.

607. Torgrud, Richard D. "The Banning of a Book," North Dakota
      Quarterly. 39:4 (Autumn 1971) 71-72.
         Torgrud discusses the censorship of the novel from senior
      English Literature classes on charges of racism. He notes that
      "although much better educated than Huck Finn, present-day
      intellectuals seem unable to reject the nonsense of their own
      time. So they ban books in the name of social progress."

--Anne Frank: The Diary of a Young Girl, by Anne Frank

608. Western, Richard D. "The Case for Anne Frank: The Diary
      of a Young Girl," In: Celebrating Censored Books, edited by
      Nicholas J. Karolides and Lee Burress. Racine, Wisc.: Wis-
      consin Council of Teachers of English, 1985. pp. 12-14.
         Western offers the following reasons for encouraging read-
      ing of the work in schools: (1) It is a primary source; (2)
      It exemplifies certain characteristics of modern fiction--the
      inward turn of narrative, the Fortinbass effect (the hard world
      of affairs, pressing in), and variations in the story of growth.
      Western also discusses the problems characterizing the book;
      i.e., it will not appeal automatically to young readers, political
      or ideological considerations, Anne's attitude toward adults,
      and Anne's sexual maturation.

--Black Like Me, by John Howard Griffin

609. Farrell, Walter C., Jr. "Black Like Me: In Defense of a Ra-
      cial Reality," In: Celebrating Censored Books, edited by
      Nicholas J. Karolides and Lee Burress. Racine, Wisc.: Wis-
      consin Council of Teachers of English, 1985. pp. 15-17.
         Farrell provides a sociological framework for the work as
      well as exploring its value in an academic setting.

--Blubber/Deenie/Then Again, Maybe I Won't, by Judy Blume
(See Also: Honey of a Chimp, by Norma Klein)

610. "A Split Decision: Judy Blume in Peoria," Newsletter on In-
      tellectual Freedom. 34:2 (March 1985) 33, 58.
          A report on the Peoria School Board's move to return three
      books by award-winning children's author Judy Blume to li-
      brary shelves, albeit restricted to older children and to those
      having parental permission to read them. The move offset the
      actions of two committees of school personnel which had recom-
      mended removal of the books because they were unsuitable for
      elementary students.

--Boys and Sex/Girls and Sex, by Wardell Pomeroy

611. Meyers, Duane H. " 'Try Not to Let Them Prevail,' " News-
      letter on Intellectual Freedom. 26:2 (March 1977) 29, 49-58.
          Meyers, associate director for management services, Okla-
      homa County Libraries System, recounts at length the system's
      struggle--taking place between December 18, 1975-April 15,
      1976--over children's right of access to library materials (in
      particular the opportunity to read two works by Dr. Wardell
      Pomeroy which provided youth-oriented sex education). A
      series of reading-and-discussion meetings constituted the core
      of the library system's attempt to educate the community re-
      garding intellectual freedom. An excerpt from Ernest Becker's
      The Denial of Death was representative of the ideas discussed
      in that project.
          "By the time the child grows up, the inverted search for
      a personal existence through perversity gets set in an indivi-
      dual mold, and it becomes more secret. It has to be kept
      secret because the community won't stand for the attempt by
      people to wholly individualize themselves. If there is going to
      be a victory over human incompleteness and limitation, it has
      to be a social project and not an individual one. Society wants
      to be the one to decide how people are to transcend death; it
      will tolerate the causa-sui project only if it fits into the stan-
      dard social project. Otherwise there is the alarm of 'anarchy!'
      This is one of the reasons for bigotry and censorship of all
      kings over personal morality: people fear that the standard
      morality will be undetermined--another way of saying that
      they fear they will no longer be able to control life and death.
      A person is said to be 'socialized' precisely when he accepts
      to 'sublimate' the body-sexual character ... He can even give
      his body over to the tribe, the state, the embracing magical
      umbrella of the elders and their symbols, that way it will no
      longer be a dangerous negation for him. But there is no real
      difference between a childish impossibility and an adult one;
      the only thing that a person achieves is a practical self-deceit--
      what we call the 'mature character.' "

--Brave New World, by Aldous Huxley

612. Beckham, Richard H. "Huxley's Brave New World as Social
     Irritant: Ban It or Buy It?" In: Celebrating Censored Books,
     edited by Nicholas J. Karolides and Lee Burress. Racine,
     Wisc.: Wisconsin Council of Teachers of English, 1985. pp.
     18-20.
          Essentially a critique of the book; however, Beckham does
     set forth a number of themes and rhetorical questions which
     would lend themselves to a classroom discussion. In addition,
     he cites the chief objections to the work as summarized in a
     September 1981 article appearing in the Newsletter on Intel-
     lectual Freedom (p. 127): "the book is depressing, fatalistic,
     and negative, and it encourages students to adopt a lifestyle
     of drugs, sex and conformity, reinforcing helpless feelings
     that they can do nothing to make an impact on their world."

--Candy, by Terry Southern and Mason Hoffenberg

613. Sachs, Ed. "I Want Candy," Focus/Midwest. 3:2 (1964) 11-
     13, 23-24.
          Upon learning that Candy is not being sold in Chicago,
     Sachs investigates the nature of police censorship in that city.
     After interviews with police and city officials, the publishers,
     and various book retailers, he posits that Chicago may be "the
     most severe city in the United States" in restricting print ma-
     terials--a "New Boston."

--The Catcher in the Rye, by J. D. Salinger

614. Booth, Wayne C. "The Catcher in the Rye; Censorship and
     the Values of Fiction," The English Journal. LIII:3 (March
     1964) 155-64. Reprinted in: Celebrating Censored Books,
     edited by Nicholas J. Karolides and Lee Burress. Racine,
     Wisc.: Wisconsin Council of Teachers of English, 1985. pp.
     21-26.
          Booth delineates various strategies for combating censorship.
     Turning to The Catcher in the Rye as a case in point, he
     notes that "a full catalog of [the protagonist's] virtues and
     good works would be unfair to the book, because it would sug-
     gest a solemn kind of sermonizing very different from the
     special Catcher brand of affectionate comedy. But it is im-
     portant to us in talking about possible censorship of the book
     to see its seeming immoralities in the context of Holden's deep
     morality."

615. MacLeod, Lanette. "Censorship History of Catcher in the Rye,"
     PNLA Quarterly. 39 (July 1975) 10-13.
          MacLeod states that a historical approach "can lead to an
     understanding of the facets of censorship as it occurs and of
     the methods of defending such works of literary merit and con-
     troversial explosiveness."

616. Schlatter, Franklin D. "The Catcher in the Rye--What Are
      We Counting?" In: Celebrating Censored Books, edited by
      Nicholas J. Karolides and Lee Burress. Racine, Wisc.: Wis-
      consin Council of Teachers of English, 1985. pp. 27-28.
          Schlatter notes that the inclination of censors to suppress
      the work is based upon a fundamental desire to misinterpret
      its message. He concludes that "The Catcher in the Rye is
      Holden's record of his troubles. Those who want to learn from
      the book will find there is much to be learned. But our learn-
      ing will depend on what things we count and our reasons for
      counting them."

617. Symula, James F. Censorship of High School Literature: A
      Study of the Incidents of Censorship Involving J. D. Salinger's
      "The Catcher in the Rye," Buffalo, N.Y.: State University
      of New York, 1969. Ed.D. dissertation, available from Uni-
      versity Microfilms, no. 69-19,035.
          Symula draws several general conclusions from his study:
      (1) censorship is based on ignorance; (2) in choosing literature
      for classroom use, the English teacher has a tremendous re-
      sponsibility to the student; (3) English teachers must fight
      censorship; (4) there is a great need for honest reporting of
      the facts which surround an incident of censorship.

      --The Chocolate War/After the First Death/The Bumblebee Flies
      Anyway/I Am the Cheese, by Robert Cormier

618. Ellis, W. Geiger. " 'Dare We Disturb ... ?' A Defense of
      Robert Cormier's Novels," In: Celebrating Censored Books,
      edited by Nicholas J. Karolides and Lee Burress. Racine,
      Wisc.: Wisconsin Council of Teachers of English, 1985. pp.
      29-31.
          That Robert Cormier's novels should need defending is
      ironic, according to Ellis, considering the quality of his writ-
      ing, the nature of the man himself, and the thematic content
      of his novels. The bulk of the article explores these factors
      as a means of rebuffing the censorship Cormier's work has
      suffered.

      --The Death of a President, by William Manchester

619. Bennett, Arnold. Jackie, Bobby & Manchester; the Story Be-
      hind the Headlines! New York: Bee-Line Books, 1967.
          Bennett chronicles the developments leading up to the publi-
      cation of The Death of a President. He focuses on Jackie Ken-
      nedy's efforts to suppress the work.

      --Deliverance, by James Dickey

620. Beck, Robert. "The Debate in Literary Consciousness: Dickey's
      Deliverance," In: Celebrating Censored Books, edited by

Nicholas J. Karolides and Lee Burress. Racine, Wisc.: Wisconsin Council of Teachers of English, 1985. pp. 32-34.

Beck employs a two-pronged approach in his argument against censorship of the novel: (1) an analysis of its structure, and (2) its placement within the context of American literature and life. His analysis notes that "like all good novels worth multiple readings, it's about many things, but principally it's about survival of the body through a terrible ordeal and the deliverance back into everyday society after terrible knowledge. Many of the concerns, images, and fields of interest found in Dickey's poetry continue in Deliverance. There is the fascination with cover of costume and nakedness, meanness and decency, sexuality, the glory and non-humanness of nature, the surprising mysteries at the heart of everyday life."

--Don't Blame the People, by Robert Cirino

621. Cirino, Robert. "Commercial Outlets Wouldn't Publish My Book," Grassroots Editor. 12:5 (September/October 1971) 4-6, 18.

Cirino recounts the problems encountered in attempting to get his book, Don't Blame the People--an indictment of the right-wing bias of the mass media--published.

--Down These Mean Streets, by Piri Thomas

622. Levine, Alan H. " 'Impressionable Minds' ... 'Forbidden Subjects': A Case in Point," Library Journal. 98 (February 15, 1973) 595-601; School Library Journal. 19 (February 1973) 19-25.

Levine analyzes the controversy ensuing out of the removal of the autobiography from Queens, New York, school libraries. He delineates the legal issues relevant to the incident as well as the arguments for and against retaining the book. He concludes, "No, the banning of a library book cannot be described as a rational act. But it must be challenged if its sinister consequences are not to destroy our schools. If school boards are permitted a free hand in what they claim are 'educational decisions,' to whom may parents, students and professionals look when their libraries and their curricula are stripped of books which happen to be in political disfavor with a shifting majority of the school board? Who will prevent our nation's schools from becoming instruments of majoritarian propaganda? If, as appears to be the case, school boards are especially responsive to demands that schools not carry books which honestly deal with race relations in America, will minorities ever be able to secure the promise of the school desegregation cases? If we concede to school boards the power to exclude all but the current orthodoxy from the classrooms and libraries of our schools, will we not be granting them awesome power over the minds of our future citizens?"

623. Levine, Alan H. "School Libraries: Shelving East Harlem,"
      Civil Liberties. (January 1973)
         The attorney for the plaintiffs analyzes the Down These
      Mean Streets case (Flushing, N.Y., 1972). He depicts the
      case as essentially a power struggle between two groups to
      determine ultimate control of the school board; the fate of the
      book--the pretext for the conflict--was of secondary importance.

      --The Electric Kool-Aid Acid Test, by Tom Wolfe

624. Beck, Terry. " 'Messing Up the Minds of the Citizenry en
      Route'--Essential Questions of Value: The Electric Kool-Aid
      Acid Test," In: Celebrating Censored Books, edited by
      Nicholas J. Karolides and Lee Burress. Racine, Wisc.: Wis-
      consin Council of Teachers of English, 1985. pp. 35-39.
         Beck argues in favor of utilizing the book in a classroom
      setting because it presents, for teenagers--through subject
      matter they can "relate to"--three broad and important sub-
      jects for study and discussion: (1) the American approach to
      the English language, complete with a wide number of literary/
      rhetorical devices and techniques; (2) a historical/sociological
      study of the birth and development of the "counter culture";
      (3) an evaluation of the values associated with the drug culture
      and with the values of contemporary American culture in gen-
      eral--indeed, with values in the widest sense.

      --Family Matters: Concepts in Marriage and Personal Relation-
      ships, by Rebecca M. Smith and Mary Lin Apicelli

625. Edwords, Frederick, et al. "Students Speak Out Against Text-
      book Censorship," The Humanist. 47:2 (March/April 1987)
      23-26, 34.
         A report on the controversy arising out of the Buffalo Board
      of Education's proposal in November 1986 to delete the home
      economics text, Family Matters: Concepts in Marriage and Per-
      sonal Relationships, from the approved textbook list. The text
      of the statements in defense of the work made by eight stu-
      dents from Buffalo City Honors High School at a December 10
      meeting of the board are included.

      --Fanny Hill, by John Cleland

626. "Case 4: John Cleland's Fanny Hill," In: Freedom and Cul-
      ture: Literary Censorship in the 70s. Belmont, Calif.: Wads-
      worth, 1970. pp. 140-153.
         A collection of viewpoints surrounding the Supreme Court
      case, A Book Named John Cleland's Memoirs of a Woman of
      Pleasure v. Attorney General of the Commonwealth of Massa-
      chusetts (1966). It is considered a landmark case in that the
      value theory (i.e., the presence of "some redeeming value"),
      coupled with the protection under the First Amendment, not

only exonerated the book--long regarded as "hard core" porno-
graphy--but set a precedent for the critical testimony of ac-
knowledged experts in the field to override more popular criteria. Includes: (1) Justices William O. Douglas and Tom
Clark: The Memoirs of a Woman of Pleasure Case Opinions;
(2) Charles Rembar: from The End of Obscenity; (3) John
Ciardi: What Is Pornography?

627.   Quennell, Peter. "Introduction" to John Cleland's Memoirs of
        a Woman of Pleasure. New York: Putnam, 1963. pp. v-xiv.
            Quennell surveys the history and literary aspects of the
        work. He cites the case of Commonwealth v. Holmes (1821) in
        which Peter Holmes was indicted for offering the work for sale;
        this case is acknowledged to be the first on record involving
        the suppression of a literary work on grounds of obscenity.
        Quennell also includes a report on the New York Supreme
        Court's decision in the early sixties to allow publication and
        distribution of the Putnam edition; Justice Arthur Klein's opinion
        is printed in full.

628.   Rembar, Charles. The End of Obscenity: The Trials of Lady
        Chatterley, Tropic of Cancer and Fanny Hill. New York: Ran-
        dom House, 1968. pp. 222-490.
            The collection of chapters surveys the work's court history,
        culminating in the landmark Supreme Court case. Rembar also
        includes anecdotes, historical information, and other material
        relevant to the intellectual freedom perspective maintained
        throughout the narrative.

        --A Farewell to Arms, by Ernest Hemingway

629.   Meriwether, James B. "The Dashes in Hemingway's A Farewell
        to Arms," The Papers of the Bibliographical Society of America.
        58 (Fourth Quarter 1964) 449-457.
            Meriwether discusses a copy of the first American edition
        of the novel into which Hemingway had penciled those obsceni-
        ties expurgated by the publishers.

630.   Rovit, Earl. "Upholding Moral Principles: A Farewell to Arms,"
        In: Celebrating Censored Books, edited by Nicholas J. Karolides
        and Lee Burress. Racine, Wisc.: Wisconsin Council of Teachers
        of English, 1985. pp. 40-41.
            Rovit cites the work's relevance to young readers, who are
        in the process of emerging from the taken-for-granted sureties
        of childhood dependence, as ample justification for retaining it
        within school curricula. He concludes that "Hemingway's A
        Farewell to Arms places a challenge on its principal characters
        that goes one step beyond Crane's A Red Badge of Courage.
        Independence is only the first stage in the progress toward
        responsible maturity. Catherine Barkley and Frederic Henry
        must also measure out the extent to which their newly achieved

independence must be surrendered in their attainment of a
mutual love. For if one of the aims of adolescence is independent, free-standing self-reliance, a second aim--and one which
may often be on a collision course with the former--is that
union of independencies in a mature love-relationship which requires an open acceptance of vulnerability and dependence.
This is, of course, one of the most painful and difficult of human laws to learn and truly accept. It is to the enormous
credit of A Farewell to Arms that this inexorable moral principle
is unflinchingly, movingly dramatized at the very core of the
novel."

--Forever, by Judy Blume

631. Battaglia, Frank. "If We Can't Trust; The Pertinence of Judy
      Blume's Forever," In: Celebrating Censored Books, edited by
      Nicholas J. Karolides and Lee Burress. Racine, Wisc.: Wis-
      consin Council of Teachers of English, 1985. pp. 42-44.
         While Battaglia is an unabashed apologist for the work, he
      acknowledges that Forever has its weak points. These flaws,
      however, do not justify censorship in any form. He concludes,
      "I think the book does hope to offer wisdom to an emerging
      adult about becoming 'completely vulnerable' to another person.
      Katherine's mother tells her: 'It's up to you to decide what's
      right and wrong ... "I'm not going to tell you to go ahead but
      I'm not going to forbid it either. It's too late for any of that.
      I expect you to handle it with a sense of responsibility though
      ... either way.' Mrs. Danziger has just said she might have
      made different choices for herself today, and so the question
      of right and wrong is truly open in her statement. But even
      a parent with certainty needs to recognize a point when a child
      has to make his or her own decisions."

--Go Ask Alice (author anonymous)

632. Rumsey, Jean P. " 'Whatsoever Things are Pure ...' A Case
      for Go Ask Alice," In: Celebrating Censored Books, edited
      by Nicholas J. Karolides and Lee Burress. Racine, Wisc.:
      Wisconsin Council of Teachers of English, 1985. pp. 45-47.
         Rumsey refutes the major criticisms of the book--language,
      drugs, sexual violence, trashy/without educational value. She
      considers its prime strength to be its effectiveness in portray-
      ing an adolescent's struggles toward maturity. She concludes,
      "Should Go Ask Alice be taught now? The white heat of the
      sixties is over. The problem drug in Wisconsin is alcohol, not
      acid. Some may find the book somewhat dated as did my friend
      who taught in a small town in northeastern Wisconsin. Time
      that could have been spent in discussing issues of substance
      was spent in explaining drug jargon. Still, the struggle of
      the young to become adults is hardly over. 'Home,' considered
      as a nucleus of values that is supposed to sustain students as

they grow older, or go elsewhere, may not suffice. How are
we to prepare our students to deal with these problems? It
is that problem which Go Ask Alice addresses, and students
can learn from her mistakes."

--God's Little Acre, by Erskine Caldwell

633. Caldwell, Erskine. "My Twenty-Five Years of Censorship,"
      Esquire. 50:4 (October 1958) 176-178.
      Caldwell recounts efforts to suppress his novel. He con-
      cludes, "Is censorship necessary in any form? It is arguable
      that it is not.... If there must be some testing ground, I
      would suggest that a panel of educators, lawyers, churchmen,
      and critics might be set up to examine a book before it is
      brought into court.
      "But censorship is inherently dangerous because when you
      start controlling what people can read, you are starting to con-
      trol what they can think. Then you no longer have a de-
      mocracy.... From a creative point of view, the threat is
      that when another author hears of a persecution for obscenity,
      he may crawl into a hole, and cut himself down to mouse size,
      in a kind of mental flinch from the criticism he might arouse."

--The Good Earth, by Pearl Buck

634. De Smet, Imogene. "An Apologia for Pearl Buck's The Good
      Earth," In: Celebrating Censored Books, edited by Nicholas
      J. Karolides and Lee Burress. Racine, Wisc.: Wisconsin
      Council of Teachers of English, 1985. pp. 48-51.
      De Smet argues that The Good Earth needs to be read for
      its humanitarian values rather than being banned from library
      shelves and English department curricula. She concludes,
      "Anyone who condemns the book on the grounds that it does
      teach concubinage and wife-abuse is not a critic but a caviller."

--The Grapes of Wrath, by John Steinbeck

635. Burress, Lee. "The Grapes of Wrath; Preserving Its Place in
      the Curriculum," In: Celebrating Censored Books, edited by
      Nicholas J. Karolides and Lee Burress. Racine, Wisc.: Wis-
      consin Council of Teachers of English, 1985. pp. 52-55.
      Burress concludes his critique by stating, "It is difficult
      to understand how any American high school or college could
      forbid the teaching or use of the book while maintaining a
      claim to act as a proper agency for the education of the young
      in this democratic republic."

636. Davis, Robert C., editor. Twentieth Century Interpretations
      of The Grapes of Wrath: A Collection of Critical Essays.
      Englewood Cliffs, New Jersey: Prentice-Hall, 1982.
      A wide-ranging selection of topics have been included in

the anthology. A number of the contributions address the
controversial aspects of the work; e.g., its anti-establishment
tone; the author's sympathies with unified labor activities.

637. Donohue, Agnes McNeill, editor. A Casebook on The Grapes
      of Wrath. New York: Cromwell, 1968.
          The book is divided into three sections: "The Grapes of
      Wrath as a Social Document"; "The Grapes of Wrath as Litera-
      ture"; and "Problems for Study and Writing." The first part
      consists of eight articles, chronologically arranged, which deal
      with The Grapes of Wrath as social commentary and the excited
      responses--many of a hostile nature--to its publication in 1939
      and later in California, Oklahoma, and elsewhere in the United
      States. These articles reveal that Steinbeck was alternately
      labeled propagandist, Communist, socialist, smutmonger, porno-
      grapher, rabble rouser.

638. French, Warren, editor. A Companion to The Grapes of Wrath.
      New York: Viking, 1963.
          A collection of essays concerning various social and aesthe-
      tic issues embodied in the novel.

639. Schockley, Martin. "The Reception of The Grapes of Wrath
      in Oklahoma," American Literature. XV (January 1944) 351-
      361. Reprinted in: John Steinbeck--The Grapes of Wrath:
      Text and Criticism, edited by Peter Lisca. New York: Viking,
      1972. pp. 680-691.
          Shockley surveys efforts to suppress the work in that state.

--A Hero Ain't Nothing But A Sandwich, by Alice Childress

640. Zidonas, Frank. "A Hero Ain't Nothing But A Sandwich,; A
      Rationale for Classroom Use," In: Celebrating Censored Books,
      edited by Nicholas J. Karolides and Lee Burress. Racine,
      Wisc.: Wisconsin Council of Teachers of English, 1985. pp.
      56-58.
          Zidonas focuses on four areas--point of view, characteriza-
      tion, language, and themes--in order to illustrate the master-
      ful craftsmanship characterizing the novel. He notes a host
      of topics which would lend themselves to classroom discussion.
      He concludes, "Why should students read this novel ... given
      that it is about drug addiction and that the language is not
      standard English and is occasionally vulgar? The reasons for
      doing so are compelling. It is an optimistic, even humorous,
      book. It is skillfully crafted. It is realistic without being
      grim. But, more important, it presents a Black family with a
      strong commitment to individual responsibility, a family that is
      warm and caring. It's a novel that depicts a striking array
      of Blacks--from the mean and radical to the professional and
      saintly. And the drugs (and their users) are depicted as of-
      fensive and trouble-causing; they are not made to appear at-
      tractive."

--Honey of a Chimp, by Norma Klein

641. Clark, Elyse. "A Slow, Subtle Exercise in Censorship," School
      Library Journal. 32:7 (March 1986) 93-97.
      Clark, a middle school librarian at the Hanover (Pa.) Public
      School District, delineates the controversy surrounding the de-
      cision of administrators to remove the following books from the
      library shelves of all elementary libraries: Norma Klein's
      Honey of a Chimp and Judy Blume's Blubber, Deenie, Starring
      Sally J. as Herself, Tiger Eyes, and It's Not the End of the
      World. She notes the consequences of this incident:
      "I feel my job now entails something of the role of police
      officer. When students defy the order and try to peek into
      the restricted titles, should I report them to the principal for
      disobeying orders? Helpers often look through the books, or
      shelve them by mistake on the open shelves. The atmosphere of
      freedom in our library has been replaced by one of moderate ten-
      sion and confusion. Students reading the titles are skeptical
      about adults who are so threatened by these books. I can't esti-
      mate how many students won't be able to read the books because
      their parents don't care enough to sign the permission forms, or
      because they don't want to be singled out. For many students,
      it's too much of a hassle to bother with the forms.
      "Ultimately, as has happened in other libraries, the censors
      will win as the books fall into disuse. The chill factor has ex-
      tended to the present and future ordering of new books. My
      own professional integrity has been called into question and,
      in the future, will be scrutinized more closely. The way is
      paved for continued infringements on academic freedom, not
      only for librarians, but for teachers and students as well."

--I Know Why the Caged Bird Sings, by Maya Angelou

642. Edwards, June. "I Know Why the Caged Bird Sings by Maya
      Angelou; Awareness of Displacement: A Reader's Rationale,"
      In: Celebrating Censored Books, edited by Nicholas J. Karoli-
      des and Lee Burress. Racine, Wisc.: Wisconsin Council of
      Teachers of English, 1985. pp. 61-63.
      In the face of right-wing objections--foul language, reli-
      gious blasphemy, and sexual looseness--Edwards delineates the
      contributions this work can make to the educative process.
      She focuses on four particular strengths: (1) it is about sur-
      vival and hope, (2) privileged white students can learn how it
      feels to live as a black in a racially bigoted world, (3) its his-
      torical insights, and (4) it encourages an open-minded toler-
      ance for differing values.

--If Beale Street Could Talk, by James Baldwin

643. McBride, William G. "If Beale Street Could Talk; A Rationale

for Classroom Use," In: Celebrating Censored Books, edited
by Nicholas J. Karolides and Lee Burress. Racine, Wisc.:
Wisconsin Council of Teachers of English, 1985. pp. 59-60.
    McBride addresses the most notable objections to the novel;
i.e., the language is straightforward, often profane; the tone
is frequently bitter; sexual scenes are specific; orthodox religion is treated lightly; the social system is decried by minorities. He concludes, however, that values portrayed in
the book should outweigh the objections.

--It's OK If You Don't Love Me, by Norma Klein

644. Karolides, Nicholas J. "It's OK If You Don't Love Me; Evaluat-
      ing Anticipated Experience for Readers," In: Celebrating Cen-
      sored Books, edited by Nicholas J. Karolides and Lee Burress.
      Racine, Wisc.: Wisconsin Council of Teachers of English, 1985.
      pp. 64-67.
          Karolides' analysis touches upon perceived flaws as well as
      strengths of the book. He asserts that most criticisms--e.g.,
      language, characterization--ignore the author's method, pur-
      pose, and ultimate statement.
          "The method is based in effect on a principle of honesty
      comparable to a code manifested by Jody in the book. Klein's
      premise of young adult sexuality, their concerns, imaginings,
      and experimentation, has validity in our late twentieth century
      reality. Portraying them thus, depicting their insecurities,
      their innocence under the veneer, their searchings, has com-
      parable validity. In this context her book becomes an effort
      to inform, to develop insights and values. She does not pro-
      mote insensitivity or license--to the contrary. Also, there is
      no voyeurism in the sex situations. Her characters grope to-
      wards valuing each other, valuing their emotions and bodies.
      But it's not exactly groping in the dark. The trials and er-
      rors include stumbling, but the moves grow out of open dis-
      cussion and increasing knowledge. The characters model this
      standard for the readers. As the readers experience vicari-
      ously the chameleon emotions, as they consider the viewpoints
      which Jody contemplates, as they respond to her choices and
      understand her betrayal and its repercussions, they can begin
      to establish appropriate behavior built from preconsidered
      values."

--Jake and Honeybunch Go to Heaven, by Margot Zemach

645. Brandenhoff, Susan E. "Jake and Honeybunch Go to Heaven:
      Children's Book Fans Smoldering Debate," American Libraries.
      14:3 (March 1983) 130-132.
          An account of the controversy over the Chicago, San Fran-
      cisco and Milwaukee libraries' refusal to purchase the book.
      The publisher claims censorship; librarians feel the book is
      undistinguished and reinforces racial stereotyping of blacks.

Brandenhoff solicits several points of view on the book with the
hope of airing some of the strongly held feelings sustaining
the controversy.

--Johnny Got His Gun, by Dalton Trumbo

646. Cook, Bruce. Dalton Trumbo. New York: Scribner, 1977.
      The work provides biographical information which is in-
dispensable in shedding light on the controversy surrounding
Johnny Got His Gun.

647. DeMuth, James. "Johnny Got His Gun; A Depression-Era Clas-
      sic," In: Celebrating Censored Books, edited by Nicholas J.
      Karolides and Lee Burress. Racine, Wisc.: Wisconsin Council
      of Teachers of English, 1985. pp. 68-70.
      DeMuth notes that this novel is unique in that the author
himself conspired in its suppression during the early years of
World War II. According to DeMuth, "It took the aggression
of Nazi Germany, the attack on Pearl Harbor and the invasion
of Soviet Russia to convince Dalton Trumbo that war could be
the necessary means of defending ideas, values and life."
However, the critique reflects that the selective pacifism of
the book will always be relevant in the face of phony wars
fought for hypocritical ideals.

--Lady Chatterley's Lover, by D. H. Lawrence

648. "Case 2: D. H. Lawrence's Lady Chatterley," In: Freedom
      and Culture: Literary Censorship in the 70s. Belmont, Ca.:
      Wadsworth, 1970. pp. 93-116.
      A collection of viewpoints surrounding the U.S. District
Court case, Grove Press v. Christenberry, 1959. Includes:
(1) Malcolm Cowley and Alfred Kazin: Defending Lady Chatterley's Lover; (2) Post Office Department: Prosecuting Lady
Chatterley's Lover; (3) Judge Frederick van Pelt Bryan: Majority Opinion, Grove Press v. Christenberry; (4) Judge Leonard P. Moore: Reluctant Concurrence, Grove Press vs. Christenberry; (5) D. H. Lawrence: Pornography and Obscenity;
(6) D. H. Lawrence: A Propos of Lady Chatterley's Lover.

649. Kauffmann, Stanley. "Lady Chatterley at Last," New Republic.
      140 (May 25, 1959) 13-16.
      Kauffmann discusses the implications of the publication of
the unexpurgated version of the work for the first time in
America. He notes that "the novel's publication inevitably
raises the issue, not only of intrinsic literary merit but of censorship." He goes on to say that "undoubtedly there are members of society who might be seriously affected by exposure to
pornographic materials, but it is hardly rational to gear society
to the level of its weakest members, like a wartime convoy. In
any event, can such highly susceptible persons be protected

merely by censoring books and films? ... Some of the censor's
best blows are struck, I believe, by his enemies, because they
cannot agree on one basic principle: all censorship--of any
kind--is untenable and immoral. It is they, the opponents,
anxious to prove that they are 'decent' even though they are
liberal, who hamstring themselves. They oppose, let us say,
restrictions on serious literature but they affirm stoutly that
there must be some control over trash. (And who is to dif-
ferentiate? Suppose there are people who want to read trash.
What about their civil liberties?) Or certain works may be
circulated to adults but not to children, the decisive factors
being availability and price. Trade books and the theatre
must not be censored, low-priced, paper-bound books and films
must be controlled."

650. Rembar, Charles. The End of Obscenity: The Trials of Lady
      Chatterley, Tropic of Cancer and Fanny Hill. New York:
      Random House, 1968. pp. 15-160.
         The collection of chapters surveys the work's court history,
      culminating in the landmark Supreme Court decision. Rembar
      also includes anecdotes, historical information, and other ma-
      terial relevant to the intellectual freedom concerns of the nar-
      rative.

651. "Sex and the Novel: American Censorship of Lady Chatterley's
      Lover," In: Literary Censorship: Principles, Cases, Problems.
      San Francisco: Wadsworth, 1961. pp. 92-138.
         This collection of arguments concerning the U.S. District
      Court case, Grove Press v. Christenberry, includes many en-
      tries not available in the 1970 update, Freedom and Culture.
      They are as follows: (1) Judge Charles E. Clark--from U.S.
      Court of Appeals Majority Opinion, Grove Press v. Christen-
      berry; (2) Harry T. Moore--Lady Chatterley's Lover as Ro-
      mance; (3) Bergen Evans--from "The Storm Over Lady Chat-
      terley's Lover"; (4) John Benedict--from "The 'Lady Chatter-
      ley's Lover' Case"; (5) Eliseo Vivas--from D. H. Lawrence,
      The Failure and Triumph of Art; (6) Stanley Kauffmann--from
      " 'Lady Chatterley' At Last."

      --Land of the Free, by John Hope Franklin

652. Scheiber, Harry N. "The California Textbook Fight," Atlantic.
      220:5 (November 1967) 38, 40, 43-44, 46-47.
         The article chronicles the controversy surrounding the use
      of Land of the Free in eighth-grade American history classes.
      Scheiber concludes,
         "Whether or not the Land of the Free episode is over, its
      history to date suggests a number of important lessons. In
      the first place, the right has demonstrated once again that it
      commands both ample funds and sufficient public relations ex-
      pertise to conduct a highly effective campaign against textbooks

that offend conservative concepts of patriotism. Nor has the
right been lax in perceiving new opportunities to exploit mass
media: many of California's local radio stations devote hour
after hour of air time to programs that consist of telephone
conversation with any and all listeners who wish to call and
talk, and there has been no lack of talk--mostly uninformed--
about Land of the Free ... The Land of the Free episode suggests that the professional associations of academicians (composed
mainly of college professors who seldom experience personally
the impact of textbook-adoption pressures) should take the
initiative to assure expert and informed discussion of textbooks
in the public schools ... Finally, what is the proper role of
the publishers of textbooks and the authors who write them?
In California, which now makes up about a tenth of the
American schoolbook market, the state board of education
not only purchases textbooks outright from publishers in
finished (manufactured) form, but for reasons of economy, it
will often purchase rights to the printer's plates and then
manufacture its own finished books. In the process, minor
changes often are necessary to conform to the state printer's
manual. In the case of Land of the Free, the procedures established to permit routine changes of these kind became the
vehicle for a full-scale review of the book's content."

--The Learning Tree, by Gordon Parks

653.   Findlay, Gilbert Powell. "Gordon Parks' The Learning Tree:
       Autobiography and Education," In: Celebrating Censored
       Books, edited by Nicholas J. Karolides and Lee Burress. Ra-
       cine, Wisc.: Wisconsin Council of Teachers of English, 1985.
       pp. 71-73.
          Findlay sets forth an impassioned defense of the work's
       value in an educational setting. He concludes, "The Learning
       Tree is a compelling history of growing up, available to any-
       one who can identify with a universal exploration of human ex-
       perience. No matter if a reader's time, race, religion, gender,
       or social environments are different. Any book about growing
       up is a story of learning, the hard choices, here guided by
       the love and faith of family, in search of the sources of identity
       and even more realistic and mature understanding. This book
       allows the reader to share insight into why a Gordon Parks is
       'miraculously' transformed from a cypher on the plain of Kansas
       to a man prepared for his success in such a variety of crea-
       tive expressions. The autobiographical The Learning Tree is
       also a moral fable. Gordon Parks said 'look at me and know
       that to destroy me is to destroy yourself ... I too am America.' "

--Little Black Sambo, by Helen Bannerman (See also: Sylves-
ter and the Magic Pebble)

654.   Yuill, Phyllis J. Little Black Sambo: A Closer Look. New
       York: The Racism and Sexism Resource Center for educators,

The Council on Interracial Books for Children, 1976.
The story of the work, particularly attempts to suppress
it. Appendices includes: (1) The Story of Little Black Sambo;
(2) Publishing History of Little Black Sambo in the United
States; (3) Other Books by Helen Bannerman; (4) Recommendations of Little Black Sambo in Bibiographies of Children's Literature; (5) Illustrators of U.S. Editions.

655. Yuill, Phyllis. "Little Black Sambo: The Continuing Controversy," School Library Journal. 22:7 (March 1976) 71-76.
Yuill surveys the work's past brushes with censorship.
She notes that it "seems to remain a popular example of the
dilemma faced by responsible librarians, teachers, and parents
when reevaluating children's books in relation to today's height-
ened social awareness."

--The Little Red Schoolbook, by Soren Hansen

656. Castan, Frances. "A Teacher vs. a Town," Scholastic Teacher.
(April/May 1974) 22-23ff.
Castan provides an account of the controversy in Berkeley
Springs, West Virginia, over the use of the book in the local
schools.

--The Lord of the Flies, by William Golding

657. Slayton, Paul. "Teaching Rationale for William Golding's Lord
of the Flies," In: Celebrating Censored Books, edited by
Nicholas J. Karolides and Lee Burress. Racine, Wisc.: Wisconsin Council of Teachers of English, 1985. pp. 74-76.
Slayton addresses the features of the work which have
aroused the ire of would-be censors--"vulgar" language, the
sexual symbolism of the killing of the sow, children killing
children, a belief that it deals with Satanism. He concludes
that these points pale in relation to the novel's assets; i.e.,
its appeal to youth, its acclaim as a modern classic of literature,
the fact that it deals with a significant universal theme with
obvious contemporary ramifications, and its having been rendered
in an exemplary style and manner.

--Love Story, by Eric Segal

658. Cline, Ruth K. J. "Love Story by Eric Segal; A Rationale
for Classroom Use," In: Celebrating Censored Books, edited
by Nicholas J. Karolides and Lee Burress. Racine, Wisc.:
Wisconsin Council of Teachers of English, 1985. pp. 77-78.
Cline's apology for the work focuses on style, themes, and
its utility for students, with particular attention paid to the
objections raised by censors in these areas. She concludes,
"This novel has enough appeal that it will continue to be read
and enjoyed by many readers. The values in the novel outweigh the problems of explicit language which have been

discussed. Knowing which students will be shocked by the language, the teacher can guide readers to the book who will not be distracted by this."

--Maggie: The Girl of the Streets, by Stephen Crane

659. Stallman, Robert W. "Stephen Crane's Revision of Maggie: The Girl of the Streets," American Literature. 26 (January 1955) 528-536.
   An account of how Crane modified the 1893 edition of his work in order to guarantee its publication.

--Male and Female Under 18 (textbook)

660. "Federal Court Reverses School Library Censorship," Newsletter on Intellectual Freedom. 27:5 (September 1978) 113, 125-128.
   On July 5, 1978, U.S. District Court Judge Joseph L. Tauro barred the Chelsea, Massachusetts, school committee from removing the anthology from the Chelsea High School library. The article reproduces the bulk of Tauro's opinion in the case. He argues, "The library is 'a mighty resource in the marketplace of ideas.' Minarcini v. Strongsville City School District, supra at 582. There a student can literally explore the unknown, and discover areas of interest and thought not covered by the prescribed curriculum. The student who discovers the magic of the library is on the way to a life-long experience of self-education and enrichment. That student learns that a library is a place to test or expand upon ideas presented to him, in or out of the classroom.
   "The most effective antidote to the poison of mindless orthodoxy is ready access to a broad sweep of ideas and philosophies. There is no danger in such exposure. The danger is in mind control."

--Manchild in the Promised Land, by Claude Brown

661. Beckham, Sue Bridwell. "Manchild in a World Where You Just Might Make It; Rationale for Teaching Claude Brown's Manchild in the Promised Land to High School Students," In: Celebrating Censored Books, edited by Nicholas J. Karolides and Lee Burress. Racine, Wisc.: Wisconsin Council of Teachers of English, 1985. pp. 79-81.
   Beckham succinctly summarizes her case for the work in the following statement: "High school students can find everything Claude Brown offers in sociology textbooks, drug education programs and linguistic training, but no lesson is so well taught as it is with concrete examples, and no textbook is so vivid as Claude Brown's prose."

662. Whaley, Elizabeth G. "What Happens When You Put the Manchild

in the Promised Land? An Experience With Censorship," English Journal. 63:5 (May 1974) 61-65. Reprinted in: Newsletter on Intellectual Freedom. XXIII:6 (November 1974) 141-142, 157-159.

Whaley recounts the uproar ensuing out of the use of the novel in a black literature class in a New Hampshire academy. The following statement, given at a meeting of the school's trustees, represents her position as the instructor under fire: "I chose Manchild in the Promised Land by Claude Brown as the finest example of contemporary life in the Harlem ghetto and I stand solidly behind that choice. I cannot imagine teaching a course in Black Literature to college preparatory juniors and seniors in high school and not including that book. The fact that certain local people think the book is 'filthy and rotten' does not impress me. I think these people may all be fine persons, but they are not aware, evidently, of what good literature is. But more pertinent perhaps than that, they are not aware of what today's high school student is like--how he perceives his own world, the world around him, and how maturely he is able to read about and discuss a multiplicity of contemporary problems."

--Molly Pilgrim, by Barbara Cohen

663. Cohen, Barbara. "Censoring the Sources," School Library Journal. 32:7 (March 1986) 97-99.

Cohen provides a diary of events surrounding the adaptation of her work, Molly Pilgrim, for a third-grade reader published by Harcourt Brace Jovanovich. She offers the following conclusions in light of her experience: "Censorship in this country is widespread, subtle, and surprising. It is not inflicted on us by the government. It doesn't need to be. We inflict it on ourselves."

--My Darling, My Hamburger, by Paul Zindel

664. Burress, Lee. "Supporting Traditional Values: My Darling, My Hamburger," In: Celebrating Censored Books, edited by Nicholas J. Karolides and Lee Burress. Racine, Wisc.: Wisconsin Council of Teachers of English, 1985. p. 82.

Burress concludes his critique with the statement, "A library that removed this book would, if consistent, have to remove hundreds of other books that have the same traditional themes and realistic manner of presentation."

--Naked Lunch, by William Burroughs

665. Ciardi, John. "The Book Banners Again (and Again and Again)," Saturday Review. 48:35 (August 28, 1965) 21.

Ciardi discusses the Boston trial of the book in which it was determined to be obscene. He concludes that "the law

itself is incapable of doing honor to itself in such trials," and
that a judge does not possess the qualifications to serve as
"a capable agent of literary criticism."

--1984, by George Orwell

666. Berninghausen, David K. "Case C: Wrenshall Bans Orwell's
      1984," In: The Flight from Reason; Essays on Intellectual
      Freedom in the Academy, the Press, and the Library.   Chicago:
      American Library Association, 1975. pp. 58-62.
          Berninghausen delineates the issues and events ensuing
      from the 1960 decision of the Wrenshall, Minnesota, school
      board to ban 1984 and fire the teacher who'd assigned it to
      his students.   After studying the decision, the Minnesota Civil
      Liberties Union issued the following resolution: "1984 is im-
      portant for the political education of all Americans because it
      illustrates what happens in a totalitarian society.   It is a very
      effective anti-Communist story and the MCLU endorses its
      educational value.   We are surprised and concerned to learn
      that any superintendent or school board would ban it from the
      curriculum or library."

667. Davis, James E. "Why Nineteen Eighty-Four Should Be Read
      and Taught," In: Celebrating Censored Books, edited by
      Nicholas J. Karolides and Lee Burress.   Racine, Wisc.:   Wis-
      consin Council of Teachers of English, 1985. pp. 83-85.
          Davis notes the grounds on which the novel has been chal-
      lenged--e.g. profanity, immorality, obscenity, Communistic
      sympathies, and a depressing tone.   He concludes his rebuttal
      by stating, "It is hard to imagine a modern novel that has more
      reasons to be read and taught.   In addition to its literary
      merit, it has special implications for our times and the society
      toward which we may be heading."

--Of Mice and Men, by John Steinbeck

668. Scarseth, Thomas. "A Teachable Good Book: Of Mice and
      Men," In: Celebrating Censored Books, edited by Nicholas J.
      Karolides and Lee Burress.   Racine, Wisc.:   Wisconsin Council
      of Teachers of English, 1985. pp. 86-88.
          Scarseth notes that while the novel contains unpleasant
      attitudes--e.g., brutality, racism, sexism, economic exploita-
      tion--it does not advocate them; rather, "it shows that these
      too-narrow conceptions of human life are part of the cause of
      human tragedy."

--One Day in the Life of Ivan Denisovich, by Aleksandr
Solzhenitsyn

669. Miller, Robert Keith. "Defending Solzhenitsyn: One Day in
      the Life of Ivan Denisovich," In: Celebrating Censored Books,

edited by Nicholas J. Karolides and Lee Burress. Racine,
Wisc.: Wisconsin Council of Teachers of English, 1985. pp.
89-92.

Miller's thorough analysis sweeps aside criticisms of the
book, concluding that it is deeply moral and one of the central documents in the intellectual history of our times. "In
short, I can imagine circumstances under which this book
might be censored for political reasons, and I can even imagine
circumstances in which instructors might feel uncomfortable
teaching a work with such a strong Christian bias, since the
discussion of religious values is often difficult in public schools.
But for this profoundly moral work to be censored for containing 'foul language' is to encourage the basest type of censor: The censor who condemns what he obviously has not
read."

670. Scammell, Michael. Solzhenitsyn: A Biography. New York:
      Norton, 1984.
      Scammell discusses attempts to censor One Day in the Life
      of Ivan Denisovich, including efforts by Ralph Parker, whose
      translation was sponsored by the Soviet government, to re-
      spond to the prudishness of Soviet sensibilities by "toning
      down some of Solzhenitsyn's saltier expressions."

      --One Flew Over the Cuckoo's Nest, by Ken Kesey

671. Quinn, Laura. "Defense of One Flew Over The Cuckoo's Nest,"
      In: Celebrating Censored Books, edited by Nicholas J. Karolides
      and Lee Burress. Racine, Wisc.: Wisconsin Council of Teachers
      of English, 1985. pp. 93-97.
      Quinn argues that the work belongs in the high school cur-
      riculum for the following reasons: (1) it opens the issue of
      social control in the truest sense of that verb; (2) it treats a
      problem that is particularly relevant to teenage readers whose
      chafing under social constraints and whose ambivalence toward
      authority is often acute; (3) it is a readable book, dramatic,
      immediate, accessible to young readers; (4) it is a work of
      substantial literary merit that features an interesting narrative
      situation--Chief Bromden, the towering Indian who has posed
      as a deaf-mute in the ward for many years, narrates the novel,
      creating a complex and ironic perspective on events and per-
      sonalities in the hospital.

672. Sutherland, Janet R. "A Defense of Ken Kesey's One Flew
      Over The Cuckoo's Nest," English Journal. 61:1 (January
      1972) 28-31.
      This English teacher's defense arose out of an attack by
      parents in Bellevue, Washington, in which she was accused of
      teaching an "indecent, obscene, racist, immoral book." She
      provides a rationale for teaching the work in high school.

--Ordinary People, by Judith Guest

673. Neuhaus, Ron. "Threshold Literature: A Discussion of Ordinary People," In: Celebrating Censored Books, edited by Nicholas J. Karolides and Lee Burress. Racine, Wisc.: Wisconsin Council of Teachers of English, 1985. pp. 98-101.
     Neuhaus discusses the most salient groups critical of the work: Fetishists, Monkey Sees, Ostriches, Dominoes, and Catchers-of-the-Raw. He concludes his defense by stating, "as 'ordinary people' we need words that can reveal insight into how we are, and where we are. Ordinary People assays out to that; it lacks the lofty level of intellectual melodrama possessed by the 'safe' book, classic or otherwise, and that's the quality that justifies making it accessible to any heart it speaks to."

--Our Bodies, Ourselves: A Book by and for Women, by The Boston Women's Health Book Collective.

674. Nilsen, Alleen Pace. "In Defense of Our Bodies, Ourselves," In: Celebrating Censored Books, edited by Nicholas J. Karolides and Lee Burress. Racine, Wisc.: Wisconsin Council of Teachers of English, 1985. pp. 102-104.
     In addition to defending the work on educational grounds, Nilsen offers the following advice to librarians and teachers: (1) do not force the book on anyone; (2) help people realize that no one book can be all things to all people; (3) help people realize the complexity of the issues that are being discussed; (4) listen sympathetically to parents and others who protest the book.

--The Permissible Lie, by Samm S. Baker

675. Baker, Samm S. "The Attempted Suppression of The Permissible Lie," Censorship Today. 1:2 (August/September 1968) 11-13.
     Baker reports on the censoring of his book by Reader's Digest Association, Inc., the parent company of Funk & Wagnalls, who owned rights to the work. Corporate censorship could increase significantly in the future in view of the fact that many book publishers are being purchased by conglomerates.

--The Scarlet Letter, by Nathaniel Hawthorne

676. Gappa, Richard. "Penance and Repentance in The Scarlet Letter," In: Celebrating Censored Books, edited by Nicholas J. Karolides and Lee Burress. Racine, Wisc.: Wisconsin Council of Teachers of English, 1985. pp. 105-107.
     Gappa feels that the work has been branded as immoral-- i.e., it mocks religion, glorifies adultery, dabbles in the occult, and negatively influences young readers--because the attackers

misread it. He notes that "while Hawthorne does examine
organized religion, the possibility of satanic influences in the
world, the complexities of adultery and the cancerous effect of
hypocrisy upon an individual, he does so in a mature and fair-
minded manner."

--A Separate Peace, by John Knowles

677.   Holborn, David G.   "A Rationale for Reading John Knowles'
       A Separate Peace," In: Celebrating Censored Books, edited
       by Nicholas J. Karolides and Lee Burress. Racine, Wisc.:
       Wisconsin Council of Teachers of English, 1985. pp. 108-110.
           Holborn recommends that the novel be read by both adoles-
       cents and adults, and that it be discussed openly. He con-
       siders its ultimate meaning to be that "War may flare out at
       various times and take on form in France or Germany, Korea
       or Viet Nam, but when we look for the causes we should look
       first within."

--Show Me!, by Hilary Davies

678.   Freedom to Read Committee, Association of American Publishers.
       "AAParagraphs: Censorship Loses A Round," Newsletter on
       Intellectual Freedom. 25:2 (March 1976) 32, 53-54.
           A report on the testimony provided in a summary examina-
       tion of the books by Massachusetts Superior Court Judge David
       S. Nelson. Acting upon a prior claim of obscenity set in mo-
       tion by a Middlesex County D.A., Nelson dismissed the pro-
       ceeding, holding that Show Me! is not obscene.

--Slaughterhouse-Five, by Kurt Vonnegut

679.   Reed, Peter J.   "Authenticity and Relevance; Kurt Vonnegut's
       Slaughterhouse-Five," In: Celebrating Censored Books, edited
       by Nicholas J. Karolides and Lee Burress. Racine, Wisc.:
       Wisconsin Council of Teachers of English, 1985. pp. 111-112.
           The bulk of the essay consists of a straightforward critique
       of Slaughterhouse-Five. Reed concludes his argument in sup-
       port of the work by stating that it "seems important not just
       in its ideas, or its morality, or as an example of modern fic-
       tion, or for what it might teach about how to write, but for
       its lesson in thinking. It is provocative, even maddening to
       some, because of irreverence. It challenges sacred cows, set
       ideas, merely traditional ways of thinking. And it does not
       do this irresponsibly, but from the foundation of a moral human
       decency. This kind of invitation to openness is surely the es-
       sence of education."

680.   Veix, Donald B.   "Teaching a Censored Novel: Slaughterhouse
       Five," English Journal. 64:7 (October 1975) 25-33.
           Veix provides methods for presenting controversial novels--

with a particular emphasis on <u>Slaughterhouse-Five</u>--to high
school English classes.

--<u>Soul on Ice</u>, by Eldridge Cleaver

681.   Church, Bud.   " 'Soul on Ice' Makes the School Board Agenda,"
       <u>Media & Methods</u>.   6 (March 1970) 54-58, 62-64.
           Church analyzes the use of Cleaver's novel in high school
       English classes. He also considers the broader perspectives of
       incorporating controversial modern works with the high school
       curricula.

--<u>Sylvester and the Magic Pebble</u>, by Jeremy Steig

682.   Fitzgerald, R. V.   "The Threat to Freedom," <u>Library Journal</u>.
       96 (April 15, 1971) 1429-1430; <u>School Library Journal</u>. (April
       1971) 31-32.
           An account of the reaction of two libraries to pressures
       from the policemen's association to remove the work; the Toledo
       Board of Education gives in to pressure, whereas the public
       library system retains it. The bulk of the article is concerned
       with delineating the differences between the public library and
       the school system in that city. Fitzgerald concludes, "It is
       indeed tragic that the majority of American citizens do not
       recognize the essential differences between our <u>constitutional</u>
       democratic government and a totalitarian government ... The
       response of the administration of the Toledo board of educa-
       tion was in the totalitarian mode: arbitrary, without open hear-
       ings, without consultation with professional librarians and edu-
       cators, without consideration of opposing views. This is not
       to say that we would wish such decisions to be left entirely
       in the hands of experts of any kind or to a vote of the majority;
       this is exactly what constitutional government is not. Were
       our precious Bill of Rights to be put to a vote of the majority
       (God forbid), most of it would be voted out, regarded by this
       unenlightened majority as ... 'Communist doctrine....' "

683.   Krug, Judith F., and James A. Harvey. "An Ox of a Different
       Color," <u>American Libraries</u>. 2 (May 1971) 532-534.
           The authors allude to the double standard practiced by some
       libraries as reflected in their willingness to censor <u>Little Black
       Sambo</u> while retaining <u>Sylvester and the Magic Pebble</u>. Such
       a tendency indicates an inability to grasp the true meaning of
       intellectual freedom. The authors provide the following pre-
       scription: "Consideration must be given to the <u>Library Bill
       of Rights</u> which clearly states that library collections should
       represent all points of view concerning the problems and is-
       sues of our times, and that no materials should be proscribed
       or removed because of partisan or doctrinal disapproval. Li-
       brarians must carefully weigh the long-range effects of remov-
       ing any library materials, no matter how legitimate the complaint.

Finally, and most importantly, librarians must reexamine their
own understanding of intellectual freedom as a concept separate
from their individual beliefs about social, political, sexual, and
religious matters. No matter how strong a librarian's personal
commitment to a particular cause, it must not influence the decision to retain or remove materials from the library collection
or intellectual freedom becomes merely a question of whose ox
is being gored."

--365 Days, by Dr. Ronald J. Glasser

684. Campbell, Scott. "Banned in Baileyville," Northeast Magazine.
      (June 27, 1982) Reprinted in: The First Freedom Today, edited
      by Robert B. Downs and Ralph E. McCoy. Chicago: American
      Library Association, 1984. pp. 86-92.
         An account of the Baileyville case. Campbell quotes liberally
      from Judge Cyr's decision in Sheck v. Baileyville. " 'As long
      as words convey ideas,' he wrote, 'federal courts must remain
      on first amendment alert in book-banning cases, even those
      ostensibly based strictly on vocabulary consideration. A less
      vigilant rule would leave the care of the flock to the fox that
      is only after their feathers.' On a somewhat less metaphorical
      note, he went on: 'The information and ideas in books placed
      in a school library by proper authority is protected speech.
      And the first amendment right of students to receive that in-
      formation and those ideas is entitled to constitutional protec-
      tion. A book may not be banned,' he continued, 'from a public
      school library in disregard of the requirements of the four-
      teenth amendment.' He went on to say that the Committee ac-
      tion appeared to be seriously deficient because of 'procedural
      irregularity, arbitrariness, vagueness and overbreadth,' and
      in ordering that the book be put back on the school library
      shelf, he became the first federal judge in history to make
      such a ruling about a book which had ostensibly been banned
      only for dirty words."

685. Fitzgerald, Frances. "A Reporter At Large; A Disagreement
      in Baileyville," New Yorker. 59 (January 16, 1984) 47-90.
         A comprehensive analysis of the Baileyville case (1981-1982),
      including its relationship to the Supreme Court's decision in
      Pico v. Island Trees.

686. "School Censorship Cases: Baileyville," In: The First Free-
      dom Today, edited by Robert B. Downs and Ralph E. McCoy.
      Chicago: American Library Association, 1984. pp. 83-85.
         A summary of the controversy in a small northeastern Maine
      community over the presence of the book in the high school
      library. In his fourteen-page decision which ordered the
      Baileyville school committee to return 365 Days to the shelves
      of the Woodland High School library, Judge Cyr questioned that
      body's judgment:

"The Committee's rationale was neither articulated nor me-
morialized. The record discloses no finding that harm might
result to students exposed to the coarse language in 365 Days.
It may be considered implicit in the Committee vote that three
of its members found the language 'objectionable,' but it does
not appear that the ban was predicated on a Committee determination that exposure might be harmful to students. Two
committee members testified that certain words in 365 Days
were considered inappropriate for use by or to students, but
no evidence has been presented that even three committee
members believed that harm might result to all students exposed to such language."

--To Kill A Mockingbird, by Harper Lee

687. May, Jill. "In Defense of To Kill A Mockingbird," In: Cele-
      Brating Censored Books, edited by Nicholas J. Karolides and
      Lee Burress. Racine, Wisc.: Wisconsin Council of Teachers
      of English, 1985. pp. 114-117.
          May's critique is prefaced by a historical survey of efforts
      to suppress the work. With respect to the censors' reactions,
      she notes,
          "Their moves to ban the book derive from their own perspec-
      tives of the book's theme. Their 'reader's response' criticism,
      usually based on one reading of the book, was personal and po-
      litical. They needed to ban the book because it told them some-
      thing about American society that they did not want to hear."

--Tropic of Cancer, by Henry Miller

688. "Case 3: Henry Miller's Tropic of Cancer," In: Freedom and
      Culture: Literary Censorship in the 70s. Belmont, Calif.:
      Wadsworth, 1970. pp. 116-139.
          A collection of essays and testimony surrounding the multi-
      tude of trials at the state and local level concerned with the
      constitutionality of the book. Includes: (1) David Littlejohn:
      The Tropics of Miller; (2) Elmer Gertz: Henry Miller and the
      Law; (3) Harry Levin: Witness: Massachusetts v. Tropic of
      Cancer; (4) Eleanor Widmer: My Day in the Censoring Tropic;
      (5) Henry Miller: Obscenity and the Law of Reflection.

689. Ciardi, John. "Tropic of Cancer," Saturday Review. 45:26
      (June 30, 1962) 13.
          Ciardi defends Tropic of Cancer not as "a great book," but
      rather "as the work of a serious artist enlarged by talent and
      passionately engaged in giving form (and thereby meaning) to
      his view of life."

690. Hutchison, E. R. "Tropic of Cancer" on Trial; A Case History
      of Censorship. New York: Grove Press, 1968.
          Hutchison documents efforts to suppress the Henry Miller
      novel since its publication in 1934, particularly through litigation.

A truly monumental work which captures the nuances of an increasingly tolerant American society during the early sixties
(the author notes that there were more than 60 legal cases
involving the book from 1961 to 1964). The appendix lists
major U.S. court cases bearing on obscenity (1812-1965).
Selected bibliography covers both Miller and censorship in
general.

691. Rembar, Charles. The End of Obscenity: The Trials of Lady
Chatterley, Tropic of Cancer and Fanny Hill. New York: Random Hill, 1968. pp. 161-215.
The collection of chapters surveys the work's court history,
culminating in the landmark Supreme Court decision. Rembar
also includes anecdotes, historical information, and other material relevant to the intellectual freedom concerns of the nar-
rative.

--Ulysses, by James Joyce

692. Ernst, Morris L. "Reflections on the Ulysses Trial and Censorship," James Joyce Quarterly. 3:2 (Fall 1965) 3-11.
Ernst recalls the James Joyce Ulysses trial of 1933 in which
he served as the defense attorney.

693. Woolsey, Judge J. M., and Judge J. W. Manton. "The Ulysses
Case Opinions," In: Freedom and Culture: Literary Censorship in the 70s. Belmont, Calif.: Wadsworth, 1970. pp. 89-
93.
A landmark decision, rendered December 6, 1933, in the
Southern District of New York, the polarities established by
Woolsey and Manton--the intention of a book taken as a whole
versus a literal interpretation of obscenity based on the presence of four-letter words--became endemic to the censorship
cases that arose over the following decades.

--The Valley of Horses, by Jean Auel

694. "Jean Auel Defends The Valley of Horses," Newsletter on Intellectual Freedom. 35:2 (March 1986) 33, 61-63.
The text of Auel's June 4, 1985, letter to librarian Putzie
Martin and the Bastrop (Texas) Public Library Board in response to a censoring attempt is reprinted in full. The author
discusses the painstaking research employed so as to achieve
an authenticity more typical of nonfiction; she includes letters
and reviews in support of her work.

Bookstores

695. Knoll, Erwin. "Bookburners," The Progressive. 49:12 (December 1985) 4.

A commentary on the torching of two adult bookstores in
Colorado Springs, Colorado, in October 1985. Knoll notes the
growing incidence of censorship nationwide and warns that
"once one acquires a taste for censorship, it can easily become
addictive."

Comic Books, Comic Strips, Political Cartoons

a. General Background

696. Busch, Brian. "Ban and Superman," Amazing Heroes. No.
      90 (March 1, 1986) 48-51.
      Busch surveys the rumblings of comic book censorship dur-
      ing the forties and fifties which stimulated the October 26,
      1954, formation of the Comics Code Authority. The article in-
      cludes a lengthy list of references to national newspaper ar-
      ticles on the subject from that period.

697. "Literature and Violence: Censorship of Comic Books," In:
      Literary Censorship: Principles, Cases, Problems. San Fran-
      cisco: Wadsworth, 1961. pp. 63-91.
      The differing viewpoints espoused by these contributors in-
      dicates that the issues posed by comic books, and arguments
      for and against censoring them, are not isolated or altogether
      unique. Includes: (1) Frederic Wertham--from Seduction of
      the Innocent; (2) Judge Jerome Frank--from U.S. Court of
      Appeals Opinion, Roth v. United States; (3) Terrence J. Mur-
      phy--from "The Evidence As To the Social Harm Caused by Such
      Potentially Objectionable Publications"; (4) American Civil Li-
      berties Union--from Censorship of Comic Books; (5) Leslie
      Fiedler--from "The Middle Against Both Ends."

698. Murrell, Jesse L. "The Greater Cincinnati Committee on Eval-
      uation of Comic Books," In: Violence and the Mass Media,
      edited by Otto N. Larsen. New York: Harper & Row, 1968.
      pp. 182-189.
      Murrell profiles the organization and its modus operandi.
      He also surveys what other localities and groups are doing with
      respect to the rating of comic books.

699. "Regulation of Comic Books," Harvard Law Review. 68 (January
      1955) 498-506.
      The article argues that "an effective system of self-limitation
      by the comic book industry would appear to be the best way to
      eliminate crime, horror, and sex in comic books."

700. Twomey, John E. "The Citizens' Committee and Comic-Book
      Control: a Study of Extragovernmental Restraint," Law and
      Contemporary Problems. 20 (Autumn 1955) 621-629.
      A survey of the Citizens' Committee for Better Juvenile

Literature of Chicago and its fight to suppress objectionable
comic book titles.

701. Twomey, John E. "New Forms of Social Control over Mass
Media Content," Studies in Public Communication. I (Summer
1957) 38-44.
Twomey surveys the crusade against the comic book medium
as reflected in the Congressional investigations, the activities
of pressure groups, and the writings of reformers such as
Fredric Wertham. He posits that this movement evolved out
of a growing climate in favor of censorship.

b. Comics Code Authority

702. "Code of the Comics Magazine Association of America, Inc.,"
In: Cartoons and Comics in the Classroom: A Reference for
Teachers and Librarians, edited by James L. Thomas. Littleton, Colo.: Libraries Unlimited, 1983. pp. 173-178.
The full text of the Code, originally adopted in 1954 and
revised in 1971 to meet contemporary standards of conduct and
morality. The enforcement of this Code is the basis for the
comics magazine industry's program of self-regulation.

703. Comics Magazine Association of America. "Role of the Code
Administrator," In: Violence and the Mass Media, edited by
Otto N. Larsen. New York: Harper & Row, 1968. pp. 244-
249.
The administrator of the Comics Code Authority, the self
regulatory system employed by the industry, recounts his experiences while serving in that capacity.

704. Maeder, Jay. "An Interview With John Goldwater, Leonard
Darvin, and Dr. Frederic Wertham," In: Comics Feature Pre-
sents An Informal History of Comics, Vol. 1. Tampa: New
Media Publishing, 1984. pp. 26-34.
Three interviews featuring, in succession, Goldwater, pre-
sident of the CCA and owner of Archie Comics, Darvin, ad-
ministrator of the CCA, and Wertham, a psychiatrist whose
Seduction of the Innocent (1954) led to the development of the
Code. Goldwater and Darvin discuss the role of the CCA:
Wertham reflects on his notoriety and claims that, while identified with censorship, he was always opposed to censorship for
adults.

705. Crawford, Hubert H. "E-C Publications," In: Crawford's
Encyclopedia of Comic Books. Middle Village, N.Y.: Jonathan
David, 1978. pp. 263-310.
Crawford examines the forces which led to the formation of
the Comics Code Authority. E-C is portrayed as receiving the
lion's share of the blame for the tastelessness characterizing
the comic books of that era due to its leadership role ensuing

out of the introduction of the "New Trend Entertainment Comics"
series. This dynamic innovation had turned a then moribund
medium around, increasing general profits as well as attracting
a new wave of criticism.

706.   Daniels, Les.   "Chapter Five: The Comics Code Controversy,"
       In: Comix: A History of Comic Books in America.   New York:
       Bonanza, 1971.   pp. 83-90.
          A historical survey of the events surrounding the creation
       of the Comics Code Authority.   A copy of the standards of
       the CCA as originally adopted in 1954 has been included.

c.   EC Comics

707.   Clifford, J. B., Jr.   "Shock Illustrated: The Rarest EC,"
       In: Comics Feature Presents An Informal History of Comics,
       Vol. 1.   Tampa: New Media Publishing, 1984.   pp. 58-63.
          Clifford reflects that Shock Illustrated was one of the ex-
       periments--in this case, "picto-fiction"--tried by EC in order
       to "escape the tender mercies of the CCA."   With these new
       titles the company attempted to zero in on older teenagers and
       adults--an audience unlikely to be interested in the watered-
       down comics allowed under the CCA.

708.   Wooley, Chuck.   "The Lost Comics Companies: A Developmental
       History of EC Comics," Comics Feature.   No. 17 (June 1981)
       64-65.
          Wooley notes the role of anti-comics crusaders and, ultimately,
       the CCA in killing the company's comic books line.   He asserts
       that "the CCA was the most stringent self-censoring agency
       ever to control an American medium, and it, along with televi-
       sion and bad publicity, almost killed the entire comics industry."

d.   Individual Titles

709.   Feltman, Lee.   "Cartoonists and Publishers Beware!"   News-
       letter on Intellectual Freedom.   26:2 (March 1977) 31, 59-60.
          Feltman discusses the implications of the Court of Appeal
       of the State of California's February 1976 ruling that if a
       publication is "susceptible" to a defamatory interpretation as
       well as an innocent one, the action will not be dismissed sum-
       marily but is indeed libelous.   Feltman agrees with the counsel
       for the publishers in the petition for certiorari to the U.S.
       Supreme Court on October 5, 1976:
          "In sum, the decision of the California Court of Appeal
       strikes at the very purpose of the constitutional privilege of
       free speech and free press in two important ways.   First, by
       a strained and tortuous interpretation of the cartoon, it de-
       crees a totally unreasonable standard for determing whether
       political and social criticism is defamatory.
          "Secondly, the California Court of Appeal requires that

petitioners, in a case involving 'public figures,' prove that
they did not make a false statement about Hartley and Union
with 'actual malice.' This is not the law, and can only serve
to create an atmosphere of fear and timidity upon those who
would give voice to public criticism."

Electronic Media

710. McDonald, Frances M. "Technology, Privacy, and Electronic
Freedom of Speech," Library Trends. 35:1 (Summer 1986)
83-104.
    Acknowledging that electronic freedom of speech is as es-
sential as print freedoms, McDonald notes that decisions being
made now have the potential for creating a society in which
all forms of communications are free or a society in which restrictions on access to information are imposed by legislators
and other government officials. Unfortunately, based on precedents set with the regulation of radio and television, tech-
nologically uninformed government officials are passing laws
without adequate attention to First Amendment freedoms and
civil liberties.

Films

a. General Background

711. Atkins, Thomas R., editor. Sexuality in the Movies. Bloomington: Indiana University Press, 1975.
    A collection of essays divided into three units: (1) attempts
at controlling films, (2) various categories of sex films, and
(3) critiques of six controversial films from the sixties and
seventies.

712. Berninghausen, David K. "Film Censorship," ALA Bulletin.
(December 1950) 447-448.
    Berninghausen documents an attack on the Peoria Public
Library by the American Legion and a local newspaper for including certain films in its collection. The confrontation had
the ultimate effect of stimulating the ALA Council to modify
the Library Bill of Rights.

713. Blumenthal, Ralph. "Porno Chic," New York Times Magazine.
21 (January 1973) 28, 30, 32-34.
    Blumenthal discusses the rising porno-film phenomenon.
The treatment received by Deep Throat in the courts constitutes a major focus of the article.

714. Carmen, Ira H. Movies, Censorship, and the Law. Ann Arbor:
University of Michigan Press, 1966.

A survey of the legal aspects of film censorship. The role of
local censorship boards is covered at length.

715. De Grazia, Edward, and Roger K. Newman. Banned Films:
Movies, Censors and the First Amendment. New York: Bowker,
1982.
The definitive study of film censorship. The work consists
of two major sections: "The Story," a historical survey of film
censorship, and "The Movies," an analysis of the censorship
of individual film titles.

716. Ernst, Morris L., and Pare Lorentz. Censored: The Private
Life of the Movies. New York: Ozer, 1971. Reprint of the
1930 publication.
The authors document censorship cases throughout the nation.

717. Linden, Kathryn B. The Film Censorship Struggle in the United
States from 1926 to 1957, and the Social Values Involved. New
York: New York University, 1972. Ph.D. dissertation, available from University Microfilms, no. 72-20, 646.
A historical survey of attempts to censor the Hollywood film
industry. Linden focuses on the social values espoused by
each side--censors and non-censors--in past confrontations.

718. Lord, Richard A. "Film Is A Four Letter Word," Memphis State
University Law Review. 5 (Fall 1974) 41-58.
Lord attempts to ascertain whether or not municipal boards
of review are constitutionally valid. He provides a historical
overview of the phenomenon.

719. Mason, John. "Obscenity in Broadcasting and Motion Pictures,"
Journal of University Film Producers Association. 23 (1971)
54-61.
Mason analyzes the significance of Roth v. United States
(1957) in the application of obscenity statutes to films.

720. Milner, Michael. Sex on Celluloid. New York: Macfadden-
Bartell, 1964.
Milner provides a wide-ranging survey of the treatment of
sex in films. Chapter 4 covers the regulation of cinematic sex,
including self-regulation, unorganized public regulation, organized public regulation, and official regulation.

721. Oberholtzer, Ellis Paxson. The Morals of the Movie. New York:
Ozer, 1971. Reprint of the 1922 publication.
Oberholtzer, then a member of the Pennsylvania State Board
of Censors, discusses the role of censorship with respect to
problematical films.

722. Randall, Richard S. Censorship of the Movies; The Social and

Political Control of a Mass Medium. Madison: University of
Wisconsin Press, 1968.
    Randall analyzes the implications of the tension between
the right of free expression and the requirements of mass
democratic society. The work is divided into the following
sections: (I) Introduction--A Medium of Controversy; (II)
The Movies and the Law; (III) Prior Censorship in Operation;
(IV) The Wider Milieu of Censorship; (V) Conclusion--Freedom
of Speech in a Mass Medium.

723. Sarris, Andrew. "Censorship: A View from New York,"
      Sight and Sound. 38 (Autumn 1969) 202-203, 219. Reprinted
      in: Andrew Sarris. Primal Screen. New York: Simon and
      Schuster, 1973. pp. 106-110.
          Because censors allowed the film industry nothing when it
      asked for very little, Sarris argues that "there can be no com-
      promise with censorship even when there is regret for some of
      the lost charm of repression and innocence."

724. Schumach, Murray. The Face on the Cutting Room Floor; The
      Story of Movie and Television Censorship. New York: Morrow,
      1964.
          A historical survey of film and television censorship. While
      the work does not include development of the past generation,
      its thorough and incisive treatment of the subject merits con-
      sideration. In Part 1 Schumach covers the developments of
      the twenties and thirties which culminated in the formulation
      of the Production Code. Particular movies that have been the
      object of controversy are analyzed in the second section. Part
      3 is concerned with the activities of pressure groups and
      government agencies. In Part 4 the blacklisting of Hollywood
      actors, writers, and producers for their espousal of left wing
      causes is covered. Part 5 discusses Hollywood's handling of
      themes of sex and violence. Part 6 covers the action of the
      courts in key movie censorship cases. Television censorship
      is covered in Part 7 and future solutions to the film censor-
      ship dilemma are considered in Part 8. The appendix includes:
      Curious Examples of Foreign Censorship, How Some Foreign
      Countries Classify Film, and the text of the Motion Picture
      Production Code.

725. Schwartzman, S. Howard. "Obscenity in the Movies," Loyola
      Law Review. 18 (1971-72) 354-374.
          Schwartzman surveys key court cases in the fifties and
      sixties concerned with obscenity in films. The cases covered
      include Burstyn v. Wilson (The Miracle), Kingsley International
      Pictures v. Regents (Lady Chatterley's Lover), and Excelsior
      Pictures Corp. v. Regents (Garden of Eden).

726. Young, Donald, et al. "Censorship or Freedom," In: The
      Annals of The American Academy of Political and Social Science;

The Motion Picture in its Economic and Social Aspects, November 1926, edited by Clyde L. King and Frank A. Tichenor. New York: Arno/New York Times, 1970. pp. 146-186. Reprint of Volume 128, Number 217 of the journal.

A collection of essays which delineate the role of censorship within the film industry as of the mid-twenties. Titles include: Social Standards and the Motion Picture; The Relation of the Motion Picture to Changing Moral Standards; How the Motion Picture Governs Itself; Official Censorship Legislation; The Work of the National Board of Review.

b. Blacklisting

727. Bessie, Alvah. "Jail, Freedom and the Screenwriting Profession," Film Comment. 3:4 (Fall 1965) 56-67.

Bessie, one of the Hollywood Ten, discusses the experiences of individuals on and off the blacklist.

728. Bessie, Alvah. "The Non-Existent Man," Contact. 2:6 (October 1960) 83-96.

Bessie analyzes the investigation carried out by the Committee on Un-American Activities. He also notes its implications with respect to his career.

729. Biberman, Herbert. "American People and Freedom of the Screen," Film Comment. 3:4 (Fall 1965) 67-69.

Biberman, one of the Hollywood Ten (cited for contempt by the Committee on Un-American Activities in 1947), argues that First Amendment rights do not apply within the film industry.

730. Cogley, John. Report on Blacklisting; Part I--The Movies. New York: Arno/ New York Times, 1972. Reprint of the 1956 edition.

Cogley reports the findings of the task force of the Fund for the Republic regarding the blacklisting phenomenon within the film industry. Appendices include: Films of "The Hollywood Ten," 1929-1949; Films of Writers, Directors and Producers Who Declared Themselves to Have Been Former Communists; Changes in the Content of Hollywood Motion Pictures, 1947-1954; Summary of Shifts in the Communist Party Line, 1929-1949.

731. Cutts, John, and Penelope Houston. "Blacklisted," Sight and Sound. 26 (Summer 1957) 15-19ff.

An analysis of the 1947 Congressional investigation; based on John Cogley's book, Report on Blacklisting (Meridian, 1956).

732. Levin, Bernard. "Seven Years' Hard," Spectator. 206 (June 30, 1961) 943-945.

A profile of the screenwriting career of Louis Pallack, focusing on his problems with the Committee on Un-American Activities.

733. MacFadden, Patrick, et al. "Blacklisted!" Take One. 1:5
     (1967) 10-15.
        A survey of blacklisting; includes personal reflections by
     Millard Lampell and Herbert Biberman.

                    c. Film Codes, Ratings, etc.

734. Alpert Hollis. "The Movies' New Sex-and Violence Ratings,"
     Woman's Day. (January 1969) Reprinted in: Mass Media and
     the Law, edited by David G. Clark and Earl R. Hutchison.
     New York: Wiley-Interscience, 1970. pp. 59-64.
        Alpert analyzes the latest classification system to be adopted
     by the film industry.

735. Bates, Roy C. "Private Censorship of Movies," Stanford Law
     Review. 22 (February 1970) 618-656.
        The author concludes that the Motion Picture Association of
     America classification system represents a form of censorship.
     He calls on the federal courts to rectify this injustice.

736. Boyd, George N. "Movies and the Sexual Revolution: Should
     the Ratings Be Revised?" Christian Century. 87 (September
     23, 1970) 1124-1125.
        Boyd evaluates the new rating system adopted by the MPAA;
     his prime criticism is that "the age restriction for R films was
     set unrealistically high."

737. Canby, Vincent. "A New Movie Code Ends Some Taboos,"
     The New York Times. CXV (September 21, 1966) 1-2.
        A report on the adoption of a new production code on Sep-
     tember 20, 1966, by the MPAA. The objectives of the code as
     well as the ten standards by which films will be judged are
     cited. By eliminating many specific taboos, the new regula-
     tions will provide the office of the Production Code Administra-
     tion with considerably more leeway in determining what is or
     is not "acceptable."

738. Farber, Stephen. The Movie Rating Game. Washington, D.C.:
     Public Affairs Press, 1972.
        Farber analyzes the Motion Picture Association of America
     Code and Rating Administration.

739. "The Journal Looks at the Film Rating Race," Journal of Screen
     Producers Guild. 18 (December 1969) 1-36.
        Various personalities outside the film community--Lou Green-
     span, Robert Steele, Anne Childress, Fredric Wertham, James
     Wall, Martin Dworkin, Art Buchwald, Gerald Kennedy, Frank
     Kelly, Richard Coe, and Bernard Kantor--answer the question,
     "What is your opinion of the rating system which was put into
     effect on November 1, 1968?"

740.   Knight, Arthur. "Gas in Good Entertainment," Saturday Review. 52 (March 1, 1969) 40.
       Knight addresses the problems inherent in the new MPAA Code.

741.   Langguth, Jack. "Doctor X," Saturday Review: The Arts. 55:49 (December 2, 1972) 6, 10-12.
       An interview with the head of the MPAA rating board, Dr. Aaron Stern.

742.   "The M-Rating Dies to Help Films Live," Business Week.   No. 2110 (February 7, 1970) 104-106.
       A report on the replacement of the "M" with the "GP" rating by the MPAA following complaints from distributors that the former was bad for business.

743.   Michener, James A.   "GMRX: An Alternative to Movie Censorship," Reader's Digest. 94:1 (January 1969) 87-93.
       Michener provides reasons for the permissive attitude which dominated moviemaking by the late sixties. He advocates public acceptance of the film industry's new rating code.

744.   Moley, Raymond. The Hays Office. New York: Ozer, 1971. Reprint of the 1945 publication.
       Moley surveys the historical development and role of the censoring agency.

745.   "New Movie Code: Clean Up or Cover Up?" Senior Scholastic. 93 (October 25, 1968) 5-8, 19.
       A discussion of the recently instituted MPAA Code; includes a historical survey of film censorship in the U.S. In response to concerns about the growing permissiveness of contemporary film, New York Magazine film critic Judith Crist states, "The films we are getting and that are to come have no holds barred as far as sex and violence and language go. [But] it's time we faced the fact that films, much like literature and drama, come out of society and mirror it, and that beyond matters of clothing and interior decoration, movies reflect and do not set patterns."

746.   Randall, Richard S.   "Classification by the Motion Picture Industry," In: Technical Report of the Commission on Obscenity and Pornography. Volume 5. Washington, D.C.: Government Printing Office, 1971. pp. 219-299.
       Randall analyzes the film rating system instituted by the MPAA in 1968 as an alternative to government censorship. He notes that "the rating system only partially defends the film medium from censorship and control. As such, it is only one control among several that operate on the medium and only one element in the public policy problem of managing the tension between freedom of speech and censorship in the medium."

747. "Revising the Rating System," Newsweek. 104 (July 2, 1984)
     45.
          A report on the institution of a new label, PG-13, within
     the existing Hollywood code.

748. Robinson, Sally. "In My Opinion: The New Movie Ratings Are
     For the Birds," Seventeen. 28 (March 1969) 22.
          A seventeen-year-old speaks out against the recently insti-
     tuted rating system. The seventeen-year-old makes the follow-
     ing observations: "... no person under sixteen can see an X
     movie, and here is where the whole classification system sinks
     rapidly in the West.
          "Who selected sixteen as the critical age? At most theaters,
     when you're over twelve and too honest to bend your knees,
     you pay the full adult price. At fourteen or fifteen many kids
     have adult responsibilities--and intelligence.... Second, how
     is this system going to be enforced? Theater owners claim
     they'll ask for proof of age--school ID's, licenses or draft
     cards. But school ID's rarely contain information about your
     age. Many kids over sixteen don't have licenses. And how
     many girls do you know who carry a draft card? Another
     problem: a fifteen-year-old girl dating a seventeen-year-old
     boy. He can't even take her to an R movie because the rules
     call for an 'adult' guardian.
          "These, however, are merely the mechanical nuisances of
     such a system. The real question is: on what basis are
     specific films going to be classified? Since this whole rating
     business is supposedly for the benefit of young people, what
     is it that we shouldn't see?... An arbitrary form of censor-
     ship isn't protection; it's just a silly obstacle. We know that
     life isn't a series of cowboy epics, situation comedies and
     kiddy cartoons. Why can't we be trusted? Why must we al-
     ways be patronized?"

749. Shalit, G. "Rating Game," Look. 34 (November 3, 1970) 82-
     89.
          Shalit discusses the implications of a self-imposed ratings
     system. The author concludes that "the rating system can
     work if intelligent people will work at it. If parents will try
     to keep an eye on their [children]. If some moviemakers will
     understand that the lurid can sink us to censorship, the
     ultimate step in ushering Government into the dark business
     of dictating what we see, feel and think."

750. Shurlock, Geoffrey, et al. "Censorship and Self-Regulation,"
     In: The Annals of the American Academy of Political and So-
     cial Science; The Motion Picture Industry, edited by Gordon S.
     Watkins. New York: Arno/New York Times, 1970. pp. 140-
     159. Reprint of the November 1947 issue of the journal.
          The unit is comprised of three essays: "The Motion Picture
     Production Code," by Geoffrey Shurlock; "Censorship At Home

and Abroad," by Luigi Luraschi; "Need for Voluntary Self-Regulation," by Ruth A. Inglis. The common thread in each of the contributions is that most censorship in the industry is self-imposed.

751. Sloan, William. "Code Control," Film Library Quarterly. 2:2 (Spring 1969) 33-36.
      The Film Library Information Council goes on record as opposed to the MPAA Code, terming it censorship.

752. "Three-and-a-Half Square," Newsweek. 68 (October 3, 1966) 22.
      A report on the institution of the new Production Code.

753. Wald, Jerry. "The Code and Common Sense," Journal of Screen Producers Guild. 8 (March 1959) 11ff.
      Wald argues that the existing Production Code is not intended to suppress quality movie making; rather, it buffers the industry from outside attempts at censorship.

754. "Where Bare Breasts Are Decent," Time. 88 (September 30, 1966) 56-61.
      The article summarizes both the evolution of American sexual mores and the role of self-imposed censorship within the Hollywood film industry. The implications of the newly developed MPAA Code are also noted: "The new code will tolerate a great deal, if not everything. In effect, it merely ratifies the changes that have taken place in American sensibilities. The old puritanical tone is virtually gone. The first principle of the old code stated that 'no picture shall be produced which will lower the moral standards of those who see it.' The new code leads off with the suggestion that movies should 'keep in closer harmony with the mores, the culture, the moral sense and the expectation of our society ... old taboos are either eliminated or modified ... There is no guarantee that movies will now be better than ever, but it is a safe guess that they will be sexier than ever--in which case Hollywood may have something to export to Sweden."

755. "X Marks the Spot," Newsweek. 73 (February 24, 1969) 101.
      A look at the impact of the rating system adopted on November 1, 1968. The article concludes its assessment of the X rating three months after the institution of the film industry's movie classification program, stating, "The general view, then, in the film industry is that, while nobody quite knows what draws an X rating, it is something to avoid. But, in the case of small, art-house films, the X rating can actually be desirable."

756. Yagoda, Ben. "How Hollywood Manipulates Film Ratings," Saturday Review. 7:12 (August 1980) 39-42.

The author argues that the arbitrary rating system has
caused a host of problems, including the decline of "G" films,
the degeneration of the "X" designation into a ghetto for exploitation films, etc. In short, the industry has adapted the
rating system to its own devices; in effectively reducing the
four ratings to two ("R" and "PG"), it has enhanced its
marketing effectiveness.

d. X-Rated Films

757. Botto, Louis. "They Shoot Dirty Movies Don't They?" Look.
     34:22 (November 3, 1970) 56, 58-60.
          A Look senior editor provides a historical survey of the
     film industry. He discusses the motivations behind and im-
     plications of the recent rise of sexploitation flicks. Botto
     alludes to the possible backlash to the increasingly libertarian
     state of affairs, citing the efforts of New York congressman
     John Murphy as an example. "Said the Congressman: 'The
     courts have made it tough to fight pornography, but they did
     not make it impossible. There are many areas in which the
     city could and should be acting.' He is appalled that
     children passing by can see the pornography on display and
     has called for the creation of an anti-smut squad within the
     Police Department."

758. "X-Rated Motion Pictures: From Restricted Theaters and
     Drive-Ins to the Television Screen," Valparaiso University Law
     Review. 8 (Fall 1973) 107-124.
          The article argues that while First Amendment Rights are
     involved, X-rated films should remain relegated to the present
     system of distribution rather than being permitted access to
     commercial television.

e. Individual Titles

--And God Created Woman

759. "Brigitte at the Bar," Time. 71 (February 24, 1958) 98.
          The article reports on the confiscation of the film by the
     Philadelphia District Attorney from two theaters while charging
     the owners with violating an anti-obscenity film provision in
     the state's criminal code. Mayor Richardson Dilworth supported
     the film's right to be shown, commenting, "[D.A.] Black thinks
     he's going to get all the votes of the women's clubs by de-
     nouncing sin." The Pennsylvania State Supreme Court slapped
     Black with an injunction requiring him to let the movie be
     shown pending further court deliberations.

--Baby Doll

760. "Should It Be Suppressed? Baby Doll," Newsweek. 48 (Decem-
     ber 31, 1956) 59.

A report on the controversy initiated by the Legion of
Decency's decision to condemn the film. Following on the heels
of Francis Cardinal Spellman's efforts to suppress the film,
Episcopal Dean James A. Pike offered an opposing view: "Baby
Doll ... raised many problems, but pornography is not the
principal one .... The church's job is not to condemn por-
trayals of real life; its job is to provide the answers for the
problems which they raise.... Until people really face the
human situation in all its ... futility without God and
ethics, its bitterness without redemption, they cannot fully
receive the Gospel; and if Christian laymen have no exposure
to or perception of these problems, they are in all the poorer
position to communicate the saving Gospel meaningfully to
others...."

--Beauties of the Night

761. "Cutting a Queen's Choice," Life. 36 (March 29, 1954) 97-98.
      The article notes that a nude bathing scene in the Rene
Clair film is acceptable to the Queen of England but not for
U.S. Censors.
      "The film contained a sequence showing Gina Lollobrigida
descending nude into a bath, and famed Director Clair had
previously raised a row when Italian authorities tried to cut
the film before its showing at the Venice Film Festival. (He
won the row, and his film won a grand prize.) Up a tree,
the British censor finally decided what the queen would
see was suitable for the British public, and vice versa, and
passed it uncut. But when the film opened here last week,
U.S. Customs had trimmed the now-celebrated sequence to [a]
chaste version...."

--The Bell Jar

762. Wald, Matthew L. "Psychiatrist Files a Libel Suit Over Film
of Plath's Bell Jar," The New York Times. CXXXVI:47,019
(January 14, 1987) A1, C19.
      A Boston psychiatrist who says she is the basis for a char-
acter in Sylvia Plath's 1961 novel has filed a suit contending
defamation, invasion of privacy, and intentional infliction of
emotional damage growing out of a 1979 film version of the
book.

--The Birth of a Nation

763. De Grazia, Edward, and Roger K. Newman. "'The Birth of
a Nation'--and of Censorship," In: Banned Films. New York:
Bowker, 1982. pp. 3-6.
      A historical survey of attempts to censor the film, from the
deliberations of the National Board of Review of Motion Pictures
in early 1915 to an anti-Klan demonstration which disrupted

a 1980 San Francisco showing. The authors note that it has been banned more often than any other film in motion picture history.

764. Griffith, D. W. The Rise and Fall of Free Speech in America. Hollywood: Larry Edmunds Book Shop, 1967. Reprint of the 1916 publication.
A substantial portion of the monograph is devoted to the controversy surrounding The Birth of a Nation.

765. O'Dell, Paul. "The Rise and Fall of Free Speech in America," Silent Picture. 9 (Winter 1970-1971) 19-20.
O'Dell examines a pamphlet written by D. W. Griffith after the release of The Birth of a Nation in which the director argues that censorship is a threat not only to artistic freedom but to knowledge.

--Caligula (See: Deep Throat)

--Citizen Kane

766. Drake, Herbert. "Citizen (Orson Welles) Kane," California Arts and Architecture. 58:7 (July 1941) 16ff.
The article recounts Welles' struggle with the film industry in making Citizen Kane.

767. Sage, M. "Hearst Over Hollywood: Matter of Orson Welles' Film, Citizen Kane," New Republic. 104 (February 24, 1941) 270-271.
Sage discusses the feud between Welles and William Randolph Hearst over the film. The author is critical of the Hays Office because it failed to support Welles' creative rights.

--Deep Throat

768. Brudnoy, David. "Comstock Lives," National Review. 32 (October 3, 1980) 1197-1198.
Brudnoy reports on the banning of Deep Throat and Caligula in Boston. A follow-up discussion is provided in the October 1980, issue of the National Review (p. 1257). He concludes, "So that's the lesson? How ya gonna keep 'em down with Disney after they have seen hard core? Not quite. The lesson is simply that x number of Americans want to see this crap and will see it, and all the moralists do by trying to censor it is to glorify. Benign neglect would have made quick hash of Caligula, and one night of Deep Throat at Quincy House won't corrupt the Harvards. No such luck. The censors bellowed, and Boston got two hefty bellylaughs for their pains."

769. Cooper, H. H. A. "Deep Throat; Not All That Easy to Swallow,"

Chitty's Law Journal. 21 (October 1973) 270-273.
   Cooper analyzes the People v. Mature Enterprises, Inc.
case, which focused on the purpose and effect of hard-core
pornography.

770. Hentoff, Nat. "How to Make the First Amendment Obscene,"
     Village Voice. 21:26 (June 28, 1976) 27-30, 32, 35; 21:27
     (July 5, 1976) 36-38, 41.
        The articles cover the conviction of actor Harry Reems for
     conspiring to transport "an obscene, lewd, lascivious, and
     filthy motion picture" across state lines. Hentoff considers
     the case to be a product of an antiobscenity campaign in
     Memphis; he decries the negative impact of using conspiracy
     as a means of obtaining obscenity prosecutions.

771. Reddy, Joseph. "Judge Tyler's New Mature Courtroom," MORE.
     3:4 (April 1973) 13-15.
        A report on the New York trial of the film in which the
     exhibitor, Mature Enterprises, Inc., was found to be guilty.

--The Fox

772. Carter, John M. "Viewpoint: Witness for Obscenity," Li-
     brary Journal. 95 (July 1970) 2431.
        A witness for the defense reports on the trial of a theater
     manager and projectionist in Jackson, Mississippi, for showing
     the film. Regarding the constitutional right of the city to
     seize movies and arrest projectionists, Carter argues "The
     defense is now in the process of appealing to the U.S. Supreme
     Court; the outcome is anybody's guess. If the ruling is al-
     lowed to stand, books could be confiscated as easily as films,
     and librarians would find that they had no protection in the
     courts."

--The French Line

773. "Russell Rumpus, Little Rock," Business Week. No. 1284
     (April 10, 1954) 172.
        A report on the banning of the Jane Russell vehicle in the
     Arkansas capitol.

--I Am Curious (Yellow)

774. Carpenter, Edwin P. "Walton's Castle: The Spectrum of 'I
     Am Curious--Yellow.'" Washburn Law Journal. 10 (Fall 1970)
     163-176.
        Carpenter disagrees with Judge Walton's determination in
     State of Kansas v. A Motion Picture Film Entitled "I Am Curious
     Yellow" that the film is obscene.

775. "Curiouser and Curiouser," Newsweek. 72 (December 9, 1968)
     111.

The article notes that the previous week's U.S. Court of
Appeals decision overruling a New York City Federal District
Court decision to ban the film "did not precisely represent a
legal landmark. But it was the stiffest test to date of the
court's obscenity standard. 'The court has just gone a little
further in saying something is not obscene,' explains leading
censorship lawyer Ephraim London. 'If this had been shown
four years ago, it never would have passed.' As a result of
the decision, the customs department will be less likely to
seize foreign films."

776. "Grove to Fight U.S. Film Seizure," Publishers Weekly. 193
(February 5, 1968) 46.
The news story notes that "Grove Press has announced its
intention to fight U.S. Customs' seizure of a Swedish film, 'I
Am Curious.' The Federal agency has branded the film as
obscene. Grove Press has acquired distribution rights to the
film in the U.S. and Canada. The upcoming censorship battle
over the film, according to Barney Rosset, Grove president,
'may win for the film industry the same freedom afforded
literature in the 'Lady Chatterley's Lover' case."

777. Jacobs, Michael A. "First Amendment Permits Showing Obscene
Film in Public Theater to Paying Adult Audience That Was Forewarned of Film's Nature," Albany Law Review. 34 (Spring
1970) 708-715.
Jacobs reviews the Karalexis v. Byrne case (1969).

778. "Karalexis v. Byrne and the Regulation of Obscenity: 'I Am
Curious (Stanley),' " Virginia Law Review. 56 (October 1970)
1205-1222.
The main issue of the case is designated to be "whether
the validity of obscenity regulation depends upon the context
of the home or merely upon the nonexistence of unrestricted
public distribution."

779. Mohan, John J., Jr. "First Amendment Protection of Public
Commercial Dissemination of Obscene Materials," Saint Louis
University Law Journal. 14 (Summer 1970) 732-740.
Mohan analyzes the significance of Karalexis v. Byrne; i.e.,
the private possession of obscene material, as decided by the
U.S. Supreme Court in Stanley v. Georgia, has been expanded
to cover its commercial distribution.

780. Pilpel, Harriet F., and Kenneth Norwick. "Federal Court Ruling Democratizes Obscenity," Publishers Weekly. 197:5 (February 2, 1970) 65.
A report on Karalexis v. Byrne case (U.S. District Court
of Massachusetts). Pilpel and Norwick note that "amid sur-
prisingly little public notice or fanfare, a special three-judge
Federal court in Massachusetts has quite recently issued an

obscenity ruling which--if upheld--could well represent the
beginning of a significant revamping of our laws on obscenity.
Indeed, so sweeping are the implications of the court's ruling
that if followed it could eliminate completely all legal limitations
on the kinds of books or movies or plays forewarned adults
may read or see so long as no 'pandering' is involved and so
long as such matter is not foisted on minors or on an unwilling
audience. In other words, the three-pronged test of 'appeal
to prurient interest,' 'patent offensiveness in the light of contemporary community standards,' and 'redeeming social importance' would not apply to forewarned adult audiences choos-
ing to view obscenity in a 'private' place."

--Inherit the Wind

781.   "Drama on Scopes Trial is Barred From Class," The New York
       Times. 133 (February 21, 1984) A14.
           A report on efforts by the Oakville Junior High School of-
       ficials to keep one of its earth science teachers, James Dicker-
       son, from showing the film to his classes. A regional ACLU
       director, Joyce Armstrong, stated, "I would think the school
       district would be on very soft ground.... School officials
       have a certain control over the curriculum, but then it reaches
       a point of academic freedom."

--King Kong

782.   "King Kong Was A Dirty Old Man," Esquire. 76 (September
       1971) 146-149.
           A pictorial account of the censoring of the film, including
       efforts to recover the censored frames.

--Lady Chatterley's Lover.

783.   "Lady Chatterley's License," Economist. 192 (July 25, 1959)
       218.
           A report on the U.S. Supreme Court's refusal to grant a
       license to the French film.

--The Language of Love

784.   Pilpel, Harriet, and Kenneth Norwick. "Courts Again Seek
       Definition of Obscenity," Publishers Weekly. 198:22 (Novem-
       ber 30, 1970) 17.
           Pilpel and Norwick comment on the U.S. Court of Appeals
       for the Second Circuit reversal of a New York City Federal
       District Court decision that the Swedish sex-education movie
       was obscene. "Whether or not we agree that the theories and
       solutions presented in 'Language of Love' accurately plumb the
       depths of that 'mysterious motive force,' the film constitutes
       'material dealing with sex in a manner that advocates ideas' ...

and the First Amendment protects the expression of ideas regardless of medium or subject."

785. "Popular Mechanics of Sex," _Time_. 96 (September 28, 1970) 58-63.
      The article focuses on Judge Leonard P. Moore's opinion in the U.S. Court of Appeals decision to extend First Amendment protection to the film.
      "After viewing the film 'in its tedious entirety,' Judge Moore and his colleagues agreed that it was protected by the First Amendment because it fell far short of the Supreme Court's standards for obscenity.... Though Moore dryly noted that Language is unlikely to be viewed 'primarily by marriage counselors and their patients in a professional setting,' he found no predominant prurience in a film that treats intercourse with all the passion of an ag-school lecture on animal husbandry.
      "In determining redeeming social value, one criterion is whether or not the sex scenes advance the 'ideas' of the film. Language is impeccable by that standard, Moore suggested, since sex is the idea."

--Last Tango in Paris

786. Ragsdale, J. Donald. Last Tango in Paris et al. v. The Supreme Court: The Current State of Obscenity Law," _Quarterly Journal of Speech_. 61 (October 1975) 279-289.
      Based upon an analysis of recent court cases, Ragsdale concludes that while a new Comstock era has not emerged, the production of aesthetically acclaimed, X-rated movies by respected directors has been noticeably inhibited.

--Limelight

787. "Limelight Out," _Time_. 61 (February 9, 1953) 96.
      A report on the banning of Limelight due to the failure to complete the investigation of Chaplin's political activities.

--Manson

788. Powers, Thomas. "Stop the Presses: Judges and the Rights of Reporters," _Commonweal_. 102 (November 21, 1975) 563-564.
      Powers discusses censorship of the film by a California judge so as to prevent possible prejudice of a jury in the trial of Lynette Fromme, attempted assassin of President Ford.

--The Miracle

789. "Chicago Police Ban The Miracle," _Publishers Weekly_. 162 (August 30, 1952) 820.
      The article covers the events surrounding the case. "Despite

the U.S. Supreme Court verdict that New York acted unconstitutionally in banning the movie, 'The Miracle,' the Chicago
police department is again attempting to prohibit it from being
shown in Chicago. The film was originally banned in Chicago
last year on the grounds that it 'features immorality' and 'exposes a religion to ridicule.' "

--Oliver Twist

790. Hart, Henry. "The Miracle and Oliver Twist," Films in Review.
      2 (May 1951) 1-6.
         An analysis of two censorship cases.

--The Outlaw

791. Dart, Peter. "Breaking the Code: A Historical Footnote,"
      Cinema Journal. 8:1 (Fall 1968) 39-41.
         Dart notes the historical significance of the Howard Hughes
      film.

--Scarface

792. Wright, C. M. "Community Stands on Its Rights," Christian
      Century. 49 (August 3, 1932) 961.
         Wright reports on the banning of the film in East Orange,
      New Jersey, due to local committee action.

--Storm Center

793. "Legion's Political Judgement," Commonweal. 64 (August 3,
      1956) 431.
         The Legion of Decency is judged to be taking on the hopeless
      task of making a moral assessment of a movie entirely apart
      from artistic considerations; i.e., Storm Center receives a
      separate categorization as a particularly objectionable film.

--Titicut Follies

794. Coles, Robert. "Stripped Bare at the Follies," New Republic.
      158 (January 20, 1968) 18, 28-30.
         Coles recounts the developments in the censorship of the
      film in Massachusetts. He concludes, "In any event, the film's
      producer and director is now in court, charged with violating
      the privacy of patients, and with a 'breach of contract.' The
      documentary wasn't supposed to turn out like that, say the
      men who allowed it to be made. The politicians, who for years
      ignored Bridgewater's problems, have someone to attack, a
      movie to vilify. The former lieutenant governor, Mr. Richard-
      son, and Bridgewater's Superintendent, Mr. Gaughan, have
      to run for cover, run for their lives. And the same politicians
      also have people to defend: the inmates whose privacy has been
      invaded.

"Titicut Follies is a brilliant work of art, and as such it
will not go unnoticed, despite the opposition to it. We are
asked not to be outraged at others--a cheap and easily spent
kind of emotion--but to look at ourselves, the rich and strong
ones whose agents hurt the weak and maimed in the name of--
what? Our freedom. Our security. Our civilization."

795.   "Privacy of Mental Hospital Inmates Will Be Protected by an
       Injunction Prohibiting Open Public Exhibition of a Motion Picture
       Depicting Hospital Conditions," Harvard Law Review. 83 (May
       1970) 1722-1731.
          The article covers the Commonwealth v. Wiseman (Massachu-
       setts, 1969) case.

   --Wages of Fear

796.   De Laurot, Edward L.   "The Price of Fear," Film Culture.
       1:3 (1955) 3-6ff.
          The author explores the implications of the cuts made for the
       U.S. premiere of the film. It is argued that this practice is
       prejudicial to the general public interest.

797.   Irvine, Keith.   "Film You Won't See: Mutilated Version of
       Wages of Fear," Nation.   181 (August 6, 1955) 109-110.
          Irvine states that the distributor's decision to cut the film
       is symptomatic of America's aversion to having reality depicted
       on the screen.

Magazines

798.   "8,000 Stores Ban Adult Magazines; Surveys Show Little Public
       Support," Newsletter on Intellectual Freedom.   35:5 (September
       1986) 147-148.
          Despite the widespread removal of adult magazines from con-
       venience stores in 1986, five different surveys suggest that
       only a minority of shopping Americans object to their sale.
       Surveys conducted by Circle K Corporation, Lawson's Mills
       Company (Cuyahoga Falls, Ohio), Gallup Organization (for the
       trade publication, Convenience Store News), and Campbell Re-
       search, Inc. (for B. Dalton) are discussed at length.

                    b. Individual Titles

   --Eros

799.   "Case 5: The Ralph Ginzburg Case," In: Freedom and Cul-
       ture: Literary Censorship in the 70s. Belmont, Calif.: Wads-
       worth, 1970. pp. 153-164.
          A two-part analysis of the Supreme Court case, Ralph Ginz-
       burg v. the U.S., notable in that Ginzburg was the first

defendant exonerated for content and convicted for advertising.
Includes: (1) Justices William J. Brennan and Hugo Black:
The Ginzburg Case Opinions; (2) Leon Friedman: The Ginz-
burg Decision and the Law.

800.   Epstein, Jason. "The Obscenity Business," Atlantic. 218:2
       (August 1966) 56-60.
          Epstein believes that the role of the Supreme Court in deal-
       ing with the growing traffic in obscenity and pornography must
       be examined in detail in order to understand its recent deci-
       sion in the Ginzburg case. He concludes that the issue at
       stake is not only individual freedom but the responsibility
       with which we use that freedom.

801.   "Ralph Ginzburg Begins Term for 1963 Porno Conviction: Is-
       sues and Court Decisions," Library Journal. 97 (May 1972)
       1650, 1652-1654.
          An historical survey of Ginzburg's court cases ensuing out
       of a 1963 conviction for distributing obscene materials through
       the mails. "Just prior to leaving for the penitentiary, he
       crumpled a small duplicate of the Bill of Rights and defiantly
       tossed it on the ground, proclaiming, 'Every day I remain in
       prison this Bill of Rights is a meaningless piece of paper.' "

       --Evergreen Review (See Also: Ramparts)

802.   Roberts, Leila-Jane. "Censorship Is Evergreen," Bay State
       Librarian. 39:3 (October 1970) 24-25.
          An account of the controversy over the magazine in the
       Winchester (Mass.) Public Library. Roberts, the director of
       the library, includes the following passages from an article in
       the local paper covering the decision of the institution to drop
       its subscription to Evergreen. "In the wake of telephone calls,
       letters and even messages from the pulpit which resulted from
       the incident, Mrs. Roberts says, 'My deep regret is that no
       one came directly to the Library.' The Trustees were also
       unhappy that the majority of people's opinions were not based
       upon knowledge of the magazine, but upon hearsay...."

       --Ms.

803.   " 'Ms.' Ordered Returned to School Library," Newsletter on
       Intellectual Freedom. 28:4 (July 1979) 69, 88-92.
          U.S. district Court Judge Shane Devine ruled that Ms. maga-
       zine was removed from the Nashua (New Hampshire) High School
       library by the school board in violation of the First Amendment.
       He ordered the board to replace issues that were removed and
       reinstate the subscription. His opinion, rendered in May 1979,
       forms the text of this article.

       --The Nation

194   Intellectual Freedom and Censorship

804. Blanshard, Paul. "Freda Kirchway and The Nation Magazine
      on Religious Freedom," The Humanist. 36:4 (July/August
      1976) 40-41.
         Blanshard recounts the controversy surrounding the banning
      of The Nation in New York public school libraries as a result
      of his criticisms of the Roman Catholic Church.

805. Blanshard, Paul. Personal and Controversial; An Autobiography.
      Boston: Beacon, 1973.
         A healthy portion of the book covers the ban on The Nation
      for publication of Blanshard's attacks on the Catholic Church
      with respect to birth control and abortion.

      --Ramparts

806. Ladof, Nina S. "Freedom to Read: A Battlefield Report,"
      ALA Bulletin. 63 (July/August 1969) 903-905.
         Ladof chronicles a demand for labeling directed at the St.
      Charles (Mo.) County Library. In response to a petition drive
      led by clergymen and organizations such as the VFW, American
      Legion and Lions Club to drop the subscription to Ramparts,
      the library issued the following seven-point statement:
      1. Labeling prevents the reader from approaching a work
          with an open mind...
      2. Ideas should be judged on their own merit, and not on
          the political beliefs of the writer...
      3. The proposed labeling interferes with the right of peo-
          ple to read freely...
      4. The proposed labeling could lead to surveillance of li-
          brary users by an interested person or groups...
      5. Labeling a writer as 'subversive' or 'un-American' vio-
          lates the basic premise of our judicial structure that a
          man is innocent until proven guilty by due process of
          law...
      6. The demands of all groups in the community for labeling
          of materials repugnant to their particular philosophy
          would have to be met on an equal basis.
      7. Finally, such labeling would be, in the broadest sense,
          un-American, since this country has always cherished,
          as one of its basic freedoms, the right of dissent.

807. Martin, Allie Beth. "Decision in Tulsa: An Issue of Censor-
      ship," American Libraries. 2 (April 1971) 370-374.
         Martin chronicles a citizen's attempts to censor Ramparts
      and Evergreen Review in the Tulsa Public Library. In light
      of the Library Commission's decision to retain both journals,
      Martin notes, "This series of events in Tulsa, Oklahoma, did
      not follow the pattern usually reported in the Intellectual Free-
      dom Newsletter. Emotionally charged reactions are frequently
      reported. Serious censorship conflicts have resulted in staff
      resignations or dismissals. Decisions have been referred to

the courts. Perhaps many other cities are experiencing the
same sequence of events as have been documented in Tulsa,
but are not reporting them since good news is not really 'news.' "

--Screw; Smut

808.   Rubin, David M. "Screw Gets Screwed: Porn Peddler Al
       Goldstein Faces 60 Years in Jail," MORE. 6:9 (September
       1976) 34-35.
          Rubin reports on the June 18, 1976, conviction of Gold-
       stein and Jim Buckley by a Wichita jury for distributing ob-
       scene material. He considers the implications of the case, cit-
       ing the words of the defense attorney that if the verdict is
       not overturned it will mean "that the government can artificially
       create a jurisdiction and then pick where you stand trial. The
       enormous expense of defending such a case will crush or liqui-
       date a publication. The government will be able to wipe out
       any organ that displeases it."

Radio (See Also: Record Industry)

                    a. General Background

809.   Connelly, Christopher. "Rock Radio: A Case of Racism?
       Industry Artists Rap Segregated Format," Rolling Stone. No.
       384 (December 9, 1982) 53-55.
          Black artists, frequently stereotyped as fitting into a
       specific stylistic category, are finding it hard to cross over
       into the broader mainstream of an increasingly fragmented
       radio audience.

810.   Goodman, Ace. "The Most Unkindest Cut of All," Saturday
       Review. 54:26 (June 26, 1971) 4.
          The article recalls instances of censorship from comedy
       programs during radio's golden age prior to the ascendancy
       of television.

811.   Harrison, Mike. "Black, White and Beige," Billboard. 92
       (November 22, 1980) 31.
          A radio personality and columnist addresses industry and
       para-industry allegations that Album Oriented Rock radio
       doesn't play black music.
          "First and foremost, the particular subgenre of AOR radio
       (and it is only a subgenre) most often subject to this allega-
       tion is not representative of the full spectrum of stations that
       either refer to themselves as AOR, or fall into the AOR family
       as it exists in these early '80s ... Secondly, on close inspec-
       tion, circumstances indicate that the motives behind the elimina-
       tion of certain artists from rock 'n' roll radio playlists is, in
       most cases, the result of loosely-defined pressure imposed by

today's highly competitive, superfractionalized market place and not by racial prejudice."

812.   Patten, McClellan. "Radio Gets the Jitters," American Magazine. 127 (March 1939) 42-43.
       Patten surveys the impact of pressure groups upon program content. He states "On guard against government censorship, radio has clamped its own hand over its own mouth in a self-censorship as rigid as, if not more rigid than, anything the government could order."

813.   "Questionable Lyrics: An Enigma," Billboard. 91 (September 22, 1979) 18.
       The consensus of a panel dealing with the topic, "Record Lyrics--Dirty, Dangerous or Dynamite," on September 10, 1979, at the National Association of Broadcasters programming conference was, "Knowing the listeners' tastes and what is acceptable to the listener is the key to walking the fine line radio programmers must walk in dealing with questionable record lyrics." This point was reinforced by individual disc jockeys and programmers such as Jim Maddox of KMJQ-FM, Houston, who warned, "You can't make up morals for others and you can go out of business if you become too pure and proper for your audience."

814.   Robinson, Glen O. "The FCC and the First Amendment: Observations on 40 Years of Radio and Television Regulation," Minnesota Law Review. 52 (November 1967) 67-163.
       Robinson analyzes the First Amendment implications of restraints placed upon these media over the past forty years.

815.   Small, William. "Radio and Television Treated Like Distant Cousins," The Quill. (September 1976), Reprinted in: The First Freedom Today, edited by Robert B. Downs and Ralph E. McCoy. Chicago: American Library Association, 1984. pp. 317-320.
       Small argues that the broadcast media should be granted the same protection under the First Amendment as the printed press.

816.   Wheeler, Tom. "Drug Lyrics, the FCC and the First Amendment," Loyola University of Los Angeles Law Review. 5 (April 1972) 329-367.
       Wheeler argues that the FCC has overstepped valid constitutional restraints with its Notice 71-205 to radio stations to discourage or eliminate the broadcasting of "drug lyrics" in the public interest.

b.   Individual Titles

--WFBQ-FM's "Bob and Tom Show"

817. Carpenter, Dan. "Cleansing the Airwaves," The Progressive.
      50:1 (January 1986) 17-18.
         A local citizens' organization based in Indianapolis, Decency
      in Broadcasting, Inc., contends that the program does not
      meet the community's moral standards and must "clean itself
      up or else." The group has also cited the station for other
      on-the-air practices.

The Record Industry
(See Also: Parents Music Resource Center)

                    a. General Background

818. Bangs, Lester. "Sex and the Art of Rock 'N' Roll," Creem.
      8 (November 1976) 38-42.
         Bangs examines the use of sexy album cover art to sell the
      vinyl contents. An annotated gallery of thirty-one classic
      covers in this genre, many of which were banned in the U.S.,
      has been appended to the article.

819. Denisoff, R. Serge. "The Censors: The Radical Right and
      the FCC," In: Solid Gold; The Popular Music Industry. New
      Brunswick, N.J.: Transaction, 1975.
         The various factors at the roots of censorship (e.g., the
      radical right, racism) and the ways in which it takes hold
      constitute the central concerns of this chapter. The role of
      the FCC in promoting censorship is also covered at length.

820. The Record; a Newsletter from the Parents' Music Resource
      Center. Arlington, Va.: Parents' Music Resource Center,
      1985-. 4x/year.
         The attractively-formatted publication focuses on the latest
      developments in the regulation and control of objectionable
      sound recordings and video clips. Tips on how to participate
      in various watchdog organizations are regularly provided.

                       b. Concerts

821. Goldberg, Michael. "Crackdown on 'Obscene' Shows; New San
      Antonio Law Aimed at Rock & Roll Concerts," Rolling Stone.
      No. 464 (January 30, 1986) 9.
         Goldberg reports on the developments--e.g., lewd behavior
      on the part of heavy metal performers--leading to the institu-
      tion of the law.

                    c. Drug-Related Songs

822. Bufford, Samuel. "Drug Songs and the Federal Communications
      Commission," Journal of Law Reform. 5 (Winter 1972) 334-350.

Bufford explores the implications of an FCC warning regarding the broadcasting of drug-related popular recordings; e.g., the extent to which the songs would receive First Amendment protection, whether the statement is precise enough to be applied in a consistent manner, etc.

823. "Constitutionality of Proscribing Drug Related Songs," New York Law Forum. 19 (Spring 1974) 902-915.
An exposition of the Yale Broadcasting v. FCC case (D.C. Cir. 1973).

d.   "Porn Rock" Controversy
(See Also: Parents Music Resource Center)

824. " 'Porn Rock' Issue Aired in Senate," Newsletter on Intellectual Freedom. 34:6 (November 1985) 189-190.
A concise report on the September 19, 1985, Senate Commerce Committee hearing.

825. "R-rated Record Albums?" Newsweek. 106 (August 26, 1985) 69.
A report on the movement to force the record industry to adopt a rating system from within.

826. Saltzman, Joe. "Porn Rock," USA Today. 114 (January 1986) 91.
The article summarizes key developments during the latter part of 1985 in the war to regulate rock music recordings.

e.   Song Lyrics

827. Belz, Carl. "Public Response to Rock," In: The Story of Rock. 2d ed. New York: Oxford University Press, 1972. pp. 56-59.
Belz focuses upon censoring activities relating to the early years of rock and roll. He notes that the level of critical intelligence expressed in such incidents was, without exception, low. Traditional rhythm-and-blues lyrics which had never before provoked public outcry now did so due to the revolutionary character of the new style.

828. Lees, Gene. "Pot Luck," Holiday. 40 (October 1966) 129-130.
Lees documents the rise in references to getting high on dope or liquor in recent pop songs. He states that the blame doesn't rest with any one group; publishers, record companies, and parents all must share the responsibility for the present situation. He considers the music business to be in sorry shape when disc jockeys become its last line of ethical defense.

829. Mullinax, Ed. "The Question of Dirty Lyrics," Billboard. 80 (April 6, 1968) 18, 23.

The WLAG manager notes that objectionable song lyrics, while not a new problem, have reached new lows. They presently cover a wide gamut of topics--lewdness, insurrection, dope addiction, and general disrespect for law and order.

830. "Regulating Rock Lyrics: A New Wave of Censorship?" Harvard Journal on Legislation. 23 (Summer 1986) 595-619.
A thorough analysis of the drive fueled by the Parents Music Resource Center to coerce the record industry into the practice of self censorship.

831. Sutherland, Sam. "Wal-Mart Pulls Albums Over Graphics, Lyric Content," Billboard. 98:31 (August 2, 1986) 1, 77.
The 800-store discount chain is reported to have removed selected albums by rock acts such as AC/DC, Black Sabbath, Judas Priest, Motley Crue, and Ozzy Osbourne, along with comedy titles by Cheech and Chong, Eddie Murphy, and Richard Pryor. A sermon by evangelist Jimmy Swaggart which was critical of both Wal-Mart and K-Mart merchandising policies is cited as a motivating force in this move. Rack jobbers and record company executives cite ongoing sensitivity in some consumer quarters as another possible factor, despite minimal pressure in recent months.

f. Individual Artists

--The Beatles (See Also: John Lennon)

832. "Beatles' U.S. Personals May Be Dented By Religioso Rhubarb & DJ Blackout," Variety. 243 (August 10, 1966) 2, 70.
The article surveys those stations that have joined in the "ban the Beatles" race. Also noted are the various pro-Beatle stands being taken around the country such as "... a statement of Richard Pritchard, a Madison, Wis., minister, who said that 'those outraged by the remarks should take a look at their own standards and values. There is much validity in what Lennon said. To many people today, the golf course is also more popular than Jesus Christ.' " The brouhaha originally erupted as a result of the reprinting of Lennon's remarks originally appearing in the London Evening Standard by Datebook: "We're more popular than Jesus now. I don't know which will go first, rock 'n' roll or Christianity."

833. Brown, Peter, and Steven Gaines. The Love You Make; An Insider's Story of the Beatles. New York: McGraw-Hill, 1983. pp. 201-204.
The authors reveal that John's "Jesus" quote--and his reaction to the flap it caused--reflected a turning point in his behavior. "(Lennon) was tired of selling out, pandering to the press and public, of suppressing his feelings and thoughts."

834. "Tex. Radio Outlets Don't Accept Lennon's Apology as Sincere;
      Ban Still On," Variety. 244 (August 24, 1966) 51.
          The heart of the Southern bible belt continues to take of-
      fense at Lennon's allegedly sacrilegious comments despite his
      later apology. "About 20 of the more than 200 Texas radio
      stations imposed a ban on the British singing group after
      Lennon's published comments that Christianity was on its way
      out.
          "Most of those keeping The Beatles off their station's air-
      waves said the ban was still on, at request of their listeners.
      Phil Ransom, news director for KLUE (Longview), said a book
      by Lennon, 'A Spaniard in the Works,' contains 'anti-Christian
      comments that would make the godless Russian leaders blush.'
      The outlet said it would not lift its ban on Beatle records."

835. Wallgren, Mark. "Yesterday ... And Today--The Beatles,"
      In: The Beatles On Record. New York: Fireside/Simon and
      Schuster, 1982. p. 164.
          Wallgren discusses the infamous "Butcher Cover," which
      served as a personal commentary by the Beatles regarding
      Capitol's habit of tearing apart their carefully crafted British
      albums solely in order to churn out more "product" for the
      States. Pictures of both the original and replacement cover
      photos have been included.

      --The Cure

836. DeCurtis, Anthony. "Cure, Arab Group Reach Accord on
      Song," Rolling Stone. n494 (February 26, 1987) 30.
          In response to complaints by the Washington-based American-
      Arab Anti-Discrimination Committee (ADC), Elektra Records
      asked radio stations not to play The Cure's "Killing an Arab,"
      and agreed to place stickers clarifying the meaning of the song
      on copies of the band's recent album, Standing on a Beach:
      The Singles. Events leading up to this announcement are
      documented at length.

837. Iorio, Paul. "Cure Song Pulled From Radio, Stickered At
      Retail After Arab Protest," Cash Box. (January 31, 1987)
      5, 22.
          While "Killing an Arab" is, in fact, a song about the futility
      of killing and was never meant to serve as a vehicle for the
      promotion of bigotry, Elektra, in the words of the band's
      manager, Chris Parry, submitted to "self-censorship." Parry
      expressed concern that the compromise with the ADC might
      "open the floodgates to a whole wave of people dissecting
      songs."

      --The Dead Kennedys

838. Morris, Chris. "Porn Charges Leveled At Punkers' LP Poster,"
      Billboard. 98:24 (June 14, 1986) 1, 85.

The Los Angeles city attorney's office filed charges on June 3 against Jello Biafra, lead vocalist of the Dead Kennedys and owner of Alternative Tentacles Records, over a 20x24-inch poster enclosed in the 1985 album, Frankenchrist. According to the RIAA, the case appears to be the first porn-oriented prosecution involving a record company since the establishment of tagging guidelines by the Parents Music Resource Center and RIAA in 1985.

--Dinning, Mark

839. Bronson, Fred. " 'Teen Angel'--Mark Dinning," In: The Billboard Book of Number One Hits. New York: Billboard Publications, 1985. p. 65.
    Bronson relates that many radio stations were reluctant to play the song. However, the tragic storyline appealed to enough listeners to propel the recording to number one on the Billboard Hot 100 for two weeks in February 1960.

--The Everly Brothers

840. Bronson, Fred. " 'Wake Up Little Susie'--Everly Brothers," In: The Billboard Book of Number One Hits. New York: Billboard Publications, 1985. p. 28.
    The author notes that Cadence Records president Archie Bleyer was opposed to releasing the song due to its suggestive lyrics: "it sounded like Susie and her boyfriend had been sleeping together at the drive-in." When released the record was, in fact, banned by some radio stations; despite this opposition it reached number one on the Billboard charts on October 14, 1957.

--The Fleetwoods

841. Bronson, Fred. " 'Come Softly to Me'--The Fleetwoods," In: The Billboard Book of Number One Hits. New York: Billboard Publications, 1985. p. 51.
    Bronson notes that the group's producer, Bob Reisdorff, considered the title originally given the song ("Come Softly") to be too suggestive and extended it to "Come Softly to Me," even though those words are never heard in the lyrics.

--Lennon, John (See Also: The Beatles)

842. Treen, Joe. "Justice for a Beatle: The Illegal Plot to Prosecute and Oust John Lennon," Rolling Stone. No. 175 (December 5, 1974) 9ff.
    Treen examines the federal government's efforts to deport the musician largely due to his role in the protest movement of the late sixties and early seventies. Treen updates the study in the November 6, 1975 issue of Rolling Stone (n199; p. 10).

--Lewis, Jerry Lee

843.   "Jerry L. Lewis Tells His Side in Open Letter," Billboard.
        70 (June 9, 1958) 2.
            Lewis attempts to explain his third marriage--to his fourteen-
        year-old third cousin, Myra--which resulted in his being boy-
        cotted by radio and concert venues on both sides of the At-
        lantic. He says, "This whole thing started because I tried
        and did tell the truth"; he then goes on to discuss the circum-
        stances of his second divorce. Lewis closes by stating, "I
        hope that if I am washed up as an entertainer it won't be be-
        cause of this bad publicity, because I can cry and wish all I
        want to, but I can't control the press or the sensationalism
        that these people will go to, to get a scandal started to sell
        papers."

844.   Tosches, Nick. "Golgotha," In: Hellfire: the Jerry Lee Lewis
        Story. New York: Dell, 1982. pp. 147-171.
            This unit outlines the details of the scandal arising out of
        Lewis' marriage to his third cousin.

--MGM Records, Artist Roster of

845.   Davis, Clive, with James Willwerth. Clive: Inside the Record
        Business. New York: William Morrow, 1975. pp. 273-275.
            Davis discusses the implications of the decision by Mike
        Curb, then MGM Records president, to drop all artists from
        his label's stable who allegedly had anything to do with drugs
        (including song lyric references). He concludes that "the issue
        seems very obvious to me. It should not be confused with
        the separate responsibility radio stations have in the use of
        public airwaves. You might not be able to show Serpico or
        Mean Streets on television, but you don't censor their release
        as films. Either we care fully about art and freedom of ex-
        pression, or we have no business making records (or publish-
        ing books, or creating films). There is little room for com-
        promise here."

--McGuire, Barry

846.   Bronson, Fred. " 'Eve of Destruction'--Barry McGuire," In:
        The Billboard Book of Number One Hits. New York: Bill-
        board Publications, 1985. p. 183.
            Bronson notes that the song, "which summed up ills both
        foreign and domestic in less than three minutes, was contro-
        versial enough to be banned by some radio stations, although
        many withstood a wave of conservative complaints about the
        lyrical content." Despite (or perhaps because of) the furor,
        the recording reached number one on the Billboard Hot 100
        during the week of September 25, 1965.

847.   " 'Destruction' " Ban Doesn't Worry Me," Melody Maker. 40
       (September 18, 1965) 17.
       McGuire comments on the suppression of his hit song on
       the airwaves.

       --Melanie

848.   Bronson, Fred. " 'Brand New Key'--Melanie," In: The Bill-
       board Book of Number One Hits. New York: Billboard Publica-
       tions, 1985. p. 304.
       The article covers the controversy surrounding the song,
       which was number one between December 25, 1971-January 14,
       1972 on the Billboard Hot 100. "Though Melanie knew that the
       'key' and 'lock' were prime Freudian symbols, she was still
       unprepared for the barrage of interpretations that greeted the
       song. In fact, some misguided radio stations went so far as
       to ban it from the airwaves."

       --The Rolling Stones

849.   Bronson, Fred. " 'Ruby Tuesday'--The Rolling Stones," In:
       The Billboard Book of Number One Hits. New York: Bill-
       board Publications, 1985. p. 218.
       Bronson recounts the story behind the rise of the intended
       "flip" side, "Ruby Tuesday," to the number one position.
       " 'Let's Spend the Night Together' was the intended "A"
       side of the first Rolling Stones single of 1967, but American
       radio stations were reluctant to broadcast its blatantly sexual
       message. So was Ed Sullivan, who had no desire to help stake
       the Stones' reputation as the dirty bad boys of rock and roll.
       When they appeared on his live television program January 15
       to promote their new single, he insisted they change the words
       to the less specific 'Let's Spend Some Time Together'....
       "Radio station program directors couldn't ask Jagger to
       change the words, so they flipped the disc and played the cool,
       pastoral lament of 'Ruby Tuesday'...."

850.   " 'Off-Color' Lyrics Spark Temporary 'Stones' TV Crisis,"
       Variety. 245 (January 18, 1967) 1ff.
       A report on the refusal of CBS to allow the band to perform
       the lyrics of "Let's Spend the Night Together" (as copyrighted)
       on the Ed Sullivan Show.

851.   Peck, Abe. "Stones Lyric Protest," Rolling Stone. No. 278.
       (November 16, 1978) 39.
       A report on Reverend Jesse Jackson's attempt to have "Some
       Girls" banned. The article is appended by an editorial which
       states that race and sex are not the real issues, but rather
       free speech; Jackson would do well, in the opinion of this
       magazine, to address problems of a more serious nature.

852. Williams, Jean. "Stones, Stations Face Pickets Irate About
      Stones' Records," Billboard. 90 (November 25, 1975) 64.
         The article documents efforts by Reverend Jesse L. Jackson
      and Operation PUSH to have Some Girls removed from the
      market due to alleged racist insinuations in the title song.

      --Summer, Donna

853. Esposito, Jim. "Donna Summer and Sex Rock," Oui. 5 (Sep-
      tember 1976) 87-88ff.
         Esposito chronicles the rise of disco diva Summer on the
      strength of her controversial paean to sexual release, "Love
      to Love You, Baby."

      --Taylor, Johnnie

854. Jerome, Jim. "'Disco Lady' Has Made Preacher Johnnie Taylor
      a Rich Man--Now What's This About Dirty Lyrics," People.
      16:29 (July 19, 1976) 22-23.
         Jerome outlines the controversy concerning the alleged
      sexual imagery of Taylor's million-selling single.

      --The Village People

855. Widner, Ellis. "Village People's 'YMCA' Stirs Controversy
      Breeze in Oklahoma," Billboard. 90 (November 25, 1978) 36,
      38.
         The article documents comments from YMCA personnel con-
      cerned about the adverse publicity which the group's hit will
      provide that organization.

      --The Weavers

856. Dunaway, David King. "Songs of Subversion: How the FBI
      Destroyed The Weavers," Village Voice. 25 (January 21, 1980)
      39-40ff.
         An in-depth examination of the federal government's anti-
      pathy for the group's brand of social protest music.

857. The Weavers: Wasn't That A Time! MGM/UA Home Video
      Presentation, 1981. Color; 78 min. MV500218. Available in
      the VHS and Beta formats.
         Members of the group reflect back on their career as pioneer
      folk popularizers in the fifties. Much attention is paid to the
      role of the McCarthy witch-hunts in terminating the quartet's
      run as bestselling recording artists.

      --Williams, Maurice, and the Zodiacs

858. Bronson, Fred. "'Stay'--Maurice Williams and the Zodiacs,"
      In: The Billboard Book of Number One Hits. New York:
      Billboard Publications, 1985. p. 80.

The article indicates that the song had to be re-recorded partly due to the presence of an objectionable lyric line. In the words of producer Phil Gernhard, "It said, 'Let's have another smoke' ... (The) radio wouldn't play anything that encouraged young people to smoke cigarettes." In its revised form the song reached number one on the Billboard Hot 100 for the week of November 21, 1960.

The Telephone

859. "Foes of 'Junk Calls' Go Into Action," U.S. News and World Report. 84:12 (March 27, 1978) 67.
A report on the recently launched investigation by the FCC that is looking into the possibility of banning or restricting unsolicited phone calls by salesmen. State legislatures and public-utility commissions are also alleged to be taking action.

860. "Planned Parenthood Complains About Censorship," Newsletter On Intellectual Freedom. 26:2 (March 1977) 30, 60.
Planned Parenthood of New York City accuses the telephone company in January of "arbitrary" and "discriminatory" censorship for its refusal to allow the organization to list its services in an ad in the 1977 Manhattan Yellow Pages. The telephone company responded that it followed state regulations prohibiting the advertisement of specific medical procedures by licensed doctors or by third parties on their behalf.

Television
(See Also: Accuracy in Media; Films; Radio)

a.   General Background

861. Alward, Jennifer. "Memoirs of a Censor," Take One. 4:10 (June 30, 1975) 14-16.
A censor for CBS examines television censorship. She notes that advertisers, local affiliates, writers, producers, directors, organized pressure groups, Nielsen ratings, the FCC, Congress, and critics have all shaped the nature of television programming.

862. Ashmore, Harry S. Fear in the Air; Broadcasting and the First Amendment: The Anatomy of a Constitutional Crisis. New York: Norton, 1973.
A collection of papers presented at a two-day conference held in January 1972 at the Center for the Study of Democratic Institutions. The work surveys the alterations of First Amendment theory under the impact of licensed broadcasting; defines the new issues arising out of the presidential challenge to journalism's historic adversary role, and the rising populist

demand for right of access to communications channels; spells
out the inadequacy of formal regulation by the FCC, and of
self-regulation bounded only by marketplace considerations;
considers the possible alternative of surveillance by a non-
governmental National News Council; and recounts the stormy
effort to augment commercial broadcasting with a public-service
network. The text of these papers had appeared previously
in the May/June 1973 issue of Center Magazine.

863.   Baer, Randy C., and Christopher Baffer. "TV Censorship of
       the Movies," Take One. 4:10 (June 30, 1975) 16-19.
           The article reveals what goes on in the process of editing
       films for broadcast on television.

864.   Barthel, Joan. "The Panic in TV Censorship," Life. 67:5
       (August 1, 1969) 51-54.
           Barthel reports on how the networks have dealt with intima-
       tions of censorship by the FCC and Congress.

865.   Boldt, David. "Blue-Pencil Men: TV Censors Work Hard
       Screening Racy Humor of Bold Comedy Shows," Wall Street
       Journal. 173:20 (January 29, 1969) 1, 15.
           An inside look at the role of network censors in the produc-
       tion of program material.

866.   Chancellor, John. "Electronic Journalism," Playboy. 19:1
       (January 1972) 121, 216-217.
           The former NBC news anchorman discusses the impact of
       the Nixon Administration's program of press intimidation. He
       concludes, "... there is no shortage of politicians willing to
       say that the divisions in our society are the result of the new
       media telling it like it isn't; powerful men in both parties will
       do that if they get into political trouble. There is no shortage
       of true believers, right-wing and left-wing, who condemn the
       media because the centrist American press does not share nor
       fully reflect their views. And there is no shortage of weak,
       venal and incompetent newspaper and television news programs,
       particularly on a local level, that make thoughtful citizens
       question their sources of information.
           "This is a distressing combination, especially in a time of
       intense social change. It has been said that journalism should
       give men a picture of the world upon which they can act.
       That has never been more difficult than it is today. The most
       important element of journalism is trust. Trust between sources
       and journalists, trust between journalists and the public. And
       trust, alas, is what we seem to have too little of these days."

867.   Diamond, Edwin. "God's Television," American Film. 5 (March
       1980) 30-35. Reprinted in: Television and American Culture,
       edited by Carl Lowe. New York: Wilson, 1981. pp. 78-87.
           A profile of TV ministries. Diamond credits their success

to an ability to satiate the spiritual hunger as well as materi-
alistic and entertainment cravings of the viewers. He concludes that "the tent preacher or sawdust-trail evangelist who
aspires to a more powerful pulpit has long been a staple of
the American novel and melodrama. Soon you may be watching it on the dial, in real life. In the thirties, a time of
great unrest and social change, the demagogic voice of Father
Coughlin, the radio preacher, came out of the Midwest with
its mixed messages of populism, faith, and hate. The eighties
may be a time of change and unrest once again, with more
people pursuing fewer resources. In an uncertain time of
energy shortages and inflationary pressures, oversimplistic
appeals from telegenic operators may take hold and grow in
the darker ground of the American spirit."

868. Epstein, Edward J. "What Happened vs. What We Saw; The
      War in Vietnam," TV Guide. 21:39 (September 29, 1973) 6-10;
      21:40 (October 6, 1973) 20-23; 21:41 (October 13, 1973) 49-54.
          Epstein notes that while TV was largely responsible for
      disillusionment with the war, the medium was also guilty of
      creating--or, at least, reinforcing--the illusion of American
      military omnipotence on which much support of the war was
      based.

869. Gunther, Max. "TV and the New Morality," TV Guide. 20:42
      (October 14, 1972) 8-10, 12; 20:43 (October 21, 1972) 27-28,
      31-32; 20:44 (October 26, 1972) 50-52, 54.
          The series of articles examines the effect of the appearance
      of more permissive programming on television; e.g., criticism
      from some politicians, individuals, and groups such as Morality
      in Media.

870. Lewis, Gregg A. Telegarbage: What You Can Do About Sex
      and Violence on TV. Foreword by Jim Johnson. Nashville:
      Thomas Nelson, 1977.
          Lewis argues that the minds of TV viewers are being pro-
      grammed by an unprecedented array of sex and violence. Ac-
      cordingly, the work attempts to "reach into the dormant nerve
      centers of the Christian and arouse him once again to the
      battle that must be waged. It is an attempt to disturb the
      complacent custodian of moral values--the Christian--and move
      him off his favorite TV chair to join that battle." In short,
      a handbook for the development of a grass-roots protest move-
      ment.

871. Miner, Worthington. "The Terrible Toll of Taboos," Television.
      18 (March 1961) 42-47.
          Miner discusses the impact of television censorship.

872. Phillips, Kevin. "An Argument to Regulate TV Networks," TV
      Guide. 22:39 (September 28, 1974) A5-A6.

Phillips argues: "given the obvious bias writ large in network actions over the last decade, plus seeming responsive-
ness to private interests as opposed to national welfare,
can we afford to let the networks go their unregulated
merry way? Barbers who shape our hair are regulated; why
not people who shape our minds? Politicians who shape our
destinies are subject to increasing conflict-of-interest regulation; and why not TV networks who shape a much larger
amount of our destiny?

b. Cable Programming

873. Baker, Warren E. "The Background and Status of CATV
Industry Regulations," TV and Communications. 4:12 (December 1967) 58, 60, 65.
Baker argues that the FCC's regulation of CATV is primarily
geared toward providing the networks with a competitive edge.

874. Meyersom, M. I. "Cable's New Obnoxiousness Tests the First
Amendment," Channels of Communications. 4 (March/April
1985) 40-42.
Meyerson surveys the upsurge of cable programming which
is offensive to many subscribing communities. The implications
of this development are also noted.

875. Kamen, Al. "Law on 'Indecent' Cable Shows Voided; High
Court Restrains States' Regulation of Programming Schedules,"
Washington Post. 110:109 (March 24, 1987) A1, A12.
By a 7-2 vote, the Supreme Court struck down a Utah law
that prohibits "indecent" programs on cable broadcasts except
during the hours from midnight to 7 a.m. The Utah officials,
conceding that the March 23, 1987, ruling thwarted their drive
against sexually explicit material, said that their only hope
may be a change some day in the composition of the high court.

c. Public Television

876. Berman, Harriet K. "Federal Meddling; Censoring Public TV,"
Civil Liberties. 297 (July 1973) 1-2.
Berman documents the censoring activities of the Corpora-
tion for Public Broadcasting and the Public Broadcasting
Service.

d. Self Censorship Within the
Television Industry

877. Chester, Giraud, Garnet R. Garrison, and Edgar E. Willis.
"Self-Regulation in Broadcasting," In: Television and Radio.
5th ed. Englewood Cliffs, N.J.: Prentice-Hall, 1978. pp.
148-168.
A concise overview of the principles and practices of self-

regulation with respect to broadcasting. The full text of the
NAB's Television Code is included; the Radio Code, a shorter
document, is omitted due to its similarity to the one governing
TV. The chapter also covers the role of a Code Authority
Director, network and station codes, and unwritten codes and
pressures (e.g. blacklisting).

878.   "Time of the Bloop," Newsweek. 67 (January 24, 1966) 54-55.
       An analysis of the widespread self-censorship within the
medium. The article notes that blooping (the noise made when
the erase head of the tape recorder censors out the audio
portion of the TV picture) "is only the latest electronic mani-
festation of television's self-censorious attitude. At a time
when books, movies and the theater are relaxing restrictions
and expanding their fields of coverage, TV still kills shows
because of subject matter and story line. Homosexuality is
taboo, as is any violence considered 'excessive.' And each
network has its own guardians of the public morality, called,
variously, reviewers, supervisors of broadcast standards and
practices, or continuity acceptance men." In defense of the
medium's censorious ways, CBS's William H. Tankersley passes
the buck to the audience. "We bend with the times and the
changing mores.... People expect television to be an island
of serenity in a troubled sea."

                    e.   Individual Cases

--"Amerika" (mini-series)

879.   Irvine, Reed. "The 'Amerika' Series Spoils A Good Idea,"
       Conservative Digest. 13:2 (February 1987) 59-64.
       The chairman of Accuracy in Media notes the criticisms of
both the left and conservatives with respect to the controversial
mini-series, "Amerika," scheduled for airing in February 1987.
His main point is that the ABC network--via poor casting,
scripting, etc.--blew its opportunity to produce a powerful
film showing why the U.S. needs a defense capable both of
halting the external encirclement that is proceeding apace and
of protecting us against nuclear blackmail.

--Editorializing

880.   Martin, Thomas. "How to Get Fired by a TV Station," TV
       Guide. 18:28 (July 11, 1970) 22-25.
       The account of an award-winning TV editorialist who is
fired by his station for alienating local businessmen. The
broader implications of this case with respect to freedom of
speech are discussed.

--Maude

881. Nicholas, David. " 'We Regret That Maude Will Not Be Seen...,' "
      TV Guide. 21:9 (March 3, 1973) 6-8.
          A report on the decision of CBS affiliates in Peoria and
      Champaign, Illinois, not to broadcast a two-part program in
      the "Maude" series due to objections to the abortion theme.

--The Merv Griffin Show

882. Ace, Goodman. "The Dirty Five-Letter Word," Saturday Re-
      view. 53 (January 24, 1970) 10.
          A report on the decision of CBS to edit out requests to
      the audience--by both Elke Sommer and Carol Burnett on The
      Merv Griffin Show--to write letters appealing for peace. Ace
      comments on the hypocrisy inherent in TV programming deci-
      sions.

--Monty Python's Flying Circus

883. Hertzberg, Hendrick. ("Monty Python v. American Broadcast-
      ing Company, Inc."), New Yorker. 52:6 (March 29, 1976) 69-
      70ff.
          Hertzberg reports on the uproar ensuing from ABC's deci-
      sion to edit--without permission of the producer--portions of
      the program. "The first 'Wide World of Entertainment' special
      went over ABC on October 3rd (1975), but the Pythons them-
      selves didn't see it until the end of November, when Nancy
      Lewis took a tape of it to London to show them. They didn't
      like it. It was obvious to them that the cuts--twenty-two
      minutes in all--had been made solely to remove 'offensive' ma-
      terial, not to tighten the shows up or make them funnier."

--Pollution Documentaries Broadcast on WJXT-TV (Jacksonville)

884. "Devil in Duval County; Firing of WJXT-TV Reporter for Pol-
      lution Documentaries," Time. 96 (August 17, 1970) 42-43.
          The article addresses the factors--alienation of powerful
      politicians, major industries, the Chamber of Commerce, etc.--
      leading to reporter Charley Thompson's dismissal. The article
      notes that "[Thompson] began to worry when the station's ad
      director sarcastically offered him a list of WJXT's customers
      'so I could hit them systematically instead of one by one.'
      The herd kept pressing, and several weeks ago Thompson was
      fined for doing his job too well. 'I've covered civil rights
      marches and jail riots,' says the bewildered Young Goodman
      Thompson, who also picked up 18 decorations in Viet Nam.
      But this conservation thing is the one that really scared the
      hell out of me.' "

--The Smothers Brothers Comedy Hour

885. Collier, Peter. "A Doily for Your Mind," Ramparts. 7 (June
      1969) 44, 46, 48-50.

Collier recounts the censorship of the program by CBS; he relies heavily upon the insights supplied by Tommy Smothers.

Theater

a. General Background

886. Witham, Barry B. "Play Jury: Censorship in the 1920's," Educational Theatre Journal. 24 (December 1972) 430-435.
     Witham chronicles the activities of New York's Play Jury, instituted by the theatrical community as a means of forestalling possible attempts by outside agencies such as the city or state to regulate its productions.

b. Individual Titles

--Animal Farm, by George Orwell

887. Kleinman, Dana. "A Mixed Reaction to Ban on Orwell," New York Times. 135 (May 29, 1986) C19.
     Kleinman reports that producers, publishers, actors and others involved in the arts responded with a mixture of anger and resignation at the decision to withdraw a stage production of George Orwell's "Animal Farm" from an international theater festival in Baltimore. She cites the reaction of Robert S. Brustein, artistic director of the American Repertory Theater at Harvard University: "It is both sad and outrageous that any work of the theater should be cancelled or modified through pressure from left or right ... Just as it would be important to protect a Soviet play from right-wing sources in the country, it is important to protect 'Animal Farm' from influence from the Soviets. We are subjected to many pressures in the arts these days from ideological groups, it's important for the theater community to stand fast."

--The Birds, by Aristophanes

888. Ciardi, John. "On Purifying the Antiquities or the Greeks Had More Words for It than You Are Going to Hear in Ypsilanti, at Least While Bert Lahr Is On Stage," Saturday Review. XLIX:33 (August 13, 1966) 22.
     A commentary on Ypsilanti's presentation of the play, starring Bert Lahr, which features an excised version of the William Arrowsmith translation.

--Br'er Rabbit's Big Secret, by Joel Chandler Harris

889. "Br'er Rabbit Banned," AP News (File 259/DIALOG Information Services, Inc.) No. 0246898 (December 10, 1986) 376 (word count).

Officials for the Savannah-Chatham County school system
cancelled performances of a play about Br'er Rabbit, a character in the Uncle Remus tales of Joel Chandler Harris. School
spokesman Barry Ostrow said, "The main concern was to prepare the teachers and children for something that is very different. They needed to be coached on dialect and language
not considered acceptable. The children needed to be taught
a historical perspective."

890. "Play on Br'er Rabbit is Banned in Atlanta," The New York
      Times. 136 (December 11, 1986) A24.
      The article reports on the cancellation of a planned per-
      formance of the play for second graders by officials at the
      Savannah-Chatham County school system. The director of
      the Savannah Theater Company, Ken Watkins, who was staging
      the play, said: "They felt there were things children wouldn't
      understand--the tar baby would be taken as a racial slur.
      Other than that, I think they were bothered by poor gram-
      matical slang."

--Che!, by Lennox Raphael

891. Hughes, Catharine. "Nudity, Obscenity and All That," The
      Christian Century. LXXXVI:43 (October 22, 1969). 1349-1350.
      Hughes discusses the closing of the off-off-Broadway pro-
      duction for presenting "consentual sodomy, public lewdness
      and obscenity." She does not find the nudity or language
      offensive or objectionable in moral terms; rather, it is offensive
      and counterproductive in artistic terms.

--A Clockwork Orange, by Anthony Burgess

892. "(Schools--Philadelphia, Pennsylvania)," Newsletter on Intel-
      lectual Freedom. XXVII:2 (March 1978) 31.
      Philadelphia students were unable to perform in a special
      stage production of A Clockwork Orange for fellow students
      enrolled in a program stressing academic and cultural enrich-
      ment. The director of the program, Rebecca Segal, stated,
      "This is decision-making, not censorship ... I have to run a
      program and I have to pick and choose what is best for my
      program. I do not think this play is a proper vehicle for the
      classroom because it is terribly violent. Kids see enough of
      that in their neighborhoods."
      Many students reacted differently. Maurice Henderson
      noted that "We were trying to portray youth of the future and
      what would happen if we don't stop violence now." Frieda
      Wone felt the play stressed "freedom of choice" and the main
      character "no longer had the ability to choose between right
      and wrong."

--Hamlet; Macbeth; Romeo and Juliet, by William Shakespeare
(See also: Romeo and Juliet)

893. "Edited Shakespeare Stirs Educators to Probe Books," Houston
      Post. (January 26, 1985) 9G. (Source: United Press Inter-
      national/VU Text; Document Number 3822)
          Virginia educators are angered that Scott, Foresman and
      Co. had omitted scenes from Romeo and Juliet, Hamlet and
      Macbeth in a Shakespeare textbook without noting it in the
      text or telling school officials. Margaret Marston of Arlington,
      a member of the board and on President Reagan's National
      Commission on Excellence in Education, suspects publishers
      omitted the sections because of pressure groups opposed to
      sexual overtones in school books. "They [high school stu-
      dents] see more racy material on TV than in a Shakespeare
      play ... It is imperative that the lines remain intact. The
      publishers have the responsibility to note that they have re-
      moved them."

      --Macbeth (See: Hamlet)

      --The Moon Children

894. "(Students' Rights--Trenton, New Jersey)," Newsletter on
      Intellectual Freedom. XXVII:4 (July 1978) 94.
          In April 1978 New Jersey Superior Court Judge George Y.
      Schoch rejected arguments that the students' freedom of speech
      was infringed when the principal, George Petrillo, ordered
      "vulgarisms" deleted from a play about campus protests in the
      1960s. In a letter to the Princeton Packet, which editorialized
      in favor of the principal's decision, Greg Davidson, a member
      of the cast and a junior at the school, challenged the qualifica-
      tions of the principal to label the play "obscene, bad, and
      blasphemous." "Mr. Petrillo's lack of a degree in dramatic
      criticism is noted, and as far as I know, no church has yet
      ordained him. Was it fair for him to say these things?"
          Davidson also noted that "whereas the paper had editorialized
      in favor of the school's enforcing 'generally held' moral stand-
      ards, it had failed to editorialize on the 'generally held'
      moral right of human beings to freedom of speech."
          Reported in the Newark Star-Ledger (April 11/12, 1978)
      and The New York Times (April 12, 1978).

      --One Flew Over the Cuckoo's Nest, by Ken Kesey

895. "(Students' Rights--Rutland, Vermont)," Newsletter on Intel-
      lectual Freedom. XXVI:4 (July 1977) 112.
          Thomas Chesley, superintendent of the Rutland Public
      Schools, ruled in March 1977 that Rutland High School Principal
      William Timbers was carrying out a "proper discharge of his
      duties" when he banned a production of the dramatic version
      of Kesey's play by seniors. Timbers' reasons for banning the
      play included: "the inappropriateness of the bureaucracy of
      mental institutions for entertainment; the play's one-sided

depiction of mental health services and its tendency to dis-
parage the efforts and procedures of mental health agencies;
the tasteless dialogue; and the inability of students to portray
mentally ill people."

--Romeo and Juliet, by William Shakespeare (See also: Hamlet)

896.   Hentoff, Nat. "Romeo, Romeo, I Can Hardly Hear You," Wash-
       ington Post. 107 (November 23, 1984) A27.
       The editorial criticizes the bowdlerizing of Shakespeare's
       Romeo and Juliet by the largest textbook publisher in the U.S.
       Hentoff notes that "The publisher is Scott, Foresman, and the
       anthology containing the bleached love story is Arrangement
       in Literature. Arrangement, indeed. Gone is Juliet's aria:
       'Spread the close curtain, love-performing Night/That runaway's
       eyes may wink and Romeo/Leap to these arms untalk'd of and
       unseen.' No longer is Romeo impatient to 'lie' with Juliet.
       Cooled down by Scott, Foresman, he wants only to 'be' with
       her ... [a] Minneapolis high school told its teachers to inform
       the students that there is more to 'Romeo and Juliet' than
       meets the innocent eye in this smoothly arranged Scott, Fores-
       man anthology. But as for those who felt injury had been
       done to young Montague and Capulet, the president of the
       firm, Richard Morson, instructed reporter Wendy Tai that
       Scott, Foresman publishes for a national market. And some
       regions, he said, may take more kindly to certain kinds of
       editing, as he put it, than other regions. 'One person's
       selection,' Morgan helpfully added, 'is another person's cen-
       sorship.' "

897.   Sugawara, Sandra. "Textbook Publisher Censors Shakespeare,"
       Washington Post. 108 (December 18, 1984) C1.
       Sugawara reports on the decision of Scott, Foresman to
       strike hundreds of lines from Shakespeare's plays out of text-
       books used in the state's high schools due to the publisher's
       fear that the material is too provocative for young minds.
       Marlene Blue, a member of a textbook advisory committee for
       Fairfax County, noted, "When all publishers do it, you have
       no option ... And that's what's so infuriating. It's as if they
       [the publishers] have become the arbiter of what children are
       to read and not read.
       "You're talking about the quality of education. It should
       be the teacher's decision to cut certain areas, not the pub-
       lishers."

--Runaways, by Elizabeth Swados

898.   "Students Sue on Ban of School Play," The New York Times.
       133 (February 21, 1984) A15.
       The article reports that six students from the high school
       in Union District 32, East Montpelier, have taken their school

board to Federal District Court, contending that a board decision to prohibit a school production of the play violated their
rights under the First Amendment. John Mattera, the teacher
who chose and would direct the play, claims that it "offers a
healthy dose of reality to the youth and to the community....
It's the most educationally sound play that we have ever done
at U-32."

--A Theological Position

899. "(Festivals, etc.--Los Angeles, California)," Newsletter on
      Intellectual Freedom. XXVII:3 (May 1977) 65-66.
      Prominent religious leaders began circulating petitions in
March 1978 to protest alleged anti-Catholic and pornographic
dramatic productions connected with the city-funded Garden
Theater Festival. In response, the city council decided to
hold up for at least a month a decision on a $30,000 appropria-
tion requested to pay performers at the July festival in Barnsdall Park. One play, A Theological Position, while presented
at the Odyssey Theater in West L.A. with private funding,
was advertised in a Garden Theater Festival program booklet.
In a March 13 editorial, the Los Angeles Times condemned attempts at censorship. "The festival is a celebration of all the
arts ... that takes over Barnsdall Park for three weeks each
summer ... Now it is under attack because one of its printed
flyers last year mentioned an unrelated production at an unrelated theater fifteen miles away ... Another charge leveled
at the Barnsdall Park festival is that three comedians last
year--among hundreds of performers--made a few off-color or
anti-religious jokes during their turns on stage....
      "We missed the [performance of 'two dirty religious plays']
but looked at the scripts, which are unpleasant. Many people
have reason to be offended by the plays' dearth of judgment
and taste. But we propose that censorship doesn't make art
better, either. We prefer to leave all these questions to the
artist and the beholder, and to recognize things for what they
are."
      The story was originally covered in the March 8 and 12
issues of the Los Angeles Times.

--Vanities, by Jack Heifner

900. "(Schools--Potomac, Maryland)," Newsletter on Intellectual
      Freedom. XXVIII:3 (May 1979) 50-51.
      A performance of the off-Broadway hit by drama students
in Marguerite Coley's class at Winston Churchill High School
resulted in the establishment of an administrative screening
committee for plays and a letter of censure in Coley's personnel
file. Coley noted that "she and her seventeen students had
decided to produce a 'meaningful' performance because they
were tired of the usual 'pablum' ... the drama examines

misplaced human values and the roles of women in society."
The sole performance of the drama got an enthusiastic reception from most Churchill students. Senior Jay DeVore ex-
claimed, "It was fantastic ... The story paralleled high school
culture and had a message for the larger society."

Carpenter, Edwin P. 774
Carter, John M. 772
Cary, Eve 225
Casagrande, Richard E. 213
Castagna, Edwin 38
Castan, Frances 656
Chancellor, John 866
Chaplin, Charlie 787
Chepesiuk, Ron 367
Chesley, Thomas 895
Chester, Giraud 877
Childress, Alice 640
Christianson, Reo M. 61
Church, Bud 681
Ciardi, John 665, 689, 888
Cirino, Robert 572, 621
Clair, Rene 761
Clark, Charles E. 651
Clark, David G. 269, 734
Clark, Elyse 328, 641
Clay, Richard H. C. 204
Cleaver, Eldridge 681
Cleland, John 626-628
Clifford, George 279
Clifford, J. B. 707
Cline, Ruth K. J. 658
Cloonan, Michele V. 600
Clor, Harry M. 62, 247, 435
Clymer, Adam 531
Coe, Richard 739
Cogley, John 730, 731
Cohen, Barbara 663
Coles, Robert 794
Coley, Marguerite 900
Collier, Peter 885
Collins, Blanche 355
Colorado 159
Combee, Jerry H. 27
Commager, Henry Steele 51, 234, 592
Comstock, Anthony 3; 436, 450, 534, 535, 786
Conley, Heather 515
Connelly, Christopher 809
Conway, Flo 536, 540, 543, 544, 547
Cook, Bruce 646
Cooke, Robert F. 400
Cooper, H. H. A. 769
Corliss, Richard 489, 509
Cormier, Robert 618

Coughlin, Father 867
Cowley, Malcolm 297, 648
Coyne, John R. 437
Crane, Stephen 630, 659
Crawford, Hubert H. 705
Crist, Judith 47, 745
Cunningham, Gregg 159
Curb, Mike 845
Curran, Father 28, 29
Cushing, Robert G. 398
Cyr, Judge 684, 686

Daily, Jay 48, 302
Damaska, Mirjan 395
Daniel, Clifton 255, 578
Daniels, Bruce E. 579, 580
Daniels, Les 706
Daniels, Walter 591
Dante 594
Darling, Richard L. 552
Dart, Peter 791
Darvin, Leonard 704
Davidson, Greg 894
Davies, Hilary 678
Davis, Clive 845
Davis, James E. 38, 127-130, 132, 142, 149, 153, 163, 189, 323, 425, 458, 486, 561, 667
Davis, Keith E. 400, 401
Davis, Robert C. 636
Davis, Rod 516
DeCurtis, Anthony 836
De Grazia, Edward 339, 715, 763
De Laurot, Edward L. 796
Del Frattore, Joan 158
Dempsey, David 355
DeMuth, James 647
Denisoff, R. Serge 819
Dennis, Everette E. 6
Dershowitz, Alan 568
De Smet, Imogene 634
Detty, Elizabeth W. 199, 325
Devine, Shane 803
De Vore, Jay 900
Dewhurst, Colleen 413
Diamond, Edwin 867
Dickerson, James 781
Dickey, James 620
Dienes, C. Thomas 2

Geller, Evelyn 319
Gernhard, Phil 858
Gerson, Lani 358, 606
Gertz, Elmer 688
Gilligan, Carol 394
Gilmore, Donald M. 6, 64, 269
Ginger, Ann Fagen 344
Ginzburg, Ralph 5
Glasser, Ira 221
Glasser, Ronald J. 684-686
Glatthorn, Allen 128
Glenn, Charles 136, 194
Glikes, Ervin A. 407
Goldberg, Michael 821
Goldfarb, Ronald L. 256
Golding, William 657
Goldstein, Al 808
Goldstein, Michael J. 400
Goldstein, Stephen R. 207, 222
Goldwater, John 704
Goodman, Ace 810
Goodman, Fred 520
Gordon, Andrew C. 282
Gordon, Maryl 480
Gore, Daniel 313
Green, Michelle 408
Greenspan, Lou 739
Grey, David L. 6
Griffin, John Howard 609
Griffith, D. W. 764, 765. See
    also: Birth of a Nation
Guest, Judith 673
Gunther, Max 869
Guth, James L. 476

Haag, Ernest van der 47
Haber, David 186
Hagist, Barbara 304
Haiman, Franklyn 19, 253
Hale, John P. 28
Hand, W. Brevard 192
Haner, Steve 499
Haney, Robert W. 450
Hansen, Soren 656
Harrington, Richard 521
Harris, Joel Chandler 889, 890
Harris, Richard 12
Harrison, Mike 811
Hart, Harold H. 47
Hart, Henry 790
Harter, Stephen 337

Hartogs, Renatus 65
Harvey, James A. 683
Hausknecht, Murray 440
Havemann, Joel 290
Hawthorne, Nathaniel 676
Haymes, Don 160
Hearn, Michael 604
Hearst, William Randolph 767
Hefner, Christie 7; 409
Hefner, Hugh 569
Heifner, Jack 900
Heinz, John P. 282
Heller, Joseph 80
Hemingway, Ernest 629, 630
Henderson, Maurice 892
Hentoff, Nat 20, 47, 161, 168,
    309, 326, 522, 597, 605,
    770, 896
Hertzberg, Hendrik 410, 883
Hirschoff, Mary-Michele Upson
    223
Hoff-Wilson, Joan 46
Hogan, Robert F. 129, 146
Hohenberg, John 573
Holborn, David G. 677
Holbrook, David 441
Hole, Carol 341, 345
Holland, Bill 523
Holland, Norman N. 394
Holmes, Oliver Wendell 2
Holmes, Peter 627
Horowitz, Bernard 398
Horowitz, Irving Louis 287
Hough, Maxine L. 356
Hove, John 148
Howard, James L. 401
Howard, Joseph 47
Howe, Irving 440
Hoyt, Edwin P. 49
Hoyt, Mary Finch 524
Hoyt, Olga G. 49
Huffman, John L. 232
Hughes, Catharine 891
Hughes, Douglas A. 60
Hughes, Howard 791
Hull, Judge 193
Hutchison, Earl R. 269, 690,
    734
Huxley, Aldous 592, 612

Inglis, Ruth A. 750

Laxalt, Paul 588
Lear, Norman 565, 570-571. See
  also: People for the American
  Way
Ledbetter, James 463
Lee, Harper 687
Lee, Robert W. 196
Leech, Margaret 535
Leerheen, Charles 569
Lees, Gene 828
Lelyveld, Arthur 47
Lennon, John 832-834, 842. See
  also: The Beatles
Lepper, Derek J. 400
Lerner, Max 47
Levin, Harry 556, 688
Levin, Jack 402
Levin, Marc 283
Levine, Alan H. 221, 225, 622-623
Levine, Ellen 410, 419
Levy, Leonard W. 22, 251-252
Lewis, Anthony 257
Lewis, Felice Flanery 595
Lewis, Gregg A. 870
Lewis, Jerry Lee 843-844
Lewis, Nancy 883
Liebman, Robert C. 498
Lillienstein, Maxwell 7; 411
Linden, Kathryn B. 717
Liptzin, Myron B. 401
Lisca, Peter 639
Little, Thomas F. 491
Littlejohn, David 688
Locke, Bernard 398
Lollobrigida, Gina 761
Lord, Richard A. 718
Lorentz, Pare 716
LoSciuto, L. 399
Luraschi, Luigi 750
Lynn, Barry W. 404, 407
Lynn, Kenneth S. 603
Lyons, Gene 184

Maddox, Jim 813
Madison, James 27
Maeder, Jay 704
Manchester, William 619
Mann, Jay 394, 401
Manton, J. W. 693
Maritain, Jacques 190
Marshall, E. 464

Marshner, Connaught 412, 530
Marston, Margaret 893
Martin, Allie Beth 807
Martin, Thomas 880
Marty, Martin E. 565
Mason, John 719
Massey, Morris E. 397
Massing, Michael 470
Mattera, John 898
May, Jill 687
Mayer, Milton 564
McAteer, Ed 531
McBride, William G. 643
McCarthy, Eugene 47
McCarthy, Joseph 857
McClellan, Grant S. 51
McCormick, John 52
McCoy, Ralph E. 346, 574a,
  574. See also: Robert B.
  Downs
McDonald, Frances M. 710
McGhehy, M. A. 198
McGuire, Barry 846, 847
McInnes, Mairi 52
McKeon, Richard 53
MacLeod, Celeste 344
MacLeod, Lanette 615
Meese, Edwin 588. See also:
  Meese Commission
Melanie 848
Meriwether, James B. 629
Merritt, LeRoy C. 347
Meyers, Duane H. 611
Meyerson, M. I. 874
Michalsky, Walt 557
Michener, James A. 741
Mill, John Stuart 4, 549
Miller, Arthur B. 265
Miller, Henry 438, 688-691
Miller, Nancy 292
Miller, Norman R. 211
Miller, Robert Keith 669
Milner, Michael 720
Milton, John 4, 549
Miner, Worthington 871
Minnery, T. 513
Minor, Dale 284
Mishkin, Edward 5
Mitchell, Arlene Harris 604
Mohan, John J. 779
Moley, Raymond 744

American Legion 103; 320, 712, 806
American Library Association 4, 37-38, 103; 274, 301, 309, 312,
   351-352, 361, 365, 372, 374, 390, 437, 473-474, 712. See also:
   individual divisions by name
American National News Service 103
American Newspaper Publishers Association 103
American Renewal Foundation 103
American Revolution 3
American Society of Newspaper Editors 244
Americans for Constitutional Freedom 39; 103
"Amerika" 879
And God Created Woman 759
Anderson v. Celebrezze 70
Animal Farm 887
Anne Frank see The Diary of Anne Frank
anti-censorship viewpoints 334-350, 549-571. See also: prepara-
   tions for dealing with the censor
Archie Comics 704
Areopagitica 4, 549
Arkansas 773
Arkansas Act on Creationism in Schools 183-185
Arlington, VA 893
Arrangements in Literature 896
Ashland, OR 555
Ashley, Benedict M. 139
Association for Education in Journalism and Mass Communication 103
"Authority Song" 522

B. Dalton 798
Baby Doll 760
Back in Control (Orange, CA) 103
Baileyville, ME 684-686
Baltimore 887
Banned Books 132; 594
Banned Films 132
Baton Rouge, LA 163
"Beat It" 522
The Beatles 832-835
Beauties of the Night 761
The Bell Jar 762
Bellevue, WA 672
Bergen Co., NJ 154
Berkeley Springs, WV 656
Best Short Stories of Negro Writers 76
Bethal School District No. 403 v. Fraser 220
The Bible 594
Bicknell v. Vergennes Union High School Board of Directors 78, 172
Bill of Rights 1, 3; 6, 564, 682, 801
Bill of Rights Newsletter 203
Billboard 839, 840, 846, 848, 858

Evergreen Review   802, 807
Everly Brothers   840
Excelsior Pictures Corp. v. Regents   725. See also: Garden of
    Eden
The Exorcist   79

faculty rights   203-215, 237-239
Fairfax County   897
fairness doctrine   555, 577-586
Family Matters   625
Fanny Hill   89; 626-628. See also: A Book Named...
A Farewell to Arms   629-630
Farmingdale, NY   317
Federal Bureau of Investigation   383
Federal Communications Commission   34; 555, 575-576, 579, 583, 814,
    816, 819, 822-823, 859, 861-862, 864, 873
Federal Communications Commission v. League of Women Voters of
    California   122
Federal Communications Commission v. Pacifica Foundation   111
federal statutes   111-125
Feminists Against Pornography   103
Feminists Anti-Censorship Task Force   103
film codes, ratings, etc.   724, 734-756
Film Library Information Council   751
films   574a, 711-797, 863
films censored in the U.S. (individual titles)   134-136
Final Report of the Attorney General's Commission on Pornography
    7; 417-418. See also: Meese Commission
The Fleetwoods   841
Florida Coalition for Clean Cable   103
Flushing, NY   see   Queens
Foreign Agents Registration Act   119
Forever   631
Fourteenth Amendment   3; 25, 226-227
The Fox   772
Frankenchrist   838
free press vs. fair trial   254-261
Freedom and Culture   651
Freedom Council   541
Freedom of Expression Foundation   103
Freedom of Information Act   289-293
Freedom of the Press   574b
Freedom to Read Foundation   38, 103
Freedom to Read Statement   4; 364
Freespeech Committee   39
The French Line   773
Funk & Wagnalls   675

gag orders   see   free press vs. fair trial

152910

Z65B.U5 H64
Hoffmann, Frank W., 1949-
Intellectual freedom and
censorship : an annotated
bibliography

DISCARDED BY

MACPHÁIDÍN LIBRARY

CUSHING-MARTIN LIBRARY
STONEHILL COLLEGE
NORTH EASTON, MASSACHUSETTS 02357